T0319967

The Internationalisation of Business R&D

NEW PERSPECTIVES ON THE MODERN CORPORATION

Series Editor: Jonathan Michie, *Director, Department for Continuing Education and President, Kellogg College, University of Oxford, UK*

The modern corporation has far reaching influence on our lives in an increasingly globalised economy. This series will provide an invaluable forum for the publication of high quality works of scholarship covering the areas of:

- corporate governance and corporate responsibility, including environmental sustainability
- human resource management and other management practices, and the relationship of these to organisational outcomes and corporate performance
- industrial economics, organisational behaviour, innovation and competitiveness
- outsourcing, offshoring, joint ventures and strategic alliances
- different ownership forms, including social enterprise and employee ownership
- intellectual property and the learning economy, including knowledge
- transfer and information exchange.

Titles in the series include:

The Modern Firm, Corporate Governance and Investment
Edited by Per-Olof Bjuggren and Dennis C. Mueller

The Growth of Firms
A Survey of Theories and Empirical Evidence
Alex Coad

Knowledge in the Development of Economies
Institutional Choices Under Globalisation
Edited by Silvia Sacchetti and Roger Sugden

Corporate Strategy and Firm Growth
Creating Value for Shareholders
Angelo Dringoli

The Internationalisation of Business R&D
Edited by Bernhard Dachs, Robert Stehrer and Georg Zahradnik

The Internationalisation of Business R&D

Edited by

Bernhard Dachs

AIT Austrian Institute of Technology, Austria

Robert Stehrer

The Vienna Institute for International Economic Studies (wiiw), Austria

Georg Zahradnik

AIT Austrian Institute of Technology, Austria

NEW PERSPECTIVES ON THE MODERN CORPORATION

Edward Elgar

Cheltenham, UK • Northampton, MA, USA

Published by
Edward Elgar Publishing Limited
The Lypiatts
15 Lansdown Road
Cheltenham
Glos GL50 2JA
UK

Edward Elgar Publishing, Inc.
William Pratt House
9 Dewey Court
Northampton
Massachusetts 01060
USA

A catalogue record for this book
is available from the British Library

Library of Congress Control Number: 2013949883

This book is available electronically in the ElgarOnline.com Business Subject Collection, E-ISBN 978 1 78347 090 7

ISBN 978 1 78347 089 1

Printed and bound in Great Britain by T.J. International Ltd, Padstow

Contents

Contributors

Bernhard Dachs

Bernhard Dachs is Senior Scientist at the Innovation Systems Department of AIT Austrian Institute of Technology, Vienna. He graduated in economics from the Vienna University of Economics and Business in 1996 and also holds a doctorate in economics (University of Bremen). He joined AIT in 2000. Bernhard Dachs' areas of expertise are the economics of innovation and technological change, in particular with regard to the internationalisation of R&D, innovation in services, and the analysis of national and international technology policy. To date, his work has been mostly empirical and applied. Papers based on this research has been published a number of international peer-reviewed journals.

Doris Hanzl-Weiss

Doris Hanzl-Weiss is Staff economist at The Vienna Institute for Internation-al Economic Studies (wiiw) where she is key expert in the area of industrial structural change and sectoral analysis in transition countries. In that function she worked on the manufacturing sector as well as on energy and services. She has been engaged in various research projects, e.g. for DG Enterprise (on EU manufacturing supply chains) and participated in a large research project within the 7th Framework programme on a world input-output database (WIOD). Ms. Hanzl-Weiss is currently mainly engaged in the research on the Slovakian economy, industrial development and also takes part in the FP7-project 'Growth-Innovation-Competitiveness. Fostering Cohesion in Central and Eastern Europe' (GRINCOH). She graduated in economics at the Vienna University of Economics and Business.

Franziska Kampik

Franziska Kampik is Credit Risk Manager at the Volksbank AG in Vienna. Before that, she worked at the Austrian Institute of Technology, where she has been engaged in various research projects for the European Comission. In her research she mainly focused on the internationalisation of R&D and inno-vation activities of multinational firms. Franziska Kampik graduated in economics at the Vienna University of Economics and Business.

Sandra Leitner

Sandra M. Leitner is an economist at the Vienna Institute for International Economic Studies (wiiw) in Vienna, Austria and a lecturer at Johannes Kepler University Linz, Austria. She holds a PhD in economics awarded by the University of Maastricht, the Netherlands and an MSc in Contemporary Asian Studies from the University of Amsterdam, the Netherlands. Her areas of research and expertise revolve around the economics of innovation and technical change and include issues of growth and business cycle theory, entrepreneurship, investment theory, labor markets and capital markets. She contributed to several EU framework projects (e.g. Micro-Dyn, WIOD) and projects for the EU Commission on issues of innovation and employment.

Thomas Scherngell

Thomas Scherngell is researcher at the Innovation Systems Department of AIT Austrian Insitute of Technology and holds a post-doc fellowship (2011-2012) at the University of Macau, China. He received a venia docendi (habilitation) in Economic Geography and Regional Science from the Vienna University of Economics and Business in 2012. He received his M.A. in Economic Geography (Mag., 2003), and his PhD (Dr. rer. Nat, 2006) from the University of Vienna. Prior to working at AIT, Thomas Scherngell was a full time university assistant at the Department of Economic Geography and GIScience at the Vienna University of Economics and Business (2002-2007). He is an expert in economics of innovation and technological change as well as in regional science and spatial analysis. Over the past five years, his research focus was on the structure and dynamics of R&D networks, with a special focus on networks constituted under the heading of the European Framework Programmes (FPs). Further he has been working extensively on spatial analysis methods, with a special emphasis on spatial econometric methods, spatial interaction modelling, Social Network Analysis (SNA) and methods from statistical physics.

Robert Stehrer

Robert Stehrer is Senior Economist and Deputy Scientific Director at the The Vienna Institute for International Economic Studies (wiiw) and lecturer in economics at the University of Vienna. He studied economics at the Johannes Kepler University Linz, Austria, where he also worked as Assistant Professor and lecturer, and Sociology at the Institute for Advanced Studies (IAS) in Vienna. He holds a Ph.D. (Dr. rer.soc.oec) in economics and the venia docendi in economics from the University of Linz. His fields of research are international economics, technical change and labour markets.

Rajnish Tiwari

Rajnish Tiwari is Senior Research Fellow and Project Leader at the Institute for Technology and Innovation Management of the Hamburg University of Technology. He studied Business Administration at University of Hamburg specializing in International Management and Business Informatics. Rajnish holds a Ph.D. (Dr. rer. Pol.) in Innovation Management from Hamburg University of Technology, where he also teaches Intercultural Communication and Management. Main fields of his research are internationalisation of research and development, emergence of lead markets in developing countries, and frugal innovations. He has also published extensively on foreign direct investments by Indian companies in Germany.

Waltraud Urban

Waltraut Urban graduated in economics at the University of Vienna in 1973. She then became a lecturer at the Institute of Economics of the Vienna University of Technology. In the late 1970s, she joined the industrial department of the Austrian Institute of Economic Research (wifo), where she got interested in the newly industrialising economies (NIEs) in Asia. With the beginning of the economic reforms and the rise of China in the 1980s, her focus of interest shifted there. After several years as a researcher at the Austrian Institute for International Affairs (oiip), she joined the Vienna Institute for International Economic Studies (wiiw) in 1995, where she specialised in the Chinese economy and industrial restructuring in the Central- and East European countries. She has specialised on macroeconomic and industrial development in China, Asian regional economic cooperation and the relation between China and the EU. In 2011, she retired from her post at wiiw and is now a freelance economist. Besides, she is fellow at the Austrian Institute for Research on China and Southeast Asia. She has taken part in many international research projects, published many articles and given numerous lectures on China, including courses at various universities.

Georg Zahradnik

Georg Zahradnik is Junior Scientist at the Innovation Systems Department of AIT Austrian Institute of Technology, Vienna. He graduated in economics at the Vienna University of Economics and Business. He is experienced in data gathering and databases, econometrics, and has worked on the internationalisation of research activities, the European ICT sector and on sectoral innovation systems in Europe. He has been involved in a number of consultancy and research projects for Austrian as well as international clients.

Acknowledgements

This book is based on the results of the study 'Internationalisation of business investments in R&D and analysis of their economic impact' commissioned by the European Commission, DG Research and Innovation, Unit C6-*Economic analysis and indicators*, headed by Mr. Pierre Vigier. The authors want to thank the staff of the European Commission for their comments and suggestions, including Benat Bilbao Osorio, Sylvia Jahn, Callum Searle, Agnieszka Skonieczna, and Lüdger Viehoff (all DG Research and Innovation), Thomas Brännström (DG Enterprise and Industry), Maria Del Sorbo, Alexander Tübke, and Peter Voigt (all DG IPTS). Special thanks go to Matthieu Delescluse, who supported the project as project officer.

Our work has also been supported by correspondents from various universities and research organisations: Brian Wixted and J. Adam Holbrook, (CPROST, Canada), Yuanjia Hu (University of Macau, China), Woosung Lee (STEPI, Korea), and Vitaly Rud (National Research University Higher School of Economics, Russia) helped us to clarify data availability for their countries. Renate Prasch (wiiw), Monika Schwarzhappel (wiiw) and Rafael Lata (AIT) helped in the data collection and data analysis.

Special thanks also goes to Matthias Weber, Head of the Business Unit Research, Technology and Innovation Policy of AIT Austrian Institute of Technology, who has generously supported the production of this book.

Finally, we want to thank the representatives of the national statistical offices who have supported data: Erich Greul and Andreas Schiefer (Statistik Austria), Roger Kalenga-Mpala and Ward Ziarko (SPP Politique scientifique / POD Wetenschapsbeleid, Belgium), Joanne Hans (Statistics Canada), Hana Peroutkova (Czech Statistical Office), Andreas Kladroba (Stifterverband für die Deutschen Wissenschaft, Germany), Marianna Édes (Hungarian Central Statistical Office), Ziv Gorodisky (Central Bureau of Statistics of Israel), Christianne Micallef (Statistical Office Malta), Miriam López Bahut (Instituto Nacional de Estadistica, Spain), Sandra Dovärn (Statistics Sweden), Elisabeth Pastor (Office fédéral de la statistique OFS Économie, État et société (SUKO), Switzerland), Isabelle Desnoyers-James (OECD), Jim Nicholls (Office for National Statistics, United Kingdom). We also acknowledge the support by EUROSTAT, in particular by Szymon Bielecki, Sergiu-Valentin Parvan, Reni Petkova, Veijo-Ismo Ritola, and Manfred Schmiemann.

Abbreviations

BERD	Business enterprise research and development
CMEA	Council for Mutual Economic Assistance
EC	European Commission
ERP	Enterprise Resource Planning
EU	European Union
EU-12	Bulgaria, Cyprus, Czech Republic, Estonia, Latvia, Lithuania, Hungary, Malta, Poland, Romania, Slovenia and Slovakia
EU-15	Austria, Belgium, Denmark, Finland, Germany, Greece, France, Ireland, Italy, Luxembourg, Netherlands, Portugal, Spain, Sweden and the United Kingdom
EU-25	EU-27 countries excluding Bulgaria and Romania
EU-27	EU-12 and EU-15 countries
EUROSTAT	Statistical office of the European Union
FATS	Foreign Affiliates Statistics
FDI	Foreign direct investment
GBAORD	Government budgetary appropriations or outlays for R&D
GDP	Gross Domestic Product
GERD	Gross domestic expenditure on R&D
ICT	Information and communications technology
IT	Information technology
ITDH	Hungarian Investment and Trade Development Agency
JV	Joint venture
KIBS	Knowledge intensive business services
KIS	Knowledge intensive services
LKIS	Less knowledge intensive services
M&A	Mergers and acquisitions

MAJÁK	Hungarian Vehicle Development Cluster
MNC	Multinational Corporation
MNE	Multinational Enterprise
MOST	Ministry of Science and Technology
NACE	Statistical Classification of Economic Activities in the European Community
NAFTA	North American Free Trade Agreement
NBS	National Bureau of Statistics
NOHAC	North Hungarian Automotive Cluster
OECD	Organisation for Economic Co-operation and Development
OECD AFA	OECD Activities of Foreign Affiliates
OECD IDI	OECD International Direct Investment Statistics
OECD NESTI	OECD Working Party of National Experts on Science and Technology Indicators
OECD STAN	OECD Structural Analysis Database
OEM	Original equipment manufacturer
PANAC	Pannon Automotive Cluster
PPS	Purchasing Power Standard
R&D	Research and development
RETC	Renewable Energy Technology Center
RTR	Renault Technology Romania
SCADA	Supervisory Control and Data Acquisition
STI	Science, technology and innovation
OECD TIP	OECD Working Party on Innovation and Technology Policy
UCI	Ultimate controlling institutional unit
ULC	Unit labour costs
UNCTAD	United Nations Conference on Trade and Development
USD	United States dollar
VA	Value added
WDI	World Development Indicators
WEF	World Economic Forum
WTO	World Trade Organisation

1. Introduction

Bernhard Dachs, Robert Stehrer and Georg Zahradnik

THE TOPIC

In a seminal paper on research and development (R&D) in large multinational enterprises (MNEs), Pari Patel and Keith Pavitt concluded in 1991 that the production of technology remains 'far from globalized', but concentrated in the home countries of the enterprises (Patel and Pavitt 1991, p 17). In their words, research and development is 'an important case of non-globalisation'. Patel and Pavitt argued that the technological performance of large firms is inextricably connected with and strongly dependent on the scientific and technological capabilities of universities and other firms in the home country.

About 20 years later, a vast amount of evidence draws a different picture of R&D internationalisation: Enterprises not only produce and sell, but increasingly also develop goods and services outside their home countries, a development that became known as the internationalisation of business R&D in the literature (OECD 2008; Dunning and Lundan 2009; Hall 2010).

Today, it seems to be the rule, rather than the exception, that large European firms perform R&D activities at different locations inside and outside the Single Market. Alike, MNEs from the United States have considerably extended their R&D activities in the European Union, and new players from emerging economies are entering the scene: Brazil, the People's Republic of China (referred to as China in the book), India and other emerging economies have come into focus as host countries for R&D activities of US and European MNEs in recent years.

AIM AND APPROACH OF THIS BOOK

This book presents a comprehensive picture of the current state of the internationalisation of R&D in the business sector. Internationalisation of R&D at universities or public research centres as well as changes in the international mobility of students and researchers are left out. Moreover, there is no discussion of policy issues related to R&D internationalisation in this book. Excellent contributions on this topic are provided by Archibugi and Iammarino (1999), UNCTAD (2005), the CREST Working Group (2007), or De Backer and Hatem (2010). Recent surveys of policy initiatives in this field can be found in TAFTIE (2009), Verbeek et al. (2009), and Schwaag Serger and Wise (2010).

The various chapters describe the main patterns in R&D internationalisation across countries and sectors, examine the drivers of the process, and reveal impacts of R&D internationalisation on home and host countries applying both qualitative and quantitative analysis. Complementary case studies give further insights into the process of R&D internationalisation at country and sectoral level pointing towards heterogenous patterns and differences with respect to drivers and impacts.

The book is based on the results of the project 'Internationalisation of business investments in R&D and analysis of their economic impact' funded by the European Commission, DG Research and Innovation, over the period 2010-2012 (Contract No. RTD/DirC/C3/2010/SI2.561034). The aim of this project was to build a new and comprehensive database of bilateral data on trans-border R&D expenditure collected from EUROSTAT, the OECD, and national statistics and the analysis of this data. The European Commission has kindly agreed to the publication of the results of this project in this book.

OUTLINE OF THE BOOK

The book starts with a discussion of the motives of firms to locate R&D activities abroad by Bernhard Dachs in Chapter 2. These motives turn out to be diverse, determined by host and home country conditions, specific firm strategies as well as the complexity of many new technologies. Internationalisation is, on the one hand, driven by the aim of multinational firms to exploit their market potential with respect to technologies and products in foreign markets. R&D labs abroad help adapt these technologies and products to host country conditions. On the other hand, firms increasingly also perform more basic R&D abroad, harnessing more beneficial and conducive conditions for R&D in a particular location like the availability of R&D staff, or proximity to universities and firms with superior expertise in a particular field.

Despite the increasing importance of R&D internationalisation, data on the process is still incomplete, inconsistent and therefore sometimes difficult to interpret. In Chapter 3, Georg Zahradnik and Waltraut Urban discuss the most important issues concerning data availability, data quality and problems in international comparability. In a case study, the authors look at data on R&D activities of foreign-owend firms in China for which the data collection ·and analysis requires particularly careful interpretation.

The term 'internationalisation' suggests a trend that encompasses the whole world. However, despite this notion, R&D internationalisation still predominantly takes place between high-income countries and in high-technology sectors. Georg Zahradnik gives an overview of the current state of R&D internationalisation in Chapter 4. Around half of total non-domestic R&D expenditure of European firms is located within Europe, mostly in neigbouring countries. In a global perspective, the United States and the European Union are the two most host important regions in terms of R&D expenditure of foreign-owned firms by far.

However, there is also evidence that R&D internationalisation became more 'global' in recent years, as concentration in terms of locations has decreased and the number of countries and sectors involved in R&D internationalisation has increased. Small European countries and Asian countries benefited from this trend in particular. In Chapter 5, Sandra Leitner, Franziska Kampik and Georg Zahradnik provide supportive evidence for these trends for various countries. Trends at the sectoral level – such as the rising degree of R&D internationalisation in services – are investiged by Georg Zahradnik in Chapter 6. The specific role of the European Union and the United States in the internationalisation of R&D is investigated by Bernhard Dachs in Chapter 7. The internationalisation of R&D creates relationships between countries, which can be investigated with the tools of social network analysis. Thomas Scherngell provides such an analysis in Chapter 8.

Chapters 9 to 12 look at the drivers and impacts of R&D internationalisation. In the econometric analysis of Chapter 9, Sandra Leitner and Robert Stehrer identify country size, quality and size of the workforce and sector level variables such as foreign direct investment (FDI) and domestic R&D intensity as the main determinants of inward business enterprise R&D (BERD) at country level. In addition, case study evidence points to the existence of a number of drivers which seem to be specific to bilateral relations between countries, sectoral characteristics and even specific to individual firm strategies – such as foreign take-overs, long-term specialisation patterns of countries, or agglomeration effects. As an example, Bernhard Dachs and Doris Hanzl present evidence for such drivers from the automotive industry and knowledge-intensive business services in Chapter 10.

The internationalisation of R&D gained a lot of attention in economic policy discussions in recent years, fuelled by fears of the negative consequences of 'R&D offshoring' on domestic R&D efforts and capabilities. Sandra Leitner and Robert Stehrer investigate these and other potential impacts of R&D internationalisation on the home countries in Chapter 11, generally pointing towards mutually beneficial effects of R&D internationalisation. The empirical evidence suggests that policy makers need not be too worried: econometric evidence suggests that R&D expenditure and labour productivity of foreign affiliates is positively related to labour productivity of domestic firms which indicates spillovers between the two groups. Moreover, the results of Chapter 11 indicate that R&D activities of domestic firms abroad are not subsituting similar activities at home.

With respect to impacts, Rajnish Tiwari presents the case of R&D activities of German firms in India and investigates how these activities are connected to R&D in Germany (Chapter 12). The second part of this contribution takes the opposite perspective and discusses R&D activities of Indian firms in Germany and their role in the R&D strategies of their parent companies.

In the final chapter of the book, Bernhard Dachs asks in which way the global financial crisis of 2008/09 has shaped the internationalisation of R&D. Though evidence is still scarce, it seems that the crisis has slowed down R&D internationalisation, but has not changed the main trends of the process.

REFERENCES

Archibugi, D. and S. Iammarino (1999), 'The policy implications of the globalisation of innovation', *Research Policy* **28**(2-3), 317-36.

CREST Working Group (2007), *Internationalisation of R&D – Facing the challenge of globalisation: approaches to a proactive international policy in S&T*, Brussles.

De Backer, K. and F. Hatem (2010), *Attractiveness for innovation. Location factors for international investment*, Paris: OECD.

Dunning, J., and S. M. Lundan (2009), 'The Internationalization of Corporate R&D: A Review of the Evidence and Some Policy Implications for Home Countries', *Review of Policy Research* **26**(1-2), 13-33.

Hall, B. A. (2010), 'The internationalization of R&D', Maastricht: UNU-MERIT Working Paper Series 2010-049.

OECD (2008), *The Internationalisation of Business R&D: Evidence, Impacts and Implications*. Paris: OECD.

Patel, P., and K. Pavitt (1991), 'Large Firms in the Production of the World's Technology: An Important Case of "Non-Globalisation"', *Journal of International Business Studies* **22**(1), 1-22.

Schwaag Serger, S. and E. Wise (2010), 'Internationalization of Research and Innovation – new policy developments', paper presented at the 2010 Concord Conference, Seville.

TAFTIE (2009), *Internationalisation of National Innovation Agencies*, Stockholm: VINNOVA.

UNCTAD (2005), *World Investment Report 2005: Transnational Corporations and the Internationalization of R&D*, New York and Geneva: United Nations.

Verbeek, A., Shapira, P., Edler, J., Gagliardi, D., Lykogianni, E. and M. Knell (2009), *RINDICATE. Analysis of R&D international funding flows and their impact on the research system in selected Member States*, Brussels: Report for the European Commission, DG Research.

2. Internationalisation of R&D: A Brief Survey of the Literature

Bernhard Dachs

This chapter gives an overview on the key findings of the literature on the internationalisation of R&D. I focus on three issues: first, the drivers of the process – why firms go abroad with R&D activities. Second, the effects of the internationalisation of R&D on the host countries. Third, the impacts of R&D internationalisation on the home countries of multinational firms.

This survey has two important limitations: first it will only include the literature on the internationalisation of R&D in firms, and leave internationalisation in higher education or public research centres aside. Second, the literature on foreign direct investment (FDI) and multinational enterprises is only covered if it relates to R&D. Internationalisation refers to the internationalisation of business R&D through the remainder of this chapter, unless otherwise stated.

The oldest literature on the internationalisation of R&D dates back to the end of the 1960s and the beginning of the 1970s (e. g. Dunning 1958; Brash 1966; Safarian 1966). Only few articles and surveys emerged in the 1970s (examples are Creamer 1976; Ronstadt 1977; Lall 1979) and in the 1980s and early 1990s (Behrman and Fischer 1980, Cantwell 1989, Pearce 1992). Since the year 2000, a growing body of literature provides evidence that the internationalisation of R&D is gaining momentum (OECD 2005; UNCTAD 2005; Hatzichronoglou 2008; OECD 2008a; OECD 2008b; OECD 2008c; OECD 2010). This literature is accompanied by a number of international comparisons of policies towards R&D internationalisation (CREST Working Group 2007, OECD 2008a, TAFTIE 2009, Schwaag Serger and Wise 2010).

DRIVERS OF R&D INTERNATIONALISATION

The benefits and costs associated with the internationalisation of R&D vary between firms, industries, regions or countries. It is therefore important to distinguish between these three levels. I start with a discussion of the drivers at the regional and country level and then go to the sectoral and firm level.

Drivers at the regional and country level

The host country or host region shapes the internationalisation decisions of firms by providing different framework conditions for R&D. Drivers at the regional or country level are also important from a policy perspective, because they give room for policy intervention to increase the locational advantages of regions or countries.

A first important regional or country level driver is income and market size. Income is an important driver, because high income and high income growth attracts FDI (Ekholm and Midelfart 2004; Blonigen 2005; Jensen 2006). R&D investments often follow FDI, and overseas R&D activities are, in most cases, an extension of existing overseas production and marketing activities (Birkinshaw and Hood 1998; Birkinshaw et al. 1998; Archibugi and Iammarino 1999). Moreover, firms may find it easier to cover the cost of R&D in a country with a large market where they expect larger absolute revenues than in a country with a small domestic market, even if wages are considerably lower.

Another important attractor of R&D of MNEs is a skilled workforce and the quality of the education system. In turn, skills shortage and a growing demand for engineers and scientists in the home country is often a motive for firms to go abroad with R&D. In a survey of multinational firms, Thursby and Thursby (2006) find that highly qualified R&D personnel is the most important driver for location decisions in R&D. Ernst (2006) relates the success of India and other Asian countries in attracting R&D of foreign MNEs to their expanding pool of graduates in science and technology. Hedge and Hicks (2008) demonstrate that the innovation activities of overseas US subsidiaries are strongly related to the scientific and engineering capabilities of the host countries. Kinkel and Maloca (2008) find that capacity bottlenecks are the most frequent reason why German firms move R&D to locations abroad. In the research of Lewin et al. (2009), an emerging shortage of high skilled science and engineering talent partially explains the relocation of product development from the United States to other parts of the world, most notably to Asian countries.

Potential knowledge spillovers between foreign-owned firms and host country organisations are another driver for R&D internationalisation. A discussion of spillovers is found in the second half of this chapter. Spillovers as a determinant for R&D location decisions point to the importance of the quality of university research as a driver of R&D internationalisation at the country level (Belderbos et al. 2009). Knowledge spillovers may be even more relevant at the regional than at the country level, because spillovers diminish with distance between sender and receiver (Jaffe et al. 1993; Breschi and Lissoni 2001). As a consequence, firms which want to utilize such localised knowledge spillovers have to be present where they occur, and innovative activity tends to cluster locally in industries with a high level of spillovers (Audretsch and Feldman 1996). This effect is related to institutional or technological conditions, such as tacitness of the knowledge base, but also to the existence of specialised local or regional labour markets (see the survey of Breschi and Lissoni 2001).

Differences in labour cost between the home country and locations abroad are one of the most important motives for the internationalisation of production. Empirical evidence that differences in the cost of R&D personnel are a major driver for the internationalisation of R&D, however, is weak; survey results as well as econometric studies see only a modest influence of wage differences in R&D location decisions compared to other factors (Booz Allen Hamilton and INSEAD 2006; Thursby and Thursby 2006; Kinkel and Maloca 2008; Belderbos et al. 2009). However, cost differences may become important when firms can choose between two locations that are similar in many other locational factors (Booz Allen Hamilton and INSEAD 2006; Thursby and Thursby 2006; Cincera et al. 2010).

Previous research has also pointed out that geographical proximity between host and home country leads to higher levels of cross-border R&D investments (Guellec and van Pottelsberghe de la Potterie 2001; Dachs and Pyka 2010). This distance effect is often explained by additional co-ordination cost, the cost of transferring knowledge over distance, and a loss of economies of scale and scope when R&D becomes more decentralised (von Zedtwitz and Gassmann 2002; Sanna-Randaccio and Veugelers 2007; Gersbach and Schmutzler 2011). In addition, the distance effect may also be explained by cultural, social and institutional factors. The international management literature stresses that foreign-owned firms have to master additional institutional and cultural barriers in their host countries. This disadvantage is known as the 'liability of foreignness' (Zaheer 1995; Eden and Miller 2004) or the 'liability of outsidership' (Johanson and Vahlne 2009) in the literature. Foreign-owned firms may suffer from a lack of market knowledge and understanding of customer demands, but also a lower degree of embeddedness in informal networks in the host country (see also Lööf 2009). Disadvantages from the liability of foreignness tend to decrease over time, but may even exist in long-established affiliates with a local management and staff, because the affiliate is embedded in intra-firm networks and have to stick to the rules, norms and standards of the multinational group.

The role of policy for R&D location decisions of MNEs has been investigated by a number of empirical studies (Cantwell and Mudambi 2000; Kumar 2001; Cantwell and Piscitello 2002; Thursby and Thursby 2006; Kinkel and Maloca 2008; De Backer and Hatem 2010). Two findings on the role of policy in R&D internationalisation find a wide consensus in the literature: first, special financial incentives and a positive discrimination of foreign-owned firms in general are not regarded as an appropriate instrument to attract foreign R&D. This does not mean that science, technology and innovation policy has no role in attracting foreign R&D. Measures to improve university education or to foster co-operation between firms and universities can considerably shape the attractiveness of locations by improving the capabilities of the national innovation systems and leveraging R&D efforts of firms. These measures, however, should be open to every firm, domestically or foreign-owned. Second, governments that want to attract R&D of foreign multinational firms should instead focus on the economic fundamentals and provide political stability, good public infrastructure, reasonable tax rates, and a stable legal system including the protection of intellectual property rights. This reflects the fact that the location of R&D often depends on the location of production, sales or other business functions of the firm.

Drivers at the sectoral level

A second important level for the analysis of drivers is the sector of the firm. Sectors matter in two ways: on the one hand, there are large differences between sectors in terms of foreign direct investment, and sectors with high shares of inward FDI also tend to be technologically intensive (Markusen 1995, p. 172). Hence, R&D internationalisation can mainly be observed in R&D or knowledge-intensive sectors. On the other hand, sectors matter because innovation processes differ considerably across sectors (Marsili 2001; Malerba 2005; Castellacci 2007, Peneder 2010). These intersectoral differences shape innovation behaviour of firms to a considerable degree, including decisions to locate R&D abroad, leading to different degrees of internationalisation at the sectoral level.

A first important determinant at the industry level is the degree of tacitness of the knowledge base of a sector. Tacitness results from the fact that cognitive capabilities and abstract concepts are not easy to articulate explicitly and to transfer between people (Cowan et al. 2000). A knowledge base which is highly tacit and bound to individuals may be an obstacle to internationalisation, because it makes knowledge exchange over distance costly. Tacitness, however, may also be a driver for internationalisation, because firms have to move to the place where this knowledge is available when it cannot be transferred over distance.

Second, sectoral knowledge bases also differ in their degree of cumulativeness, or, in other words, in the degree future innovation success depends on the knowledge which has been built up in the past (Marsili 2001). Cumulativeness is high in chemicals, pharmaceuticals, telecommunications and electronics, but low in mechanical engineering, food, clothing, or civil engineering (Malerba and Orsenigo 1996; Marsili 2001). A high degree of cumulativeness may require a high degree of specialisation in R&D, which gives advantages to centralised R&D. Cumulativeness may also promote R&D centralisation when strong learning effects lead to increasing returns to scale in R&D, or when the R&D process includes economies of scope and effects from cross-fertilisation. Moreover, cumulativeness of the knowledge base may also imply that R&D activities require a certain minimum scale in order to be successful.

Third, sectors also differ in terms of appropriability, the degree to which an innovation can be protected from imitation (Cohen et al. 2000; Cohen 2010). Firms in sectors with a low degree of appropriability, like many service sectors, may be reluctant to internationalise R&D because they have only weak means to prevent involuntary knowledge spillovers.

Fourth, another source for inter-sectoral differences is the firm's network of external relations with suppliers, clients, universities, public administration, etc. (Marsili 2001; Malerba 2002). Some industries, such as biotechnology or pharmaceuticals, have strong linkages to basic science, and firms in these industries may find it useful to locate R&D close to excellent research universities. Firms in other sectors, such as the automotive of the electronics industry, are closely connected to suppliers and customers through international production networks. Suppliers in these sectors may be forced to internationalise their R&D to have development capabilities in proximity to key clients. The existence of lead users or other potential co-operation partners may also pose a strong incentive to locate R&D in a particular country.

Drivers at the firm level

The third relevant level for the explanation of overall patterns of R&D internationalisation is the firm level. Internationalisation paths of two firms can be completely different – even if they are located in the same region and operate in the same industry – because firms differ in their firm characteristics (for example, size, international experience), the costs that arise for them from internationalisation, and the benefits from internationalisation and resulting motives and strategies. The interplay of these three factors, together with framework conditions from the country, regional and sectoral level, determines the degree of R&D internationalisation of firms.

Internationalisation decisions in R&D are closely connected with internationalisation decisions in production or sales for two reasons. First, internationalisation in production can be a result of superior, firm-specific assets. Firms internationalise, because they want to exploit these assets at foreign markets via their subsidiaries (Dunning 1973; Markusen 1995; Caves 1996 (1974); Markusen 2002). Dunning (1973; 1981) suggests that firms exploit these assets via FDI and not via exports or licensing because of ownership, location and internalisation advantages associated with this mode of exploitation. Thus, firm heterogeneity leads to self-selection in the internationalisation strategies of firms (Head and Ries 2003; Helpman et al. 2004; Helpman 2006). Only the most productive (and thus innovation intensive) firms expand their operations via FDI, while less productive firms choose to export or serve only domestic markets. In addition, there is also evidence for a positive relationship between innovation and exports at the firm level (Greenhalgh and Taylor 1990; Lachenmaier and Wößmann 2006; Harris and Li 2009).

Second, there is a mutual relationship between innovation and internation-al expansion because they are both driven by the same determinants. Firm characteristics that are positively related to R&D and R&D intensity drive internationalisation as well (Arvanitis and Hollenstein 2006, Cerrato 2009). Dogson and Rothwell (1994), Cohen (1995, 2010), Kleinknecht and Mohnen (2002) or the OECD (2009) have examined the determinants of R&D and innovation in detail. R&D and R&D intensity is, at first, associated with firm size. There are different advantages and disadvantages of small and large firms in the innovation process, leading to a U-shaped relationship between size and R&D (Kleinknecht 1989; Cohen 1995). Regression analysis also finds a significant and positive association between firm size and the interna-tionalisation of R&D or innovation activities (Arvanitis and Hollenstein 2006; Kinkel and Maloca 2008; Schmiele 2012). Innovativeness and R&D is also positively related to the internal knowledge and capabilities of the firm (Cohen and Levinthal 1989 and 1990; Teece et al. 1997). These capabilities enable the firm to create new knowledge, but also absorb knowledge from external sources.

Besides firm characteristics, another source of firm heterogeneity in the internationalisation of R&D are the costs of a decentralised organisation of R&D (Sanna-Randaccio and Veugelers 2007; Gersbach and Schmutzler 2011). These costs first comprise the foregone benefits of R&D centralisa-tion, including economies of scale and scope from specialisation, or a tighter control over core technologies of the firm. Second, additional costs also arise from higher co-ordination efforts and the cost of transferring knowledge within the MNE. Proximity also facilitates co-ordination of R&D and innova-tion activities with other parts of the firm, such as production and marketing, and mutual learning between these parts (Ketokivi and Ali-Yrkkö 2009). Third, a concentration of R&D activity in the home country is also favoured by various linkages between the firm and the host country innovation system. Patel and Pavitt (1999) or Narula (2002) point out that firms are strongly embedded in and dependent on their home country innovation system. The ties that bind firms to their home country include relations with other organi-sations in the innovation system such as formal R&D co-operations with domestic universities, but also informal networks that grew from doing busi-ness together in the past. Informal networks between firms may also evolve from joint training of staff at universities and labour mobility. Removing these linkages by moving R&D abroad would incur considerable costs on the firms, because they would need to re-install similar linkages with host coun-try organisations.

Finally, firm characteristics and the costs of R&D internationalisation have to be seen alongside the benefits of R&D internationalisation and the resulting strategies of the firms. A first benefit is that R&D can support over-seas production. Products and technologies often have to be adapted to consumer preferences, regulation, or environmental conditions of foreign markets in order to facilitate their exploitation in these markets. These adaptations can be done more easily in proximity to potential clients in the host countries. MNEs therefore locate design, engineering and R&D units in main foreign markets to support marketing and production facilities abroad. There are various names for this motive in the literature, including asset-exploiting behaviour (Dunning and Narula 1995), competence-exploiting subsidiary mandates (Cantwell and Mudambi 2005), home-base exploiting strategies (Kuemmerle 1999), or market-driven internationalisation of R&D (von Zedtwitz and Gassmann 2002).

A second benefit and important driver of R&D internationalisation at the firm level is access to knowledge and the creation of new knowledge abroad. This motive is known as the asset-seeking motive (Dunning and Narula 1995), competence-creating subsidiary mandate (Cantwell and Mudambi 2005), home-base augmenting strategy (Kuemmerle 1999), or global R&D strategy (von Zedtwitz and Gassmann 2002) in the literature.

Asset-seeking strategies are driven, on the one hand, by the existence of superior local knowledge and favourable framework conditions for R&D in various host countries. Some types of knowledge are tacit, bound to their local context, and transferable over distance only at high costs (Cowan et al. 2000; Breschi and Lissoni 2001). This knowledge may be found at universities and other research organisations, in clusters, or be available from clients, suppliers or competitors. Various authors describe foreign-owned subsidiaries as 'surveillance outposts' or 'antennas' (Florida 1997; Almeida 1999) that extensively monitor and assimilate knowledge from local sources. On the other hand, asset-seeking strategies may also be driven by factors related to the nature of various technologies and changing firm strategies. Narula and Zanfei (2005) for example, suggest that the increasing complexity of products is a driver of the internationalisation of R&D. Rising technological complexity increases the knowledge requirements of firms and forces them to search for new knowledge abroad. A similar argument is brought forward by Chesbrough (2003). He points out that many innovative firms have moved to an 'open innovation' model where they exploit ideas and knowledge not only provided by internal R&D, but also from a broad range of external sources and actors. In this respect, asset-seeking can be seen as a variant of 'open innovation' strategies with a focus on their geographical dimension.

There is evidence that asset-seeking strategies have become more frequent in the recent years, although asset-exploiting strategies still prevail (Narula and Zanfei 2005; Sachwald 2008). Moreover, some authors (for example Criscuolo et al. 2005) stress the fact that the two motives cannot be separated in a number of cases. Firms – intentionally or unintentionally – often follow both strategies simultaneously. Microsoft's efforts to adapt their products to the Chinese language resulted in new knowledge that could also be used in other contexts (Gassmann and Han 2004).

Finally, an important aspect of firm strategy towards R&D internationalisation is the degree of decentralisation. In order to make internationalisation of R&D possible, the head office of the MNE has to allow a higher degree of decentralisation by changing firm organisation and giving a higher degree of autonomy to the subsidiaries (Birkinshaw and Hood 1998; Birkinshaw et al. 1998; Zanfei 2000).

IMPACTS OF MNE R&D ACTIVITIES ON HOST AND HOME COUNTRIES

The technological and economic characteristics of countries provide different locational advantages and disadvantages for foreign-owned firms to set up R&D activities. However, R&D activities of MNE affiliates may also influence the innovation systems of their host and home countries to a considerable degree. The literature has identified various potential challenges and opportunities for host and home countries from the internationalisation of R&D and innovation (see Table 2.1).

Impacts of MNE R&D and innovation activities on host countries

I first discuss the perspective of the host country (the two upper segments of Table 2.1). The presence of MNE affiliates in a country can considerably raise aggregate R&D expenditure of this country over the short and medium term. Multinational firms spend huge amounts on R&D, even compared with aggregate R&D expenditure of countries (OECD 2010, p. 121). A new R&D venture of an MNE may therefore considerably affect aggregate R&D activity of the host country. MNE affiliates – in contrast to domestically owned firms – can also access financial means of their parent enterprise abroad; expansion of R&D activity is therefore not limited by a lack of internal resources or incomplete credit markets in the host country. Moreover, the threat of market entry by R&D intensive MNEs may also spur R&D activities of domestically owned firms (Aghion et al. 2009). Empirical evidence suggests that small countries benefit most in relative terms because they usually exhibit higher degrees of internationalisation in FDI than large countries (Lonmo and Anderson 2003; Costa and Filippov 2008).

A second benefit for the host country is the diffusion of information and knowledge (knowledge spillovers[1]) to host country organisations. Potential receivers of this knowledge are domestic firms, universities, or research centres. The literature gives considerable attention to knowledge diffusion and spillovers by foreign-owned firms (see the surveys by Keller (2004, 2010) or Mayer and Sinani (2009)). According to Blomström and Kokko (2003), spillovers are the strongest argument as to why countries should try to attract inward investment. Empirical evidence on the size and the effects of spillovers, however, is mixed. Meta-studies (Görg and Strobl 2001, Görg and Greenaway 2004; Mayer and Sinani 2009; Havránek and Iršová 2010) show no clear relationship between foreign presence and the performance of domestically owned firms. Görg and Strobl (2001) for example indicate that the number of studies that identify positive spillovers roughly equals those identifying no effects or even negative consequences from the presence of foreign-owned firms. In the majority of cases considered by Görg and Greenaway (2004), no significant effect of MNE presence on domestic firm productivity is observed. Veugelers (2005, p 37) finds that it is 'fair to conclude that the results on positive spillovers on host economies are not strong and robust'. Empirical evidence is clearer below the aggregate level. Recent contributions by Singh (2007), Keller and Yeaple (2009) and by Coe et al. (2009) reveal substantial spillover effects from foreign R&D stocks and the presence of foreign-owned firms at the sectoral level.

Table 2.1 Potential opportunities and challenges for national innovation systems from the internationalisation of R&D and innovation

	Opportunities	Challenges and Risks
Host country	Increases in aggregate R&D and innovation expenditure	Competition with domestically owned firms for resources
	Knowledge diffusion to the host economy	Loss of control over domestic innovation capacity
	Demand for skilled personnel	Less strategic research, less radical innovations, more adapting
	Structural change and agglomeration effects	Separation of R&D and production
Home Country	Improved overall R&D efficiency	Loss of jobs due to relocation
	Reverse technology transfer	'Hollowing out' of domestic R&D and innovation activities
	Market expansion effects	
	Exploitation of foreign knowledge at home	Technology leakage and involuntary knowledge diffusion

Source: Adapted from Sheehan (2004), UNCTAD (2005), Veugelers (2005).

A main reason for this vagueness of the results, besides measurement issues, is the fact that spillovers from foreign-owned firms to the local economy are bound to specific industry and economy-wide conditions to occur. These factors include a certain level of absorptive capacity (Cohen and Levinthal 1989, 1990; Cantner and Pyka 1998) of domestic organisations; weak instruments of foreign-owned firms to protect proprietary knowledge, which is mostly sector-specific; and the propensity of the transfer channel or type of interaction between foreign-owned firms and domestic organisations (Veugelers and Cassiman 2004).

R&D activities of foreign-owned firms in a particular country may also help to enhance the level and quality of human resources. New R&D labs by MNEs may create additional demand for researchers and give incentives to governments to improve higher education systems. MNEs are attractive employers, because they can offer international career perspectives and pay higher wages than domestically owned enterprises (Lipsey 2002; Bailey and Driffield 2007). Moreover, jobs created by foreign-owned firms appear to be more persistent than jobs generated in domestically owned plants (Görg and Strobl 2003).

Finally, foreign-owned firms can also contribute to structural change towards a higher share of technology-intensive firms and to the emergence of clusters in the host country. Structural change is related in two ways to the presence of foreign-owned firms. On the one hand, foreign-owned firms operate predominantly in technology-intensive industries. Market entrance and subsequent growth of the foreign-owned firm will therefore move the industrial structure of a country towards higher technology intensity. There is also evidence that FDI contributes to a shift in labour demand towards skilled labour in the host country (Blonigen and Slaughter 2001; Driffield et al. 2009). On the other hand, MNE subsidiaries trigger structural change because their demand for inputs favours the growth of technology-intensive suppliers in the host country. This demand may lead to the emergence of clusters and other agglomerations at the regional level in the host country (Young et al. 1994; Bellandi 2001; Pavlínek 2004). Foreign-owned subsidiaries in clusters are often strongly embedded locally, but also internationally-oriented and can therefore act as bridges for knowledge transfer between domestic organisations and abroad (Birkinshaw and Hood 2000; Lorenzen and Mahnke 2002).

I now turn to potential challenges for host countries that emerge from the presence of foreign-owned firms. One striking aspect of the literature on FDI spillovers is the number of studies that report negative effects (see, for example, Aitken and Harrison 1999; Konings 2001; Castellani and Zanfei 2002; Damijan et al. 2003; Marin and Sasidharan 2010). These negative spillovers are predominantly found in developing or transition economies. Wang (2010), for example, investigates the determinants of R&D investment at the national level for 26 OECD countries from 1996-2006 and finds that foreign technology inflows through trade and FDI had a robust and negative impact on domestic R&D. We may explain these negative impacts by increased competition in product and factor markets due to foreign presence (Aitken and Harrison 1999; Konings 2001). In the context of R&D, competition for personnel (Figini and Görg 1999; Driffield and Taylor 2000) seems to be relevant in particular. Additional demand by MNEs for skilled personnel is beneficial for the host country in the short run when there are unemployed scientists, engineers and technicians and alternative employment opportunities – for example at domestic universities – are scarce. However, it may have negative consequences for the host country when the supply for research personnel is inelastic and foreign-owned firms and domestic organisations compete for qualified staff. In the long run, the effects of the demand by foreign-owned firms on the labour market for R&D staff look more positive. Stronger demand for high-skilled labour due to market entry of foreign-owned firms and structural change may foster academic training and increase the number of graduates in science and technology in the long run. A higher skill intensity in the economy, in turn, may foster locational advantages and further increase the attractiveness of the country for inward investment. Barry (2004) illustrates such a 'virtuous circle' for the case of Ireland.

Fears that a high share of foreign-owned firms on aggregate R&D expenditure may lead to negative effects are also nurtured by more general concerns against MNE presence (see Barba Navaretti and Venables 2004; Jensen 2006; Forsgren 2008 for a summary of this discussion). This is less an academic and more a general policy discussion, so there are only very few academic papers that investigate these issues. These concerns include: the assumption that the internationalisation of R&D leads to a loss of control over domestic innovation capacity, because decisions on R&D of foreign-owned firms may not be taken by the subsidiaries themselves, but by corporate headquarters abroad; the assumption that MNEs are more 'footloose' than domestically owned firms, because they mainly pursue economic activities that can be easily transferred between countries; the assumption that foreign-owned enterprises act in ways that are not in accordance with the national interest; the assumption that an important motive for R&D internationalisation is rent-seeking in selecting locations. Another concern against foreign ownership is that R&D of foreign-owned firms is associated with a higher degree of adaptation and less basic, strategic research, because MNEs often concentrate strategic, long-term R&D in the home country; rising shares of foreign ownership on aggregate innovation activity may therefore lead to fewer radical innovations than in the case of domestic ownership.

Empirical evidence that supports these concerns is thin. Internationalisation certainly leads to a shift of control from domestic head offices to MNE headquarters abroad. However, domestic policy does not necessarily have a higher ability to influence R&D decisions when enterprises are domestically owned (Dunning and Lundan 2008, p. 249 ff). In addition, it seems that autonomy of MNE subsidiaries over their R&D activities has been rising over time (Dunning and Lundan 2009, chapter 8). The question if foreign ownership is associated with a downsizing of R&D activity has been evaluated both for take-overs as well as for all foreign-owned and domestically owned firms. In the case of take-overs, there are both, examples of downsizing as well as examples of expansion, depending on the complementarity between acquiring and acquired firms and other factors (Cassiman et al. 2005; Bertrand 2009; Bandick et al. 2010; Stiebale and Reize 2011). Studies that compare innovation input and output of domestically owned and foreign-owned firms find no negative effect of foreign ownership after controlling for firm characteristics such as size, sector, or export intensity (Sadowski and Sadowski-Rasters 2006, Dachs et al. 2010).

R&D internationalisation may also be associated with a separation of R&D and production (Pearce 2004; Pearce and Papanastassiou 2009). MNEs have various choices in the location and organisation of R&D and production which mono-national firms do not have. Research, development and production is not necessarily located in the same country, because MNEs may find it useful to develop products in one country and manufacture in another country where conditions for production seem more favourable. As a consequence, policy measures to promote R&D and product development may yield only few jobs and give only a weak stimulus to growth, when foreign-owned firms decide to produce abroad. To my knowledge, no empirical study has thoroughly examined the effects from the separation of R&D and production so far. It is, however, plausible that such a leaking-out may be stronger in small countries and in countries with a high share of foreign-controlled R&D, and weaker or even reverse when foreign-owned firms have a high degree of autonomy and strong mandates in their enterprise groups, because these firms may try to concentrate not only R&D, but also production at their location to maximise influence in their enterprise goup. The effect may level out when studied at the EU instead of the national level.

Impacts of R&D and innovation activities abroad on the home countries

The internationalisation of R&D has also implications for the home country of the multinational firm. Before I briefly discuss home country effects of R&D internationalisation, one remark is important. As Kokko (2006) points out, the decision to engage in activities abroad is a voluntary decision; thus, it can be assumed that overseas activities benefit the MNE in general.

As discussed above, a main reason for firms to go abroad with R&D activities is to get access to knowledge not available in the home country. Hence, a first main benefit for the home countries is the transfer of results from overseas R&D activities which brings new knowledge into the home country. Various studies provide evidence for such reverse knowledge transfers (Fors 1997; Feinberg and Gupta 2004; Todo and Shimizutani 2005; Ambos and Schlegelmilch 2006; Piscitello and Rabbiosi 2006; Narula and Michel 2009; Rabbiosi 2009; AlAzzawi 2011). Reverse knowledge transfer can increase overall technological capacities, help to develop new products and foster growth and employment in the home country. R&D activities abroad can therefore strengthen the growth of the parent company in the home country (Rammer and Schmiele 2008). The size of these benefits depends on the absorptive capacities and other firm characteristics of the parent company (Schmiele 2012), on the degree of complementarity between activities abroad and at home (Arvanitis and Hollenstein 2011), and on the motives for R&D

activities abroad. Todo and Shimizutani (2005) demonstrate for Japan that effects of reverse technology transfer on the productivity of firms in the home country is large when foreign-owned affiliates undertake R&D to tap into advanced knowledge abroad. Adaptive R&D however was found to improve productivity in the host country, but did not contribute to enhanced productivity in the home country. Griffith et al. (2004) find that R&D by UK firms in the US have resulted in benefits from reverse technology with the effects being larger in the case of R&D units set up to source technology. Results for Sweden, however (Fors 1997; Braconier et al. 2002) indicate that there have not been significant spillovers to the home country, possibly because much R&D has been of the adaptive type. AlAzzawi (2011) finds that R&D abroad had a positive impact on the home country's level of innovation activity in both developed and newly industrialised countries, but finds productivity benefits for newly industrialised countries only. Moreover, there seems to be a positive relationship between internationalisation and the returns from R&D at home (Criscuolo and Martin 2009; Añón Higón et al. 2011) which may further increase the benefits for the home country.

Potential challenges or costs from the internationalisation of R&D for the home country may arise when firms replace domestic R&D and innovation activities with similar activities abroad. This may lead to a 'hollowing out' (Criscuolo and Patel 2003) of domestic innovation capacity, a loss of jobs in R&D, and a downward pressure on wages of R&D personnel in the home country. Despite public discussions on the offshoring of R&D and possible consequences for home country innovation systems,[2] empirical results that confirm such 'hollowing out'-effects are rare. Studies based on patent data give no indication for a substitutive relationship between R&D abroad and home-based R&D activities (D'Agostino et al. 2013). However, data on R&D expenditure of domestic firms abroad is available only for a very small number of countries, which makes a test of the assumption difficult.

NOTES

1. The concept of spillovers found in the international economics literature differs in some respect from the concept of knowledge flows in the innovation economics literature where knowledge flows are also frequently labelled as spillovers. Spillovers in the context of the international economics literature do not exclusively focus on the transfer of information or knowledge, but also include other non-compensated effects like competition, labour market or agglomeration effects (see Harris and Robinson 2004 for a typology of spillovers). One example is a lower price level in a certain market due to increased competition after market entry of a foreign-owned firm.
2. An example is the June 2010 issue of the Journal of Technology Transfer which discusses production offshoring and its effects on US manufacturing R&D in detail.

REFERENCES

Aghion, P., Blundell, R., Griffith, R., Howitt, P. and S. Prantl (2009), 'The effects of entry on incumbent innovation and productivity', *Review of Economics and Statistics* **91**(1), 20-32.

Aitken, B.J. and A.E. Harrison (1999), 'Do domestic firms benefit from direct foreign investment? Evidence from Venezuela', *American Economic Review* **89**(3), 605-18.

AlAzzawi, S. (2011), 'Multinational corporations and knowledge flows: evidence from patent citations', *Economic Development and Cultural Change,* **59**(3), 649-80.

Almeida, P. (1999), 'Knowledge Sourcing by Foreign Multinationals: Patent Citation Analysis in the U.S. Semiconductor Industry', in J. Cantwell (ed.), *Foreign direct investment and technological change*, Cheltenham: Edward Elgar, 421-31.

Ambos, B. and B.B. Schlegelmilch (2006), 'Learning from foreign subsidiaries: An empirical investigation of headquarters' benefits from reverse knowledge transfers', *International Business Review* **15**(3), 294-312.

Añón Higón, D., Manjón Antolín, M. and J.A. Mañez (2011), 'Multinationals, R&D, and productivity: evidence for UK manufacturing firms', *Industrial and Corporate Change*, **20**(2), 641-59.

Archibugi, D. and S. Iammarino (1999), 'The policy implications of the globalisation of innovation', *Research Policy* **28**(2-3), 317-36.

Arvanitis, S. and H. Hollenstein (2006), 'Determinants of Swiss firms' R&D activities at foreign locations: an empirical analysis based on firm-level data', Zurich: Swiss Institute for Business Cycle Research (KOF) Working Paper no. 127.

Arvanitis, S. and H. Hollenstein (2011), 'How do different drivers of R&D investment in foreign locations affect domestic firm performance? An analysis based on Swiss panel micro data', *Industrial and Corporate Change*, **20**(2), 605-40.

Audretsch, D. and M. Feldman (1996), 'R&D spillovers and the geography of innovation and production', *American Economic Review* **86**(3), 630-40.

Bailey, D. and N.L. Driffield (2007), 'Industrial policy, FDI and employment: still 'missing a strategy'', *Journal for Industry, Competition and Trade* **7**(3-4), 189-211.

Bandick, R., Görg, H. and P. Karpaty (2010), 'Foreign acquisitions, domestic multinationals, and R&D', Kiel: Kiel Working Papers no. 1651.

Barba Navaretti, G. and A.M. Falzoni (2004), 'Home country effects of foreign direct investment', in G. Barba Navaretti and A.J. Venables (eds), *Multinational firms in the world economy*, Princeton and Oxford: Princeton University Press, pp. 217-39.

Barba Navaretti, G. and A.J. Venables (2004), *Multinational firms in the world economy*, Princeton and Oxford: Princeton University Press.

Barry, F. (2004), 'FDI and the host economy: a case study of Ireland', in G. Barba Navaretti and A.J. Venables (eds), *Multinational firms in the world economy*, Princeton and Oxford: Princeton University Press, pp. 187-215.

Behrman, J.N. and W.A. Fischer (1980), *Overseas R&D Activities of Transnational Companies*, Cambridge, Mass: Oelgesclagert, Gunn & Hein.

Belderbos, R., Leten, B. and S. Suzuki (2009), 'Does excellence in scientific research attract foreign R&D?', Maastricht: UNU-Merit Working Paper 2009-066.

Bellandi, M. (2001), 'Local development and embedded large firms', *Entrepreneurship & Regional Development* **13**(3), 189-210.

Bertrand, O. (2009), 'Effects of foreign acquisitions on R&D activity: Evidence from firm-level data for France', *Research Policy* **38**(6), 1021-31.

Birkinshaw, J.M. and N. Hood (1998), 'Multinational subsidiary evolution: capability and charter change in foreign-owned subsidiary companies', *Academy of Management Review* **23**(4), 773-95.

Birkinshaw, J.M. and N. Hood (2000), 'Characteristics of Foreign Subsidiaries in Industry Clusters', *Journal of International Business Studies* **31**(1), 141-54.

Birkinshaw, J.M., Hood, N. and S. Jonsson (1998), 'Building firm-specific advantages in multinational corporations: the role of subsidiary initiative', *Strategic Management Journal* **19**(3), 221-41.

Blomström, M. and A. Kokko (2003), 'The economics of foreign direct investment incentives', Cambridge (Mass.): National Bureau of Economic Research (NBER) Working Paper no. 9489.

Blonigen, B.A. (2005), 'A review of the empirical literature on FDI determinants', Cambridge (Mass.): National Bureau of Economic Research (NBER) Working Paper no. 11299.

Blonigen, B.A. and M.J. Slaughter (2001), 'Foreign-affiliate activity and US skill upgrading', *Review of Economics and Statistics* **83**(2), 362-76.

Booz Allen Hamilton and INSEAD (2006), *Innovation: Is Global the Way Forward?* Paris: INSEAD.

Braconier, H., Henrik, K. and K.H. Midelfart-Knarvik (2002), 'Does FDI work as a channel for R&D spillovers? Evidence based on Swedish Data', Stockholm: The Research Institute of Industrial Economics Working Paper no 551.

Brash, D.T. (1966), *American Investment in Australian Industry*, Cambridge, Mass: Harvard University Press.

Breschi, S. and F. Lissoni (2001), 'Knowledge spillovers and local innovation systems: a critical survey', *Industrial and Corporate Change* **10**(4), 975-1005.

Cantner, U. and A. Pyka (1998), 'Absorbing Technological Spillovers: Simulations in an Evolutionary Framework', *Industrial and Corporate Change* **7**(2), 369-397.

Cantwell, J. and R. Mudambi (2000), 'The location of MNE R&D activity; the role of investment incentives', *Management International Review* **40**(1), 127-48.

Cantwell, J. and R. Mudambi (2005), 'MNE competence-creating subsidiary mandates', *Strategic Management Journal* **26**(12), 1109-128.

Cantwell, J. and L. Piscitello (2002), 'The location of technological activities of MNCs in European regions: The role of spillovers and local competencies', *Journal of International Management* **8**(1), 69-96.

Cassiman, B., Colombo, M.G., Garrone, P. and R. Veugelers (2005), 'The impact of M&A on the R&D process. An empirical analysis of the role of technological- and market-relatedness', *Research Policy* **34**(2), 195-220.

Castellacci, F. (2007), 'Technological regimes and sectoral differences in productivity growth', *Industrial and Corporate Change* **16**(6), 1105-145.

Castellani, D. and A. Zanfei (2002), 'Multinational experience and the creation of linkages with local firms. Evidence from the electronics industry', *Cambridge Journal of Economics* **26**(1), 1-25.

Caves, R. (1996), *Multinational enterprises and economic analysis*, Cambridge: Cambridge University Press.

Cerrato, D. (2009), 'Does innovation lead to global orientation? Empirical evidence from a sample of Italian firms', *European Management Journal* **27**(5), 305-15.

Chesbrough, H.W. (2003), *Open innovation: The new imperative for creating and profiting from technology*, Boston: Harvard Business School Press.

Cincera, M. Cozza, C. and A. Tübke (2010), 'The main drivers for the internationalization of R&D activities by EU MNEs', Seville: JRC-IPTS Working Papers on Corporate R&D and Innovation no 2010-02.

Coe, D.T., Helpman, E. and A.W. Hoffmaister (2009), 'International R&D spillovers and institutions', *European Economic Review* **53**(7), 723-41.

Cohen, W.M. (1995), 'Empirical studies of innovative activity', in P. Stoneman (ed), *Handbook of innovation and technological change*, Oxford: Blackwell, pp. 182-264.

Cohen, W.M. (2010), 'Fifty years of empirical studies of innovative activity and performance', in B.A. Hall and N. Rosenberg (eds), *Handbook of economics of innovation*, Amsterdam: Elsevier, pp. 129-213.

Cohen, W.M. and D. Levinthal (1989), 'Innovation and learning: the two faces of R&D', *Economic Journal* **99**(September), 569-96.

Cohen, W.M. and D. Levinthal (1990), 'Absorptive capacity: a new perspective on learning and innovation', *Administrative Science Quarterly* **35**(1), 128-52.

Cohen, W.M., Nelson, R.R. and J. Walsh (2000), 'Protecting their intellectual assets: appropriability conditions and why U.S. manufacturing firms patent (or not)', Cambridge (Mass.): National Bureau of Economic Research (NBER) Working Paper no. 7552.

Costa, I. and S. Filippov (2008), 'Foreign-owned subsidiaries: a neglected nexus between foreign direct investment, industrial and innovation policies', *Science and Public Policy* **35**(6), 379-90.

Cowan, R., David, P.A. and D. Foray (2000), 'The explicit economics of knowledge codification and tacitness', *Industrial and Corporate Change* **9**(2), 211-53.

Creamer, D.B. (1976), *Overseas research and development by the US multinationals*, New York: The Conference Board.

CREST Working Group (2007), *Internationalisation of R&D – facing the challenge of globalisation: approaches to a proactive International policy in S&T*, Brussles: CREST.

Criscuolo, C. and R. Martin (2009), 'Multinationals and U.S. productivity leadership: Evidence from Great Britain', *Review of Economics and Statistics* **91**(2), 263-81.

Criscuolo, P., Narula, R. and B. Verspagen (2005), 'Role of home and host country innovation systems in R&D internationalisation: a patent citation analysis', *Economics of Innovation and New Technology* **14**(5), 417-33.

Criscuolo, P. and P. Patel (2003), 'Large Firms and internationalisation of R&D: Hollowing out of National Technological Capacity?', paper presented at the SETI Workshop: Rome.

D'Agostino, L.M., Laursen, K. and G.D. Santangelo (2013), 'The impact of R&D offshoring on the home knowledge production of OECD investing regions', *Journal of Economic Geography* **13**(1), 145-75.

Dachs, B., Kampik, F., Peters, B., Rammer, C., Schartinger, D., Schmiele, A. and G. Zahradnik (2010), *Foreign corporate R&D and innovation activities in the European Union*. Background report for the 2010 Competitiveness Report, Brussels: European Commission.

Dachs, B. and A. Pyka (2010), 'What drives the internationalisation of innovation? Evidence from European patent data', *Economics of Innovation and New Technology* **19**(1), 71-86.

Damijan, J.P., Knell, M., Majcen, B. and M. Rojec (2003), 'The role of FDI, R&D accumulation and trade in transferring technology to transition countries: evidence from firm panel data for eight transition countries', *Economic Systems* **27**(2), 189-204.

De Backer, K. and F. Hatem (2010), *Attractiveness for Innovation. Location Factors for International Investment*, Paris: OECD.

Dogson, M. and R. Rothwell (1994), 'Innovation and the size of the firm', in M. Dogson and R. Rothwell (eds), *The handbook of industrial innovation*, Cheltenham: Edward Elgar, pp. 310-25.

Driffield, N., Love, J.H. and K. Taylor (2009), 'Productivity and labour demand effects of inward and outward foreign direct investment on UK industry', *The Manchester School* **77**(2), 171-203.

Driffield, N.L. and K. Taylor (2000), 'FDI and the labour market: a review of the evidence and policy implications', *Oxford Review of Economic Policy* **16**(3), 90-103.

Dunning, J. (1958), *American investment in British manufacturing industry*, London: Allen and Unwin.

Dunning, J. (1973), 'The determinants of international production', *Oxford Economic Papers* **25**(3), 289-336.

Dunning, J. (1981), *International production and the multinational enterprise*, London: Allen and Unwin.

Dunning, J., and S.M. Lundan (2008), *Multinational enterprises and the global economy* (2nd ed.), Cheltenham: Edward Elgar.

Dunning, J. and S.M. Lundan (2009), 'The internationalization of corporate R&D: A review of the evidence and some policy implications for home countries', *Review of Policy Research* **26**(1-2), 13-33.

Dunning, J. and R. Narula (1995), 'The R&D activities of foreign firms in the United States', *International Studies of Management & Organization* **25**(1-2), 39-72.

Economist Intelligence Unit (2004), *Scattering the Seeds of Innovation: The Globalization of Research and Development*, London: Economist Intelligence Unit.

Eden, L. and S. Miller (2004), 'Distance matters: Liability of foreignness, institutional distance and ownership strategy', in M.A. Hitt, and J.L.C. Cheng (eds), *The evolving theory of the multinational firm. Advances in International Management*, Vol. 16, Amsterdam: Elsevier, pp. 187-221.

Ekholm, K. and K.H. Midelfart (2004), 'Determinants of FDI: the evidence', in G. Barba Navaretti and A.J. Venables (eds), *Multinational firms in the world economy*, Princeton and Oxford: Princeton University Press, pp. 127-50.

Ernst, D. (2006), *Innovation offshoring – Asia's emerging role in global innovation networks*, Honolulu: East-West Center Report Nr. 10.

Feinberg, S.E. and A.K. Gupta (2004), 'Knowledge spillovers and the assignment of R&D responsibilities to foreign subsidiaries', *Strategic Management Journal* **25**(8-9), 823-45.

Figini, P. and H. Görg (1999), 'Multinational companies and wage inequality in the host country: The case of Ireland', *Review of World Economics* **135**(4), p. 594-612.

Florida, R. (1997), 'The globalization of R&D: Results of a survey of foreign-affiliated R&D laboratories in the USA', *Research Policy* **26**(1), 85-103.

Fors, G. (1997), 'Utilization of R&D Results in the Home and Foreign Plants of Multinationals', *Journal of Industrial Economics* **45**(3), 341-58.

Forsgren, M. (2008), *Theories of the Multinational Firm*, Cheltenham: Edward Elgar.

Gassmann, O. and Z. Han (2004), 'Motivations and barriers of foreign R&D activities in China', *R&D Management* **34**(4), 423-37.

Gersbach, H. and A. Schmutzler, (2011), 'Foreign Direct Investment and R&D Offshoring', *Oxford Economic Papers* **63**(1), 134-57.

Görg, H. and D. Greenaway (2004), 'Much Ado about Nothing? Do Domestic Firms Really Benefit from Foreign Direct Investment?', *The World Bank Research Observer* **19**(2), 171-97.

Görg, H., and E. Strobl (2001), 'Multinational Companies and Productivity Spillovers: A Meta-analysis', *Economic Journal* **111**(November), 723-39.

Görg, H. and E. Strobl (2003), '"Footloose" Multinationals?', *The Manchester School* **71**(1), 1-19.

Greenhalgh, C.A. and P. Taylor (1990), 'Innovation and Export Volumes and Prices: A Disaggregated Study', London: CEPR Discussion Papers 487.

Griffith, R., Redding, S. and H. Simpson (2004), 'Foreign Ownership and Productivity: New Evidence from the Service Sector and the R&D Lab', London: CEP Discussion Paper 649.

Guellec, D. and B. van Pottelsberghe de la Potterie (2001), 'The Internationalisation of Technology Analysed with Patent Data', *Research Policy* **30**(8), 1253-266.

Guimón, J. (2009), 'Government strategies to attract R&D-intensive FDI', *Journal of Technology Transfer* **34**(4), 364-79.

Harris, R. and Q.C. Li (2009), 'Exporting, R&D, and absorptive capacity in UK establishments', *Oxford Economic Papers* **61**(1), 74-103.

Harris, R. and C. Robinson (2004), 'Productivity impacts and spillovers from foreign ownership in the United Kingdom', *National Institute Economic Review* 185(1), 58-75.

Hatzichronoglou, T. (2008), *The Location of investment of multinationals linked to innovation*, Paris: OECD.

Havránek, T. and Z. Iršová (2010), 'Which Foreigners Are Worth Wooing? A Meta-Analysis of Vertical Spillovers from FDI', Prague: Czech National Bank Working paper 3/2010.

Head, K. and J. Ries (2003), 'Heterogeneity and the FDI versus Export Decision of Japanese Manufacturers', Cambridge (Mass.): National Bureau of Economic Research (NBER) Working Paper 10052.

Hedge, D. and D. Hicks (2008), 'The maturation of global corporate R&D: Evidence from the activity of U.S. foreign subsidiaries', *Research Policy* **37**(3), 390-406.

Helpman, E. (2006), 'Trade, FDI and the organisation of firms', *Journal of Economic Literature* **44**(3), 589-631.

Helpman, E., Melitz, M.J. and S.R. Yeaple (2004), 'Export versus FDI with heterogeneous firms', *American Economic Review* **94**(1), 300-16.

Jaffe, A.B., Trajtenberg, M. and R. Henderson (1993), 'Geographic localization of knowledge spillovers as evidenced by patent citations', *Quarterly Journal of Economics* 108(3), 577-598.

Jensen, N.M. (2006), *Nation-states and the multinational corporation*, Princeton and Oxford: Princeton University Press.

Johanson, J. and J.-E. Vahlne (2009), 'The Uppsala internationalization process model revisited: From liability of foreignness to liability of outsidership', *Journal of International Business Studies* **40**(9), 1411-431.

Keller, W. (2004), 'International technology diffusion', *Journal of Economic Literature* **42**(3), 752-58.

Keller, W. (2010), 'International trade, foreign direct investment, and technology spillovers', in B.A. Hall and N. Rosenberg (eds), *Handbook of the economics of innovation*, Vol. 2, Amsterdam, Elsevier, pp. 794-829.

Keller, W. and S.R. Yeaple (2009), 'Multinational enterprises, international trade, and productivity growth: firm-level evidence from the United States', *Review of Economics and Statistics* **91**(4), 821-31.

Ketokivi, M. and J. Ali-Yrkkö (2009), 'Unbundling R&D and manufacturing: postindustrial myth or economic reality?', *Review of Policy Research* **26**(1-2), 35-

54.

Kinkel, S. and S. Maloca (2008), *FuE-Verlagerungen in Ausland - Ausverkauf deutscher Entwicklungskompetenz?*, Karlsruhe: Fraunhofer ISI.

Kleinknecht, A. (1989), 'Firm size and Innovation', *Small Business Economics* **1**(3), 215-22.

Kleinknecht, A. and P. Mohnen (eds)(2002), *Innovation and Firm Performance*. Basingstoke and New York: Palgrave.

Kokko, A. (2006), The home country effects of FDI in developed economies, Stockholm, EIJS Working Paper Series no. 225.

Konings, J. (2001), 'The effects of foreign direct investment on domestic firms. Evidence from firm-level panel data in emerging economies', *Economics of Transition* **9**(3), 619-33.

Kuemmerle, W. (1997), 'Building effective R&D capabilities abroad', *Harvard Business Review* **75**(2), 61-70.

Kuemmerle, W. (1999), 'Foreign direct investment in industrial research in the pharmaceutical and electronics industries – results from a survey of multinational firms', *Research Policy* **28**(2-3), 179-93.

Kumar, N. (2001), 'Determinants of location of overseas R&D activity of multinational enterprises: the case of US and Japanese corporations', *Research Policy* **30**(1), 159-74.

Lachenmaier, S. and L. Wößmann (2006), 'Does innovation cause exports? Evidence from exogenous innovation impulses and obstacles using German micro data', *Oxford Economic Papers* **58**(2), 317-50.

Lall, S. (1979), 'The international allocation of research activity by US multinationals', *Oxford Bulletin of Economics and Statistics* **41**(4), 313-31.

Lee, G. (2004). 'How the globalization of R&D competition affects trade and growth', *Japanese Economic Review* **55**(3), 267-85.

Lewin, A.Y., Massini, S. and C. Peeters (2009), 'Why are companies offshoring innovation? The emerging global race for talent', *Journal of International Business Studies* **40**(6), 901-25.

Lipsey, R.E. (2002), Home and host country effects of FDI, Cambridge (Mass.): National Bureau of Economic Research (NBER) Working Paper 9293.

Lonmo, C. and F. Anderson (2003), A comparison of international R&D performance: an analysis of countries that have significantly increased their GERD/GDP ratios during the period 1989-1999, Ottawa: Statistics Canada 88F0006XIE2003001.

Lööf, H. (2009), 'Multinational enterprises and innovation: firm level evidence on spillover via R&D collaboration', *Journal of Evolutionary Economics* **19**(1), 41-71.

Lorenzen, M. and V. Mahnke (2002), Global strategy and the acquisition of local knowledge: how MNCs enter regional knowledge clusters, Copenhagen: DRUID Working Paper 02-08.

Malerba, F. (2002), 'Sectoral Systems of Innovation and Production', *Research Policy* **31**(2), 247-64.

Malerba, F. (2005), 'Sectoral systems of innovation', in J. Fagerberg, D. Mowery and R.R. Nelson (eds), *The Oxford Handbook of Innovation*, Oxford: Oxford University Press, pp. 380-406.

Malerba, F. and L. Orsenigo (1996), 'Schumpeterian patterns of innovation are technology-specific', *Research Policy* **25**(3), 451-78.

Marin, A. and S. Sasidharan (2010), 'Heterogeneous MNC subsidiaries and technological spillovers: Explaining positive and negative effects in India',

Research Policy **39**(9), 1227–241.

Markusen, J.R. (1995), 'The Boundaries of Multinational Enterprises and the Theory of International Trade', *Journal of Economic Perspectives* **9**(2), 169-89.

Markusen, J.R. (2002), *Multinational firms and the theory of international trade*, Cambridge [Mass.]: MIT Press.

Marsili, O. (2001), *The anatomy and evolution of industries: technological change and industrial dynamics*, Cheltenham: Edward Elgar.

Mayer, K.E. and E. Sinani (2009), 'When and Where Does Foreign Direct Investment Generate Positive Spillovers? A Meta-Analysis', *Journal of International Business Studies* **40**(7), 1075-94.

Narula, R. (2002), 'Innovation Systems and "Inertia" in R&D Location: Norwegian Firms and the Role of Systemic Lock-in', *Research Policy* **31**(5), 795-816.

Narula, R. and J. Michel (2009), Reverse knowledge transfer and its implications for European policy, Maastricht: UNU-MERIT Working Paper 2009-035.

Narula, R. and A. Zanfei (2005), 'Globalisation of innovation: the role of multinational enterprises', in J. Fagerberg, D.C. Movery and R.R. Nelson (eds), *The Oxford Handbook of Innovation*, Oxford: Oxford University Press, pp. 318-48.

OECD (2005), *Measuring globalisation: OECD economic globalisation indicators*, Paris: OECD.

OECD (2008a), *The Internationalisation of business R&D: evidence, impacts and implications*, Paris: OECD.

OECD (2008b), *Open Innovation in Global Networks*, Paris: OECD.

OECD (2008c), Recent trends in the internationalisation of R&D in the enterprise sector, Paris: DSTI/EAS/IND/SWP (2006)1/Final.

OECD (2008d), *OECD Science, Technology and Industry Outlook 2008,* Paris: OECD.

OECD (2009), *Innovation in Firms. A Microeconomic Perspective*, Paris: OECD.

OECD (2010), *Measuring Globalisation: OECD Economic Globalisation Indicators 2010*, Paris: OECD.

Patel, P. and K. Pavitt (1999), 'Global Corporations and National Systems of Innovation: Who Dominates Whom?', in D. Archibugi, J. Howells, and J. Michie (eds), *Innovation Policy in a Global Economy*, Cambridge: Cambridge University Press, pp. 94-119.

Pavlínek, P. (2004), 'Regional Development Implications of Foreign Direct Investment in Central Europe', *European Urban and Regional Studies* **11**(1), 47-70.

Pearce, R. (1992), 'Factors Influencing the Internationalisation of Research and Development in Multinational Enterprises', in P.J. Buckley and M. Casson (eds), *Multinational Enterprises in the World Economy*, Cheltenham: Edward Elgar, pp. 75-95.

Pearce, R. (2004), *National systems of innovation and the international technology strategy of multinationals*, Reading: University of Reading Discussion paper 2004-06.

Pearce, R. and M. Papanastassiou (2009), 'Multinationals and National Systems of Innovation: Strategy and Policy Issues', in R. Pearce and M. Papanastassiou (eds), *The Strategic Development of Multinationals Subsidiaries and Innovation* Basingstoke: Macmillan Publishers, pp. 289-307.

Peneder, M. (2010), 'Technological regimes and the variety of innovation behaviour: Creating integrated taxonomies of firms and sectors', *Research Policy* **39**(3), 323-34.

Piscitello, L. and L. Rabbiosi (2006), *How does Knowledge Transfer from Foreign Subsidiaries affect Parent Companies' Innovative Capacity?*, Copenhagen: Druid Working Paper No. 06-22.

Rabbiosi, L. (2009), 'The impact of reverse knowledge transfer on the parent company's innovativeness : Which role for organizational mechanisms and subsidiary's characteristics?', in L. Piscitello and G. Santangelo (eds), *Multinationals and local competitiveness*, Milan: Edizioni Franco Angeli, pp. 167-95.

Rammer, C. and A. Schmiele (2008), 'Globalisation of innovation in SMEs: why they go abroad and what they bring back', *Applied Economics Quarterly* **59**(Supplement), 173-206.

Ronstadt, R.C. (1977), *Research and Development Abroad by U.S. Multinationals*, New York: Praeger Publishers.

Sachwald, F. (2008), 'Location choices within global innovation networks: the case of Europe', *Journal of Technology Transfer* **33**(4), 364-78.

Sadowski, B.M. and G. Sadowski-Rasters (2006), 'On the innovativeness of foreign affiliates: Evidence from companies in The Netherlands', *Research Policy* **35**(3), 447-62.

Safarian, A.E. (1966), *Foreign Ownership of Canadian Industry*, Toronto: McGraw Hill.

Sanna-Randaccio, F. and R. Veugelers (2007), 'Multinational knowledge spillovers with decentralised R&D: a game-theoretic approach', *Journal of International Business Studies* **38**(1), 47-63.

Schmiele, A. (2012), 'Drivers for international innovation activities in developed and emerging countries' *Journal of Technology Transfer* **37**(1), 98-123.

Schwaag Serger, S. and E. Wise (2010), *Internationalization of Research and Innovation – new policy developments*, Seville: paper presented at the 2010 Concord Conference.

Sheehan, J. (2004), *Globalisation of R&D: Trends, Drivers and Policy Implications*, Den Haag: paper presented at the IST 2004 conference.

Singh, J. (2007), 'Asymmetry of Knowledge Spillovers between MNCs and Host Country Firms', *Journal of International Business Studies* **38**(5), 764-86.

Stiebale, J. and F. Reize (2011), 'The impact of FDI through mergers and acquisitions on innovation in target firms', *International Journal of Industrial Organization* **29**(2), 155-67.

TAFTIE (2009), *Internationalisation of National Innovation Agencies*, Stockholm: TAFTIE.

Teece, D.J. Pisano, G. and A. Shuen (1997), 'Dynamic capabilities and strategic management', *Strategic Management Journal* **18**(7), 509-33.

Thursby, J. and M. Thursby (2006), *Here or There? A Survey of Factors in Multinational R&D Location*, Washington DC: National Academies Press.

Todo, Y. and S. Shimizutani (2005), Overseas R&D activities by multinational enterprises: evidence from Japanese firm-level data, Tokyo: Hi-Stat Discussion Paper Series no. 05-91, Institute of Economic Research, Hitotsubashi University.

UNCTAD (2005), *World Investment Report 2005: Transnational Corporations and the Internationalization of R&D*, New York and Geneva: United Nations.

Verbeek, A., Shapira, P., Edler, J., Gagliardi, D., Lykogianni, E. and M. Knell (2009), *RINDICATE. Analysis of R&D international funding flows and their impact on the research system in selected Member States*, Brussels: Report for the European Commission, DG Research.

Veugelers, R. (2005), *Internationalisation of R&D: Trends, Issues and Implications for S&T policies*, Background report for the OECD Forum on the internationalization of R&D, Paris: OECD.

Veugelers, R. and B. Cassiman (2004), 'Foreign Subsidiaries as a Channel of International Technology Diffusion: Some Direct Firm Level Evidence from Belgium', *European Economic Review* **48**(2), 455-76.

von Zedtwitz, M. and O. Gassmann (2002), 'Market versus Technology Drive in R&D Internationalization: Four different Patterns of Managing Research and Development', *Research Policy* **31**(4), 569-58.

Wang, E.C. (2010), 'Determinants of R&D investment: the extreme-bounds-analysis approach applied to 26 OECD countries', *Research Policy* **39**(1), 103-16.

Young, S., N. Hood, and E. Peters (1994), 'Multinational enterprises and regional economic development', *Regional Studies* **28**(7), 657-77.

Zaheer, S. (1995), 'Overcoming the Liability of Foreignness', *Academy of Management Journal* **38**(2), 341-64.

Zanfei, A. (2000), 'Transnational Firms and the Changing Organisation of Innovative Activities', *Cambridge Journal of Economics* **24**(5), 515-42.

3. Issues in Collecting Data on the Internationalisation of R&D

Georg Zahradnik and Waltraut Urban

Data on R&D expenditure of foreign-owned firms collected from national statistical offices, EUROSTAT and the OECD is the basis of the analysis of this book. This chapter summarises the experiences from the data collection. After presenting some basic definitions of R&D and innovation in the context of internationalisation of R&D, we provide a summary of the available data and discuss existing data gaps and important pitfalls that have to be taken into account when analysing data on foreign-owned R&D.

DEFINITIONS OF R&D AND INNOVATION

For the analysis of the internationalisation of business R&D a first important step is to clearly define business R&D and distinguish R&D from other types of innovation activity.

The OECD Frascati Manual defines R&D as 'creative work undertaken on a systematic basis in order to increase the stock of knowledge, including knowledge of man, culture and society, and the use of this stock of knowledge to devise new applications' (OECD 2002, p. 30). Compared to innovation, the term R&D rather refers to scientific discovery and knowledge creation than to the economic application of new knowledge. In practice, however, many firms may find it difficult to distinguish between innovation and R&D activities. Both terms are overlapping: R&D financed and performed by enterprises is always an innovation activity; in fact, R&D expenditure accounts for around half of innovation expenditure. The share is higher in countries with high average R&D intensity, such as Finland, Austria, France or Sweden, where R&D expenditure accounts for more than 60 percent of total innovation expenditure.

But not all R&D performed in a country is innovation activity, because a considerable part of total R&D is performed by universities which do not introduce new products or processes to the market. Moreover, some activities which are not R&D may be innovation activity; examples are design activities, staff training activities related to market introduction or production

27

preparations. In a number of service industries, these activities comprise the bulk of innovation expenditure.

The focus of this book is on business R&D. Following the OECD Frascati Manual (OECD 2002, p. 54), the business enterprise sector includes 'all firms, organisations and institutions whose primary activity is the market production of goods or services for sale to the general public at an economically significant price' and 'the private non-profit institutions mainly serving them'. This definition excludes the government sector, the private non-profit sector and higher education, no matter if privately or publicly funded. Public enterprises are included if they are mainly engaged in market production.

Data on R&D expenditure is usually collected separately for intramural R&D and extramural R&D. The OECD Frascati Manual (OECD 2002, p. 21) defines intramural R&D expenditures as 'all expenditures for R&D performed within a statistical unit or sector of the economy during a specific period, whatever the source of funds'. In contrast, extramural R&D expenditures are defined as 'the sums a unit, organisation or sector reports having paid or committed themselves to pay to another unit, organisation or sector for the performance of R&D during a specific period' (OECD 2002, p. 21). Generally, R&D expenditures include both, intramural and extramural R&D expenditures and follow the definition of R&D as stated above to distinguish them from other innovative activities like design or staff training (OECD 2002).

Table 3.1 Main definitions

Business Enterprise R&D	
Total BERD	Total business enterprise research and development (BERD) by domestically owned firms and foreign-owned affiliates performed in the reporting country
Inward BERD	BERD by foreign-owned affiliates in the reporting country
Domestic BERD	BERD by domestically owned firms in the reporting country
Outward BERD	BERD of domestically owned firms outside of the reporting country
Sector and industry classification	
Sector	A NACE 1.1 section (mainly two-digit level)
Industry	The data aggregated into high-, medium-high-, medium-low-, low-technology manufacturing sectors, knowledge-intensive and less knowledge-intensive services

This book frequently uses some key terms and abbreviations for different types of R&D which are summarised in Table 3.1. An important distinction is between business R&D expenditure of domestically owned firms (domestic BERD) and business R&D expenditure of foreign-owned firms (inward BERD) in a particular country. Outward BERD refers to all business R&D expenditure of domestically owned firms performed outside their home country.

METHODOLOGY, DATA SOURCES AND CHALLENGES

The increasing interest in the internationalisation of economic activity during the 1980s and 1990s brought forward various initiatives to collect data on the internationalisation of R&D, to the largest part organised by the OECD (Godin 2004). These efforts have been intensified after the year 2000, pushed forward by the OECD Working Party of National Experts on Science and Technology Indicators (OECD NESTI), and the OECD Working Party on Innovation and Technology Policy (OECD TIP) (OECD 1998; Colecchia 2005; OECD 2005; Colecchia 2006; Colecchia 2007; OECD 2008a).

Another impetus for the collection of data on the internationalisation of R&D came from the European Union. Regulation (EC) No 716/2007 requires EU member states to collect data on intramural R&D expenditure by foreign-owned affiliates for every second year and, to a limited degree, on outward BERD starting with the year 2007. The methodology used is in line with the OECD Frascati manual. Foreign affiliates are defined as 'enterprises resident in the compiling country over which an institutional unit not resident in the compiling country has control, or an enterprise not resident in the compiling country over which an institutional unit resident in the compiling country has control' (Regulation (EC) No 716/2007, Article 2 a)). The concept of the ultimate controlling institutional unit (UCI) is used to determine foreign control of an enterprise. The UCI is the institutional unit in a chain of control which is not controlled by another institutional unit (Eurostat 2007). In their Foreign Affiliates Statistics (FATS), EUROSTAT distinguishes between inward FATS data, which includes the activity of foreign affiliates resident in the compiling country, and outward FATS data, which includes the activity of affiliates abroad controlled by the compiling country (Eurostat 2007). Values for a reporting firm are allocated completely to the majority owner's country; splitting of values according to owner shares or double counting is not recommended.

Most major non-OECD countries, including Brazil, China, India and Russia, follow the guidelines for the collection of R&D data provided by the OECD Frascati Manual. The Frascati Manual, however, offers only little guidance for collecting data on R&D internationalisation. Hence, the availability of data and the level of aggregation vary significantly across these countries (OECD 2010).

Despite increasing efforts to collect data and harmonise survey methodologies, some open methodological issues remain that have to be kept in mind when interpreting the data (Colecchia 2005; Colecchia 2006; Colecchia 2007; Cozza 2010; OECD 2010):

- A first critical issue is the correct identification of the 'ultimate controller' and the ultimate country of ownership. Multi-level ownership structures of multinational corporations make is sometimes difficult to identify the ultimate controller of a firm.
- A second issue are accounting practices. R&D internationalisation takes place within large multinational firms with a presence in many countries. Thus, data on R&D expenditure of affiliates in different countries may be distorted by internal transfer pricing, non-priced transfers of R&D personnel, and possibly by problems in dividing flows of funds for R&D within the group across borders.
- Another challenge for statistics on R&D of foreign-owned firms is institutional separation. Responsibilities for collecting data on R&D expenditure and on the activities of foreign-owned firms (FDI or FATS surveys) are divided between statistical agencies and the central banks in some countries. This may result in different samples for both surveys. The collection of data on R&D expenditure of domestic firms abroad (outward R&D) seems to be a challenge in particular.
- The problem of institutional separation and different samples of foreign-owned firms multiplies when R&D inward and outward data is compared bilaterally. A study by OECD NESTI (Colecchia 2006) compared outward BERD of the US and some European countries with corresponding data for inward BERD in several European countries. The comparison showed considerable differences both in the number of foreign-owned firms surveyed and in R&D expenditure between the two data sources. A case study at the end of this chapter discusses this issue for Chinese data.
- With increased efforts put into the identification of foreign-owned firms, additional issues arise for the analysis of this data over time. We have to be careful in the interpretation of time series, because increasing levels of internationalisation for a given country or industry over time may rather be the result of increased efforts put into the collection of this data than of increased levels of internationalisation.
- Data on the R&D expenditure of foreign-owned firms in a detailed sectoral disaggregation should be interpreted with care as well. Data reported by the OECD (Colecchia 2006, p. 10) indicate that a handful of MNE subsidiaries account for a major share of R&D expenditure of foreign-owned firms in smaller countries. A change in the classification of only one of these firms may result in shifts in the sectoral composition of inward BERD.

- The statistical unit of R&D surveys is the firm and all R&D expenditure of the firm is assigned to the sector of the main economic activity of the firm. Some countries, however, further split R&D expenditure if enterprises are active in more than one product field, for example chemicals and pharmaceuticals. This may be a source of inconsistencies in international comparisons of total BERD and inward BERD at the sectoral level.
- Another challenge related to the sectoral classification of foreign-owned firms is the treatment of non-producing affiliates. If a foreign-owned affiliate generates the majority of its value added by selling the products of its parent company, it is classified as wholesale and retail trade, even if it belongs to a parent company from the manufacturing sector.
- Finally, another relevant issue is the treatment of non-R&D performers. R&D surveys only report information on R&D active firms. If a regional headquarter of a multinational firm sponsors R&D abroad, but does not have own domestic R&D activities, it is unlikely that this R&D expenditure enters the survey results.

EXPERIENCES FROM THE DATA COLLECTION

Data on R&D expenditure of foreign-owned firms collected from national statistical offices, EUROSTAT and the OECD is the basis of the analysis of this book. We collected data on inward BERD which captures R&D expenditure of foreign-owned firms in a particular host country, as well as outward BERD data which includes R&D expenditure of domestic firms abroad.

Over the last two years there has been a noticeable increase in attention of national statistical offices for R&D internationalisation, in particular in EU member countries. As mentioned before, a major impetus for the extension of survey programmes is EU regulation on FATS statistics starting with (EC) No. 716/2007 which requires EU member states to collect data on the R&D expenditure of foreign-owned firms every two years. Data from national statistical offices is considerably more actual and much more detailed in a number of countries than it was some years before. However, this is not yet fully reflected in the OECD Activities of Foreign Affiliates statistics (OECD AFA) and EUROSTAT databases. Thus, we can expect a better coverage of these databases in the near future.

Data on the **inward BERD** is available at the aggregate and the sectoral level and by the home country of the foreign-owned firm for most European countries. In contrast, there is considerably less data available for non-European countries: Only incomplete data on inward BERD could be collected for China and Israel. No data was available for South Korea, Russia, India, and Brazil. This is a major shortcoming and a serious obstacle to a global analysis of R&D internationalisation, since emerging economies may rapidly gaining importance in the process.

In most countries, inward BERD data is collected by business sector R&D surveys. From our perspective, this is the preferred organisational form, because it ensures the comparability of the data with total BERD or sectoral BERD. Separate R&D surveys for multinational firms (like in Israel) should only be considered as a second-best strategy.

Sectoral data is mostly available at NACE two-digit level. For a few selected industries (mainly pharmaceuticals and aeronautics), some statistical offices also provide data at the NACE three-digit level. The availability and quality of inward BERD data is better for manufacturing than for service industries. In our opinion, this is a second major shortcoming of the available data. Some countries exclude the service sector for some or all years (Denmark, Spain, Finland, the Netherlands, Bulgaria, Hungary and Turkey), while others only report data for broad service sector aggregates. Moreover, there are considerable differences in the share of service industries on inward BERD, and their development over time between countries which may also raise concerns about data quality. From our perspective, it is difficult to tell if these differences reflect a different economic structure or different survey designs.

In many countries, inward BERD data is also available in a split by the home country of the foreign-owned firm. National statistical offices tend to offer this data in more detail than OECD and EUROSTAT databases. Some smaller countries do not fully publish inward data in a home country split due to data confidentiality when there are only a few R&D active foreign-owned firms from a particular country. This is a considerable obstacle for the analysis of cross-country patterns of R&D internationalisation. Inward BERD data is also provided in a home country x sector dimension by many EU countries. Confidentiality issues are even larger in this case, and even medium-sized countries like the Netherlands have to omit data due to data confidentiality.

In some countries large changes in the shares of different home countries between two years can be observed. This may be the result of the concentration of foreign activity in a few large firms. It may, however, also be the result of a better identification of the 'ultimate controller' and the ultimate country of ownership. This is often hard to capture because of the multi-level structure of many multinational companies.

There is much less data on **outward BERD** than on inward BERD. Detailed outward BERD data is available only for two countries, the US and Japan. One reason for this poor coverage is the fact that collecting outward BERD data is more difficult than collecting inward BERD data. A firm-level survey of outward BERD addresses R&D performing firms located abroad. Statistical offices may have very little information about this population, because they typically address the firm population located within a country.

CASE STUDY: DATA ON R&D INTERNATIONALISATION IN CHINA

This section takes a closer look at some of the challenges in collecting data on R&D activities of foreign-owned firms for the case of China. Various data sources indicate that R&D activities of foreign multinational firms in China increased considerably in recent years. However, data on outward BERD from Europe to China is scarce, and data on China's inward BERD provided by Chinese sources is difficult to compare with similar statistics provided by statistical offices in the EU and the US.

As mentioned above, only very few countries report R&D expenditure of domestic affiliates abroad (outward BERD). No more than four countries report R&D expenditure of their affiliates in China, namely Japan, the US, Sweden and Italy. Only the US and Sweden provide data for a longer period starting in 1998/1999. From this data, the following broad picture emerges: The R&D expenditure by foreign enterprises in China is rising faster than total outward BERD of the respective countries, but still takes a relative small share of around 4 percent. The relative importance of China as a location for R&D has increased most and reached the highest proportion in Japan. However, given the very small number of countries, we cannot draw any conclusions on the development of aggregate outward BERD to China and there is also no information at the sectoral level available from this data source.

Table 3.2 Outward BERD to China

billion EUR	2000	2003	2004	2007	2008	av. growth 2003-07, %
Japan		0.04	0.05	0.11		31.3
US	0.55	0.50	0.46	0.86	1.03	14.4
Sweden		0.06		0.13		21.3
Italy		0.00				
aggregated	**0.55**	**0.60**	**0.52**	**1.10**	**1.03**	**16.4**
as % of total outward BERD of the respective country						
Japan		1.6%	2.3%	5.2%		
US	2.5%	2.5%	2.2%	3.4%	4.1%	
Sweden		2.7%		4.0%		
Italy		0.1%				

Source: OECD, Eurostat, national statistical offices, own calculations.

In contrast to outward BERD by EU countries, data on inward BERD reported by the Chinese authorities is rich. There exist basically three sets of data on BERD in China. The Ministry of Science and Technology (MOST) calculates the R&D expenditure of *all business enterprises* (total BERD). However, this data set includes no corresponding data on R&D expenditure of foreign enterprises (inward BERD). The second data set is provided by the National Bureau of Statistics (NBS) for Census years only (2004, 2008/09). BERD is reported for *industrial enterprises above designated size*, i.e. enterprises from the mining and quarrying, manufacturing and the utilities sectors and with annual business revenue from principal activity of five million RMB (about 500,000 EUR) and above. Approximately 90 percent of total BERD is spent by these enterprises. Here, intramural expenditure on R&D of domestic and of foreign enterprises (inward BERD) is presented separately. However, the most detailed data on inward BERD over a longer period of time (2004-2010) are given in a third data set for *large and medium-sized industrial enterprises*, which were responsible for 80 percent of total BERD in 2008 (see Table 3.3).

All data sets show a similar strong increase of total and inward BERD. Between 2004 and 2008, inward BERD nearly tripled, growing at an annual average rate of 28.8 percent (enterprises above designated size) and 29.7 percent (large and medium-sized enterprises). These rates are significantly higher than those of aggregate *outward* BERD to China during a comparable period (16.4 percent, 2003-2007), but compare well with the average annual growth rates of the 'late-comer' Japan (31.3 percent);[1] see Table 3.2.

Data for *large and medium-sized industrial enterprises* also shows that firms funded from Hong Kong, Macao & Taiwan are typically responsible for about 30 percent of total inward BERD in China. Unfortunately, beyond this, no break-down of R&D expenditure according to source countries is given by the Chinese statistical authorities.

Obviously, there are large discrepancies between inward BERD in China reported by Chinese sources and the outward BERD to China reported by EU and US statistical offices. For comparison, we take the year 2007, for which most information on outward BERD is available. In that year, inward BERD of *large and medium sized industrial enterprises*, which will include most western firms in the country, amounted to 61.5 billion RMB (around 6.1 billion EUR). The aggregate of *outward* BERD calculated for that year is 1.1 billion EUR, which comes up to 18 percent of total *inward* BERD only – despite the fact that major investors (US, Japan) are among the reporting countries. Furthermore, considering outward BERD of the US (856 million EUR) and of Japan (110 million EUR) separately, gives shares in China's inward BERD of 14 percent for the US and of 1.8 percent for Japan. Both shares look much too small, compared for instance to survey results from a Tsinghua University research team investigating R&D activities of MNEs with business operations in China (2004-2006)[2] and general findings according to which the 'Triade' and especially the US play an over-proportionate role in R&D internationalisation. We may thus conclude, that either outward

BERD to China is significantly under-reported or inward BERD is over-estimated – or probably both. A thorough comparison of the methodologies and definitions for generating these figures is needed.[3]

Table 3.3 Inward BERD in China (billion RMB)

	2000	2003	2004	2007	2008	2009	2010	av. growth 2003-07, %
R&D expenditure of all business enterprises (domestic and foreign)[a]	53.7	96	131.4	267.9	338.2	424.9		26.7
Industrial enterprises above designated size [b]								
Intramural expenditure on R&D of all enterprises			110.5		307.3	377.7		29.2
Intramural expenditure on R&D of domestic enterprises			80.5		224.9			
Intramural expenditure on R&D of foreign-owned enterprises [c]			30		82.4	99.7		28.8
Large and medium-sized industrial enterprises [d]								
Intramural expenditure on R&D of all enterprises	35.3	72.1	95.5	211.3	268.1	321.2	401.5	29.5
Intramural expenditure on R&D of domestic enterprises			69.7	149.7	195.2	234.5	296.7	29.4
Intramural expenditure on R&D of foreign-owned enterprises [e]			25.8	61.5	72.9	86.7	104.8	29.7
Enterprises with funds from HK, Macao and Taiwan [f]			7.4	18.3	22.4	31.2	35.7	31.7
out of this: wholly foreign-owned			3.2	8.1	10.2	14.2	16	33.6
Foreign Funded Enterprises [f]			18.3	43.2	50.6	55.4	69.1	28.9
out of this: wholly foreign-owned			5.9	14.7	16.5	20.3	26.5	29.2
Intramural expenditure on R&D of all *wholly foreign-owned* enterprises			9.1	22.8	26.7	34.6	42.5	30.8
Exchange rate RMB/EUR, annual average [g]		9.36	10.29	10.42	10.22	9.53	8.98	

Sources: a) National Bureau of Statistics of China (NBS) and Ministry of Science and Technology of the People's Republic of China (MOST). b) MOST, annual business revenue from principal activity of five million RMB (about 500 million euro) and above; data for 2004 are identical with industrial census 2004, enterprises above a designated size, First National Economic Census of the State Council of the People's Republic of China. c) Foreign funded enterprises plus enterprises with funds from Hong Kong, Macao and Taiwan. d) NBS, Basic Statistics on Science and Technology Activities of Large and Medium-sized Industrial Enterprises and Basic Statistics on R&D Activities of Large and Medium-sized Industrial Enterprises by Registration Status; 2004: First National Economic Census of the State Council. e) Comprises enterprises with funds from Hong Kong, Macao and Taiwan plus foreign funded enterprises. f) Joint Ventures, cooperative enterprises, wholly foreign-owned enterprises and share-holding corporations. g) NBS.

Ad hoc, the following reasons for a possible over-estimation of China's inward BERD seem plausible:

- In case of a Chinese-Foreign Joint Venture (JV), the full amount of R&D expenditure of that firm may be reported as inward BERD by the Chinese Statistical Office. JVs still comprise more than half of all foreign enterprises in China. To avoid that problem, some researchers take only wholly foreign-owned firms into account (In 2007, inward BERD would thus come up to 22.8 billion RMB, i.e. around 2.3 billion EUR instead of 6.1 billion EUR, see Table 3.2).

- 'Round-tripping': this refers to the practice of Chinese investors to set up special purpose entities in territories outside China, including Hong Kong, for the purpose to invest in China and so benefit from financial incentives offered to foreign investors. This may lead to an overestimation of foreign activity.

- Deliberate over-reporting: as R&D activities often are a necessary condition for government support, foreign enterprises declare part of their activities related to product development as R&D.[4]

- Sometimes no clear distinction is made in Chinese reporting between realised and prospective R&D expenditure.

CONCLUSIONS

Based on the experiences from the data collection we identify four areas where improvements in data quality and availability can considerably increase our knowledge of the internationalisation of business R&D:

First, we believe that *less – not more – detailed data* may give a more complete picture of R&D internationalisation. With an increasing level of detail of the data reported by EU member states over the last years, confidentiality issues further increased and became a main constraint when analysing data on R&D of foreign-owned firms. Data on inward BERD by firms from non-European countries (except the US), for example, is only poorly available in many small EU member states because there are usually only a handful of R&D active foreign-owned firms from a particular home country. As a result, many results are confidential. Another example is inward data in a country x sector split, which may very useful for analytical purposes, but also leads to a large number of confidential values, even in medium sized reporting countries. Thus, we propose to publish (but not collect) data only in larger aggregates to avoid confidentiality issues.

Statistical agencies can overcome this issue by providing data in higher country group and sectoral aggregations. Rather than reporting inward BERD data for individual countries of origin (at the risk of suppressing data due to confidentiality), the statistical agencies should publish country aggregates, specifying the countries included in these aggregates. An aggregate for foreign-owned firms from Asian countries excluding Japan, for example may provide much more valuable information than data for individual countries where most information has to be suppressed because of the low number of firms. Moreover, country aggregates for the EU-27 prepared by EUROSTAT based on the national data would be extremely helpful. Such aggregates will provide valuable information on the role of the EU in the process of R&D internationalisation. It is not possible for researchers to generate such aggregates by summing up national data; though it seems very unlikely that confidentiality is an issue at the EU level.

Second, there are some serious data gaps in the *service sector*. In some countries the service sector is not included at all. More complete data on inward BERD in services, in particular in *knowledge-intensive services*, would enhance our picture of R&D internationalisation where most attention still focuses on manufacturing.

Third, we see a considerable difference in *data quality and availability* between EU and non-EU member countries, in particular emerging economies. Any measure to increase the awareness for the topic in these countries may help to improve our understanding of R&D internationalisation. Some of these countries, in particular China and India, may already be major host locations for overseas R&D of European firms – however, data to test this assumption is not available.

Finally, the *outward perspective* remains poorly covered and is not included in most reporting countries. Outward data can be substituted by the corresponding inward data (mirror flows). This is feasible for some large countries like Germany or France, which appear in nearly all inward BERD data as home countries. But even in these cases big numerical differences between reported inward and outward BERD are visible.

Constructing outward data by the corresponding (mirrored) inward data in a home country split may be helpful to see which countries have large R&D activities abroad and which have not, or to observe shifts in the distribution of outward BERD between the US, Europe and Asia. However, such an approach is only a second-best solution to outward data from enterprise surveys.

NOTES

1. The US, an 'early bird' with respect to R&D in China also realised much higher growth rates in the beginning with an annual average growth rates of outward BERD to China at about 95 percent over the period 1998-2002.
2. For a concise description of the project see Berger and Nones (2008), pp. 105 f. For more details see: Lan and Zheng (2007), pp. 35-51 and OECD (2008c), pp. 278 f.
3. A similar discrepancy can be observed regarding the number of R&D centres in China: According to the Chinese Ministry of Commerce, there were more than 936 foreign R&D centres of various forms in China by the end of 2006. According to western researchers, the number was possibly around 350-450 by early 2007 (OECD 2008b, p. 273).
4. Liefner (2006) presents the results of a survey covering 121 foreign high-tech enterprises in Shanghai in 2003. To be classified and officially acknowledged as a high-tech enterprise, the enterprise has to develop and to produce new products. But only 52 percent of the companies surveyed stated that they were in fact doing R&D (Berger and Nones 2008, p 110).

REFERENCES

Berger, M. and B. Nones (2008), 'Der Sprung über die große Mauer. Die Internationalisierung von F&E und das chinesische Innovationssystem', in M. Steiner (ed.), *Schriftenreihe des Instituts für Technologie und Regionalpolitik,* Volume 9, Graz: Leykam.

Colecchia, A. (2005), *Note on measuring the internationalisation of R&D: what role for NESTI?*, OECD Working Party of National Experts on Science and Technology Indicators, DSTI/EAS/STP/NESTI(2005)11, Paris: OECD.

Colecchia, A. (2006), *Note on internationalisation of R&D: A pilot study undertaken by the NESTI Task Force*, OECD Working Party of National Experts on Science and Technology Indicators, DSTI/EAS/STP/NESTI(2006)22, Paris: OECD.

Colecchia, A. (2007), *NESTI work on R&D internationalisation: Issues for discussion*, OECD Working Party of National Experts on Science and Technology Indicators, DSTI/EAS/STP/NESTI(2007)9, Paris: OECD.

Cozza, C. (2010), *Measuring the internationalisation of EU corporate R&D: A novel complementary use of statistical sources*, Luxembourg: JRC Scientific and Technical Reports.

Davis, K. (2010), *Inward FDI in China and its policy context*, Columbia FDI Profiles, New York: Vale Columbia Center on sustainable international investment, Columbia University.

Eurostat (2007), *Recommendations manual on the production of foreign affiliates statistics (FATS)*, Luxembourg: Office for Official Publications of the European Communities.

Godin, B. (2004), 'Globalizing S&T indicators. How statisticians responded to the political agenda on globalization', Montreal: Project on the History and Sociology of S&T Statistics Working Paper No 27.

Lan, X. and L. Zheng (2007), 'Globalisation of R&D by multinational enterprises in China', in OECD (ed), *Progress report: Review of China's innovation system and policy. Annex 2: Globalisation of R&D*, Paris: OECD.

Liefner, I. (2006), *Ausländische Direktinvestitionen und internationaler Wissenstransfer nach China untersucht am Beispiel von High-Tech Unternehmen in Shanghai und Beijing*. Münster: Lit Verlag.

OECD (1998), *The Internationalisation of Industrial R&D: Patterns and Trends*, Paris: OECD.

OECD (2002), *Frascati Manual 2002. Proposed Standard Practice for Surveys on Research and Experimental Development*, Paris: OECD.

OECD (2005), *Measuring Globalisation: OECD Economic Globalisation Indicators, Paris*, OECD.

OECD (2008a), *The Internationalisation of Business R&D: Evidence, Impacts and Implications*, Paris, OECD.

OECD (2008b), *OECD Reviews of Innovation Policy: CHINA*, Paris: OECD.

OECD (2010), *Measuring Globalisation: OECD Economic Globalisation Indicators 2010*, Paris: OECD.

4. R&D Internationalisation across Countries and over Time

Georg Zahradnik

R&D internationalisation is a highly idiosyncratic process and differs considerably between countries, sectors, and over time (OECD 2008; Hall 2010). This chapter investigates variations in the degree of R&D internationalisation across countries and over time. The first section looks at differences in R&D expenditure of foreign-owned firms (inward BERD) across countries and over time to identify the countries which are most internationalised. The following section gives insights in the shares of various home countries in total inward BERD of the EU countries. In particular, we focus on the question in which countries EU- or non-EU firms have the largest share on inward BERD and look at the most important investor country for each EU country. The following section proceeds with a cross-country analysis of the existing outward BERD data. Finally, we take a first look on the global perspective of R&D internationalisation which will be further investigated in the following chapters.

INWARD BERD ACROSS COUNTRIES AND OVER TIME

We start with a look at the largest countries in terms of inward BERD (Figure 4.1). Although data for a number of countries is missing, it is safe to say that the United States account for the lion's share of total world inward BERD with more than 30 bn EUR PPS. Germany and the United Kingdom follow with more than 5 billion EUR PPP inward BERD in 2007. Japan, France and Canada have a total inward BERD of between 4 and 5 billion EUR PPP. Behind France, a number of countries in the range of between 3 and 4 billion EUR PPP follow, including Israel, Sweden, Italy, Austria, and Belgium. In absolute numbers, inward BERD increased in every single country of Figure 4.1 between 2003 and 2007, except France and Sweden, although decreases in these countries are vanishingly small.

Two important entities are missing in Figure 4.1. First, there is no official data on R&D expenditure of foreign-owned firms for the whole European Union, just data for each member country. Based on the data from the member countries, we estimate that R&D expenditure of foreign-owned firms in the EU-27[1] accounts to more than 42.6 billion EUR in the year 2007. This is higher than the corresponding value for the US. However, this estimation also includes inward BERD between two EU member states (for example R&D expenditure of a French firm in Germany). If inward BERD by EU firms is excluded, inward BERD of the EU-27 shrinks to 22.2 billion EUR.

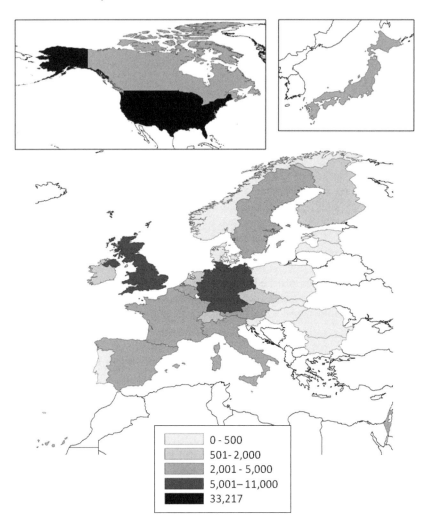

	0 - 500
	501 - 2,000
	2,001 - 5,000
	5,001 - 11,000
	33,217

Note: Malta and Switzerland 2008; Finland 2006.
Source: OECD, Eurostat, national statistical offices, own calculations.

Figure 4.1 Total inward BERD (2007, PPS million EUR)

Another important country missing in Figure 4.1 is China. As discussed in Chapter 3, there is a considerable mismatch between inward BERD in China as reported by the Chinese authorities, and outward BERD to China as reported by national statistical agencies in the EU, the US and Japan. As shown in Chapter 3, R&D expenditure by foreign-owned firms in China accounts 6.1 billion EUR according to Chinese sources. This would put China in a group with Germany and the UK in Figure 4.1, However, US firms report only 856 million EUR of outward BERD in China, and Japanese firms add another 110 million EUR. This would mean that European firms, including Swiss firms, spend around 5 billion EUR on R&D in China, which seems unrealistic. Based R&D expenditure of wholly foreign-owned firms in China and on the share of China on total US outward BERD, we estimate that outward BERD of the EU and Switzerland amounts to around 1.3 billion EUR and total inward BERD in China to be around 2.3 billion EUR in 2007. This puts China in a group with Italy, Austria and Belgium.

The intensity of R&D internationalisation at country level can be measured by overall inward R&D intensity. This indicator measures the ratio of inward BERD to total BERD (including foreign-owned and domestically owned BERD). It thus shows the relative importance of foreign-owned firms in different national innovation systems. Figure 4.2 depicts overall inward R&D intensity for different countries between 2003 and 2007. The figure reveals that the intensity of internationalisation in business R&D is increasing in the majority of countries. Only Hungary and the United Kingdom experienced a decrease in overall inward R&D intensity between 2003 and 2007. However, the internationalisation of R&D emerges only slowly, as inward R&D intensities remained stagnant in a number of countries, including large countries such as France, the US, Japan or Germany. Huge changes between 2003 and 2007 can only be observed in small countries.

There is a large variation in overall inward R&D intensity across countries – ranging from over 80 percent in Malta to less than 5 percent in Japan, Bulgaria and Latvia. As a general rule, the level of R&D internationalisation is highest in small countries. Important examples are Austria, Belgium, the Czech Republic or Ireland. In some of these small countries, R&D expenditure of foreign-owned firms is even higher than R&D expenditure of domestic firms. Smaller countries also exhibit a higher degree of openness in trade or foreign direct investment. In addition, it only takes a handful of multinational firms and their R&D investments to substantially raise overall R&D expenditure in a small country.

Large and medium-sized countries, in contrast, tend to have considerably lower levels of R&D internationalisation. The share of foreign-owned firms on total BERD is around 25 percent in Germany or Spain. In the US, around 15 percent of all business R&D expenditure can be attributed to foreign-owned firms. Japan is, as noted before, with less than five percent considerably below the US value. But there are also exceptions to the rule that the degree of R&D internationalisation decreases with country size. The United

Kingdom and Canada, on the one hand, have high levels of R&D internationalisation compared to other countries of similar size. The UK benefits from its role as the preferred location for the European headquarters of US, Asian and other non-European firms. Canada owes its high degree of R&D internationalisation mostly to its strong economic ties with the US (Hall 2010). Based on the estimate of inward BERD for the European Union (excluding intra-EU internationalisation), inward R&D intensity for the EU-27 is around 15 percent of total BERD. This is roughly the same value as for the United States, so the EU and the US have comparable levels of R&D internationalisation.

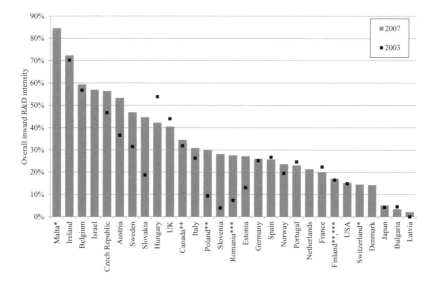

Note: No 2003 data for Malta, Israel, Netherlands, Switzerland and Denmark; * 2008 instead of 2007; ** 2006 instead of 2007; *** 2004 instead of 2003.
Source: OECD, Eurostat, national statistical offices, own calculations.

Figure 4.2 Overall inward R&D intensity[2] (2003 and 2007)

Table 4.1 shows the overall inward R&D intensity as well as the level and the trend of inward BERD for several countries between 1998 and 2007. For years prior to 1998, data is only available for a handful of countries. It is evident that overall inward R&D intensity has been growing or at least remained stable in almost all countries over the last decade. A decline of inward R&D intensity over the long run can only be found in Hungary, Spain and to a lesser extent in Italy. Large increases and decreases are mostly found in small countries and EU-12 countries.

Table 4.1 Overall inward R&D intensity[2] (2000-2007)

	2000	2001	2002	2003	2004	2005	2006	2007	Level	Trend
Ireland		66.4%		70.2%		70.3%		72.4%	High	+
Belgium	59.7%	58.9%	58.0%	56.8%	57.2%	56.8%	59.7%	59.4%	High	=
Israel							59.0%	57.0%	High	=
Czech Republic	36.9%	45.2%	43.3%	46.6%	49.6%	52.5%	59.6%	56.4%	High	+
Austria				36.7%	44.9%			53.3%	High	+
Sweden		44.7%		31.5%		41.0%		46.8%	High	=
Slovakia				18.6%	20.7%	22.7%	33.1%	44.6%	High	+
Hungary				53.9%	38.1%	43.7%	40.8%	42.3%	High	-
United Kingdom	31.3%	42.8%	40.7%	43.9%	40.4%	40.4%	39.1%	40.5%	High	+
Canada	29.2%	28.8%	31.8%	31.9%	33.5%	33.5%	34.6%		Medium	=
Italy		33.0%	27.7%	26.3%	25.8%	25.2%	26.6%	30.9%	Medium	=
Poland	12.1%	4.6%	10.6%	9.3%	16.8%	30.4%	30.1%		Medium	+
Slovenia				3.9%	36.6%		27.6%	28.2%	Medium	+
Romania					7.3%	3.9%	18.4%	27.6%	Medium	+
Estonia				13.0%	26.1%	26.6%	28.5%	27.2%	Medium	+
Germany		22.1%		25.2%		27.5%		26.0%	Medium	+
Spain		31.0%		26.7%	27.4%	26.5%	26.1%	25.8%	Medium	-
Norway				19.5%	21.4%	21.5%	21.9%	23.6%	Medium	=
Portugal		30.8%		24.6%		34.0%		23.1%	Medium	+
Netherlands	26.1%	24.7%						21.4%	Medium	=
France		23.1%	20.4%	22.4%		23.5%	22.2%	20.1%	Medium	=
Finland	12.7%	13.6%			16.4%	16.1%	17.0%		Low	=
US	13.0%	13.1%	14.2%	14.8%	14.4%	13.8%	14.0%	15.2%	Low	=
Turkey	10.6%		6.6%						Low	=
Japan	3.6%	3.4%	3.6%	4.3%	5.1%	5.1%	5.4%	5.1%	Low	=
Bulgaria				4.5%	10.2%	4.4%	4.9%	3.4%	Low	=
Latvia				0.0%	3.4%	2.0%	1.2%	2.2%	Low	=

Note: High intensity is defined as an intensity of more than 40 percent in the last year with data available, medium intensity as intensity between 20 percent and 40 percent and low intensity as intensity of less than 20 percent.
Source: OECD, Eurostat. national statistical offices, own calculations.

Another way to look at the internationalisation of business R&D is to relate inward BERD to the gross domestic product (GDP) (Figure 4.3). Gross domestic expenditure on R&D (GERD) as a percentage of GDP is the most widely used indicator in science and technology policy studies. The EU 2020 strategy sets the goal that at least 3 percent of EU GDP should be spent on R&D in the year 2020.

Foreign-owned firms contribute considerably to this goal in a number of countries. In the European Union, the share of inward BERD on GDP is highest in Sweden, Austria, and Belgium, where R&D expenditure of foreign-owned firms amounts to around one percentage of GDP. All countries with an inward BERD share of more than 0.5 percent of GDP are small and medium sized countries. The non-EU countries included – Canada, Switzerland, the US and Norway – have medium levels of inward BERD as percentage of GDP. The only exception is Israel, which has by far the highest contribution of foreign-owned firms. Israel is an important host country for R&D activities of US computer and software firms.

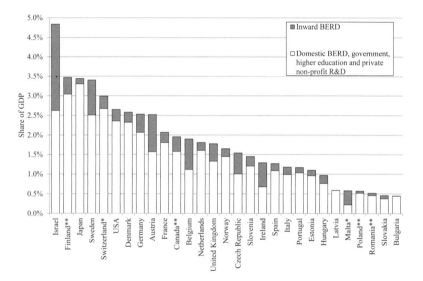

Note: No 2003 data for Malta, Israel, Netherlands, Switzerland and Denmark; * 2008 instead of 2007; ** 2006 instead of 2007; *** 2004 instead of 2003.
Source: OECD, Eurostat, national statistical offices, own calculations.

Figure 4.3 Total inward BERD and gross domestic expenditure on R&D as a % of GDP (2007)

THE MAIN COUNTRIES OF ORIGIN OF INWARD BERD

Countries vary considerably in the degree foreign-owned firms contribute to total R&D expenditure of the business sector. Moreover, there are also major differences between countries in the sources of inward BERD, or, more precisely, in the relative importance of foreign-owned firms from different countries of origin. In particular, we are interested in the relative importance of EU vs. non-EU firms, which are mainly US firms.

The share of different countries of origin on overall inward BERD is illustrated in Figure 4.4. We distinguish between EU-27 and non EU-27 member countries. Further, Germany and the United States are listed separately because of their outstanding absolute importance as home countries of MNEs performing R&D abroad. There are huge differences between countries in this indicator. Countries such as Romania, Hungary, Latvia, or Portugal have virtually no inward BERD from non-EU firms, while the opposite is true for Malta, Ireland and Bulgaria. Between these two extremes, virtually every ratio between EU and non-EU firms can be observed with Belgium, France and Sweden ranging in the middle.

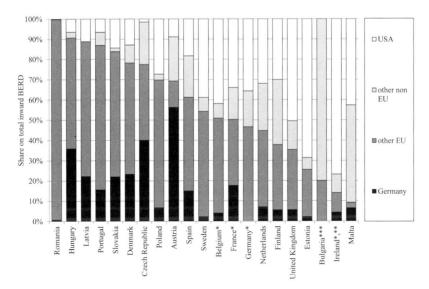

Note: * only manufacturing; ** 1999 (Greece) and 2005 (Ireland) instead of 2007; *** Germany included in other EU and the US included in other non EU.
Source: OECD, Eurostat, national statistical offices, own calculations.

Figure 4.4 Shares of investor countries on inward BERD (2007)

Inward BERD in the countries which joined the European Union in 2004 or later (EU-12 countries) mostly originates from other EU countries. The role of non-EU countries is vanishingly small for most of the EU-12 countries. Exceptions are Estonia, Bulgaria and Malta, which show considerably high shares of inward BERD from the United States. One should however keep in mind that inward BERD in absolute terms is very small in all these countries: this pattern should thus not be over-interpreted and may be traced back to only one or a few firms. This might likewise be the case in Bulgaria, where data only allows us to differentiate between EU and non-EU countries of origin. Similarly to most EU-12 countries, the major shares of inward BERD in Portugal and Denmark are from EU countries.

These variations in the importance of various countries of origin point to the importance of geography, a common language or cultural ties for the internationalisation of R&D. These factors are investigated in detail in Chapter 9 on the drivers of R&D internationalisation. Proximity – may it be socio-cultural or geographic proximity – and language is relevant for countries like Austria, Hungary and the Czech Republic, where the largest shares of inward BERD come from Germany. Large shares of inward BERD from the US in Ireland, Malta or the UK may be explained by the same language.

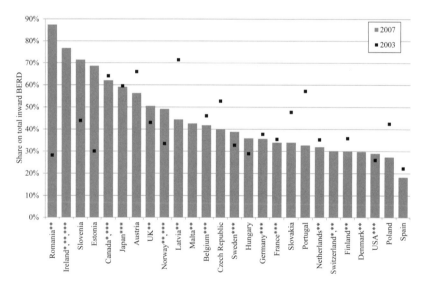

Note: * 2004 (Canada), 2005 (Ireland) and 2008 (Switzerland) instead of 2007; ** 1999 (United Kingdom), 2001 (Netherlands), 2004 (Latvia, Finland) and 2005 (Romania, Norway) instead of 2003; no data for 2003 (Ireland, Malta, Switzerland, Denmark); *** only manufacturing.
Source: OECD, Eurostat, national statistical offices, own calculations.

Figure 4.5 Share of top investor country on inward BERD (2003 and 2007)

OUTWARD BERD ACROSS COUNTRIES AND OVER TIME

In a next step, we turn to the outward perspective and look at R&D activities of firms outside of their home countries. There is considerably less data available for outward BERD than for inward BERD, and no data at all for any emerging economy. Even data for some large industrialised countries like France or the United Kingdom is missing. Therefore, the comparison is limited to only a small number of countries.

Corresponding to the overall inward R&D intensity of Figure 4.2, Figure 4.6 displays overall outward R&D intensity for all countries where data is available. This indicator is defined as outward BERD as a share of total national BERD (including domestic and inward BERD).

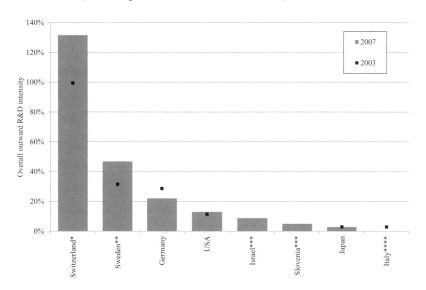

Note: * 2008 instead of 2007 and 2004 instead of 2003, ** only manufacturing included; *** no data for years before 2007; **** 2003 only year with data.
Source: OECD, Eurostat, national statistical offices, own calculations.

Figure 4.6 Overall outward R&D intensity[3] (2003 and 2007)

Similar to inward R&D intensity, the share of overall outward R&D intensity has increased in nearly all countries between 2003 and 2007. Particular attention should be given to Switzerland, where outward R&D intensity amounts to more than 130 percent of total BERD. In other words, R&D expenditure of Swiss firms abroad is higher abroad than in Switzerland.

Another country with a large outward R&D intensity is Sweden; the volume, however, is considerably lower than in Switzerland.

How can we explain the exceptional values of Switzerland and Sweden? Both countries have only a limited domestic market, but a large stock of foreign direct investment abroad and host a number of large multinational firms. These firms have a need to delocalise R&D to bring it closer to larger markets. Moreover, the literature reviewed in Chapter 2 points out that R&D activities abroad can augment and complement the domestic knowledge base, provided that knowledge flows sufficiently towards the MNEs' headquarters.

In contrast to Sweden and Switzerland, Germany and the United States, ranked third and fourth, have large domestic markets. For these countries, the second argument may be of greater importance; i.e. to use R&D abroad to augment and complement the domestic knowledge base. Outward R&D intensity of Germany and the United States is similar to their respective levels of inward R&D intensity. This indicates that the magnitude of investment in R&D abroad is similar to the level of inward R&D in both Germany and the United States.

Total outward BERD in absolute terms is depicted in Figure 4.7. It does not come as a surprise that total outward BERD is largest for the United States, as its stock of FDI abroad is the largest of all countries observed here.

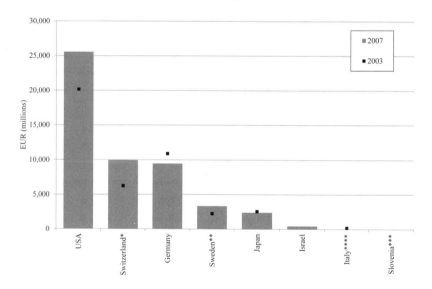

Note: * 2008 instead of 2007 and 2004 instead of 2003; ** only manufacturing included; *** no data for years before 2007; **** 2003 only year with data.
Source: OECD, Eurostat, national statistical offices, own calculations.

Figure 4.7 Total outward BERD (2003 and 2007, million EUR)

Switzerland whose outward R&D intensity is largest (see Figure 4.6) is ranked second, right before Germany and Sweden. Total outward BERD has increased significantly in the United States, Switzerland and Sweden since 2003 (Switzerland 2004) but at the same time slightly decreased in Germany and Japan. The largest increases can be found for the United States; Switzerland showed considerable increases as well.

THE GLOBAL PERSPECTIVE

Finally, inward and outward BERD data for various countries can be used to compile one picture of the global relationships in R&D internationalisation. Figure 4.8 summarises these global relations between the EU, the United States, Japan and Switzerland as measured by inward BERD. Additionally, an estimation for inward BERD in China presented in the first section of this chapter is included. The relations included in the Figure cover the lion's share of R&D expenditure of foreign-owned firms worldwide.

For the US, EU, Japan and Switzerland, we have split inward BERD into the shares of US, EU, Japanese, Swiss firms and in the share of firms from the rest of the world. These shares are marked in different colours. For China we were only able to distinguish between investments from the US, Japan and the rest of the world due to data constraints. Inward BERD of EU and Swiss firms in China is included in 'Rest of the world'. Moreover, the figure illustrates the major relations with lines. The size of each circle represents total inward BERD.

In 2007, US firms spent around 13 billion EUR on R&D in the European Union. R&D expenditure of EU firms in the US is about 9.5 billion EUR. Inward BERD from the US towards the EU-27 and vice versa, accounts for more than half of all inward BERD worldwide, if inward BERD between EU member states is excluded.

R&D expenditure of EU-27 firms in Japan (3.7 billion EUR), R&D expenditure of Swiss firms in the EU-27 (2.5 billion EUR), and R&D expenditure of Swiss firms in the US (4.5 billion EUR) are the most important ones out the remaining cross border links. Inward BERD from countries summarised under Rest of the World appears, if at all, almost entirely in the US or the EU-27.

Inward BERD in China with about 2.3 billion EUR is significantly smaller than the corresponding inward BERD in the US or the EU. However, there are major gaps in Chinese inward BERD data. US and Japanese firms account for about 40 percent of inward BERD in China, the remaining 1.4 billion EUR cannot be allocated to a specific home country and investments from EU countries are included in this value. With a maximum possible value of 1.4 billion EUR of R&D investments of EU firms in China, this value is about 10 percent of the corresponding investments of EU firms in the US.

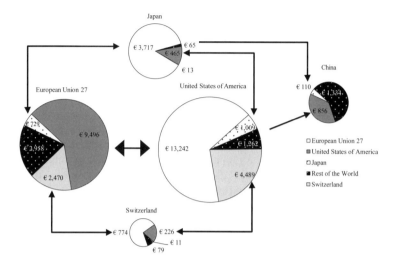

Note: 2006 (US) and 2008 (CH) instead of 2007. Circles represent the location of the R&D activity; values are based on the performing country's inward statistics. The value for EU-27 companies investing in the US includes all European except Swiss companies. EU inward data only includes countries with data available. Only manufacturing included except Switzerland and China (total business). US and JP investments in China are based on the countries' outward statistics. Rest of the World includes all other countries, in particular Canada, China, India, Korea and Australia but also all South American and African economies as well as outward BERD from offshore financial centres.

Source: OECD, Eurostat, national statistical offices, own calculations.

Figure 4.8 Overseas business R&D expenditure in manufacturing between the EU, the US, Japan, China and Switzerland (2007, million EUR)

SUMMARY AND CONCLUSIONS

This chapter presented a comprehensive overview of R&D internationalisation in the business sector at the country level. R&D expenditure of foreign-owned firms increases in the majority of countries over time. The two most important players are the European Union and the United States. Together, they account for the majority of worldwide R&D expenditure of foreign-owned firms. The share of foreign-owned firms on total business R&D expenditure tends to be higher in small countries. Data on R&D activities of domestic firms abroad is scarce. Existing data reveals that the US, Switzerland and Germany are the most active countries abroad. Swiss and Swedish firms show particularly high overseas R&D expenditure compared to R&D at home.

From a policy perspective, the analysis allows to draw some important conclusions. First, it seems that the internationalisation of R&D has the highest relevance for small countries. Inflows of inward BERD helped to raise aggregate R&D expenditure in a very short time in some of these countries. However, there may be also a downside of foreign presence, in particular when the majority of business R&D expenditure is controlled by foreign-owned firms. National policies to foster R&D and innovation often assume that R&D, innovation and production takes place nationally; this is not necessarily the case when MNEs are involved. As a consequence, national policy may face a situation where the results of R&D supported by public money are put into new products and new jobs in another country.

Moreover, the analysis has demonstrated that countries with large overseas R&D activities also show a high degree of R&D intensity at home. Examples are Germany, Sweden and Switzerland. In this perspective, fears that R&D internationalisation in the form of 'R&D offshoring' may endanger national technological capabilities are exaggerated.

NOTES

1.   Data for Cyprus, Greece, Lithuania and Luxembourg is not included in this estimation.
2.   Overall inward R&D intensity is defined as the ratio of inward BERD to total BERD.
3.   Overall outward R&D intensity is defined as the ratio of outward BERD to total BERD.

REFERENCES

Hall, B. A. (2010). 'The internationalization of R&D', Maastricht: UNU-MERIT Working Paper Series 049.

OECD (2008), *The Internationalisation of Business R&D: Evidence, Impacts and Implications*, Paris: OECD.

5. R&D Internationalisation in Belgium, the Czech Republic and Switzerland

Franziska Kampik, Sandra Leitner and Georg Zahradnik

INTRODUCTION

This chapter takes a closer look at of R&D internationalisation in three countries: Belgium, the Czech Republic and Switzerland. All three are small open economies in Europe with a considerable share of exports and inward foreign direct investment; the previous chapter has shown that this type of country benefited most from R&D internationalisation since the year 2000. Belgium and the Czech Republic are indeed among the most internationalised countries in the world in terms of inward BERD; foreign-owned firms account for more than 50 percent on total business R&D in these countries. Switzerland, in addition, is also home to a number of large multinational firms which have generated considerable outward BERD in recent years.

For all three countries, we will examine in detail the development of inward BERD over time, its sectoral distribution, the countries of origins of inward BERD, and the development of outward BERD if available.

BELGIUM

Belgium has a high degree of internationalisation in terms of foreign direct investment and exports. The largest part of business R&D expenditure is concentrated in a small number of firms; in 2001, 40 percent of all business R&D was conducted by only ten enterprises, and only two of these 10 firms were Belgian-owned (Teirlinck 2005). The largest performer of R&D in Belgium, Janssen Pharmaceutica, belongs to the American group Johnson and Johnson since 1961.[1]

In Belgium, the ratio between inward and domestic BERD barely varies over the 1998-2007 period (Figure 5.1). The share of domestic BERD is about 40 percent, while inward BERD is about 60 percent of total BERD over the years. Thus the increase of the total business expenditure in R&D since 2003 results in equal parts from increases of inward and domestic

BERD. Total BERD as share of GDP rises between 1998 and 2001, whereas the total BERD increases more than the GDP, with hardly any variations in the following years. As a result, the share of total BERD over GDP is the same in the years 1998 and 2007.

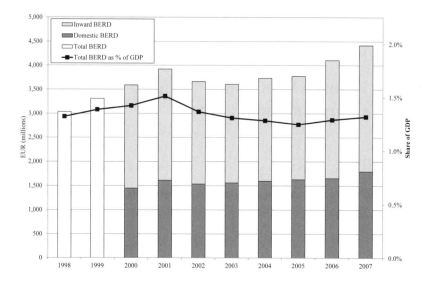

Source: BELSPO, OECD, own calculations.

Figure 5.1 Total BERD, inward BERD, domestic BERD and total BERD as % of GDP (Belgium, 1998-2007)

Inward BERD in Belgium is very much concentrated in a few high-technology sectors.[2] High-technology industries account for around half of total inward BERD in Belgium. Only one quarter of inward BERD in Belgium is outside the high-technology and medium-high technology industries.

At the level of individual industries, the pharmaceutical industry stands out as the sector with the – by far – highest share on total inward BERD (Figure 5.4). Pharmaceuticals account for a share of 36 percent of total inward BERD in Belgium, followed by Radio, TV and communications equipment with a share of 11 percent. Together, the pharmaceutical and the chemical industry account for nearly half (47 percent) of total inward BERD in Belgium. According to a study by the European Cluster Observatory (CSC 2011), Belgium and the Antwerp region in particular comprises one of the largest clusters in the chemical industry in Europe. the region is home to some of the most important manufacturers of chemical products in the world (see also EPCA 2007).

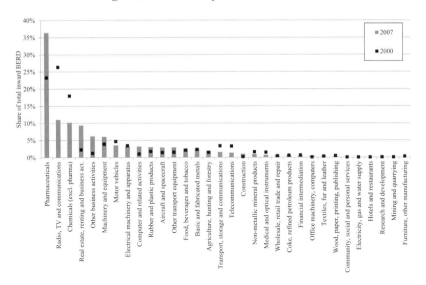

Source: BELSPO, own calculations.

Figure 5.2 Share of inward BERD in different sectors on total inward BERD (Belgium, 2000 and 2007)

We further investigate patterns of R&D internationalisation at the level of industries by calculating an indicator of inward R&D intensity, which is the ratio of inward BERD to total BERD (Figure 5.3).

There is no clear pattern which sectors reveal high inward R&D intensities and which do not: Among the 10 industries with the highest degree of internationalisation, there are knowledge intensive services, less knowledge intensive services, high-technology, medium-high-technology and medium-low-technology manufacturing. Hotels and restaurants is the sector with the highest inward R&D intensity in Belgium (99 percent) in 2007, but has only very little R&D expenditure. A much larger sector which is also largely dominated by foreign-owned firms in Belgium is other transport equipment. A high share of foreign-owned firms on total sectoral BERD can also be found in pharmaceuticals and chemicals, two of the largest sectors in terms of absolute inward BERD.

In contrast to pharmaceuticals and chemicals, there is a large number of sectors where foreign-owned firms play virtually no role as R&D performers. This includes a number of medium- and low-technology sectors, such as textiles, wood, paper, furniture, construction, non-metallic mineral products including glass and bricks, public utilities or a number service industries. Thus, R&D internationalisation predominantly takes place in a rather small number of industries, and R&D activities in large parts of the Belgium business sector are still dominated by domestic actors.

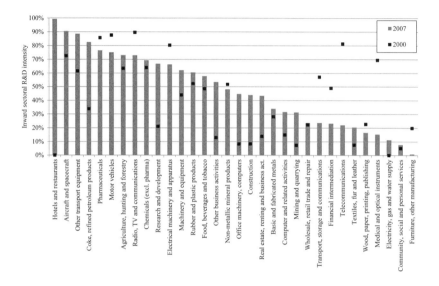

Source: BELSPO, own calculations.

Figure 5.3 Inward sectoral R&D intensity² (Belgium, 2000 and 2007)

The empirical literature reveals that the degree of R&D internationalisation between two countries depends on the distance between these two countries, cultural proximity, relative size of the home and host country, and existing FDI relationships between the two countries (Belderbos et al. 2009; Dachs and Pyka 2010).

Belgium deviates in some respect from this pattern. Unlike other European countries which receive most inward BERD from their neighbouring countries, Belgium receives the largest share of inward BERD from the US (Figure 5.4). This share is still growing. The same applies for other non-EU countries, although the share as well as the growth rate is not as pronounced as in the case of the United States. Inward BERD from the neighbouring countries Netherlands, France and Germany, in contrast, is surprisingly low and even declining. Readers may compare the figures for Belgium with those for the Czech Republic and Switzerland (Figures 5.8 and Figure 5.12). Inward BERD from the UK increased significantly. A slight increase can also be observed in the share of other European countries on inward BERD in Belgium. Therefore, the dependence of R&D internationalisation on the distance between countries, cultural proximity, and relative size of the home and host country cannot be verified for Belgium. The US accounts for nearly 40 percent of all inward BERD in Belgium; on the contrary, the neighbouring countries Germany, France and Netherlands together account for only 30 percent of inward BERD.

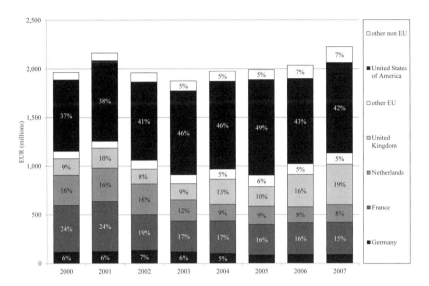

Source: BELSPO, own calculations.

Figure 5.4 Inward BERD – country of origin (Belgium, 2000-2007)

Data not presented here allows to further split inward BERD at the sectoral level into different countries of origin. The large amount of inward BERD from the US (686.9 millions EUR) can be attributed to US firms in the Belgium chemical and pharmaceutical industry. We have already mentioned the takeover of Janssen Pharmaceutica by Johnson and Johnson as one example. The largest share of French inward BERD in Belgium (90.6 percent), is in aerospace. This can be explained by the consolidation of the European aerospace industry since the 1980s.

Inward BERD from Germany, France, Netherlands and the US to a great part goes to medium-high-technology and high-technology manufacturing industries; investments from the UK are concentrated in the high-technology manufacturing industries, whereby the greatest parts go to pharmaceuticals and rubber and plastic products. There is barely any inward BERD to the service sector. One exception is are Swiss firms; the greatest share of Swiss business expenditure on R&D can be found in financial intermediation (including insurance), real estate, renting and business activities, i.e. knowledge intensive services. This fits well with the strong position of the Swiss financial services industry in outward BERD (see Figure 5.14).

CZECH REPUBLIC

Compared to Belgium and Switzerland, the internationalisation of R&D has a rather short history in the Czech Republic. After the collapse of communism in 1989, transition into a market economy started, with privatisation being one of its main tasks. The new company owners then decided over the survival of existing research and development centres of the privatised firms. Foreign investors were welcomed in this privatisation process. Thus, foreign direct investment is the second highest in the region. The Czech economy is strongly focused on the transport equipment industry, basic and fabricated metal products, rubber and other non-metallic mineral products as well as electrical equipment and electronics. Foreign direct investment also went predominantly into these industries.

Figure 5.5 demonstrates that within only ten years, both domestic and foreign inward BERD changed dramatically in the Czech Republic. Specifically, domestic BERD almost doubled from initially 284.03 million EUR in 1998 to 487.13 million EUR in 2007. Interestingly, this increase is more of a recent phenomenon and attributable to the years 2005 to 2007 only, while the period from 1998 to 2004 is characterised by relatively stable or only slightly rising domestic BERD.

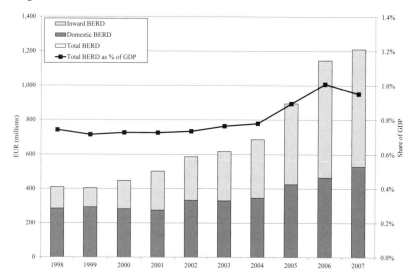

Source: Czech Statistical Office based on R&D survey and information from SBS, own calculations.

Figure 5.5 Total BERD, inward BERD, domestic BERD and total BERD as % of GDP (Czech Republic, 1998-2007)

The surge in R&D expenditure is, however, even more spectacular for inward BERD which, starting from 125.46 million EUR in 1998, already doubled within just four years (to 254.11 million EUR in 2002), almost tripled in 2004 (to 349.91 million EUR) and more than quintupled in 2007 (to 682.87 million EUR). As a consequence, the share of inward BERD in total BERD nearly doubled from initially 30 percent in 1998 to around 60 percent in 2007, reflecting the growing dominance of inward BERD in the Czech Republic and highlighting the country's rising attractiveness for R&D activities of foreign-owned firms. Moreover, these changes in domestic and inward BERD also translate into higher total BERD as a percentage of GDP. And while the share of total BERD in GDP remained fairly stable at around 0.74 percent between 1998 and 2004, it rose to approximately 1 percent in 2006, due to the joint dramatic increase in both domestic and inward BERD between 2005 and 2007.

A closer look at total inward BERD at the sectoral level reveals the strong role of the manufacturing sector which spent the lion's share of inward BERD (Figure 5.6). Starting in 2002/2003, however, the service sector gained importance, contributing ever increasing inward BERD to total BERD. Specifically, between 1998 and 2001, 90 percent of all inward BERD was attributed to the manufacturing sector while this share dropped to 73 percent in 2007.

In terms of composition of sectoral inward BERD, medium-high-tech industries and knowledge-intensive service industries account for most of total inward BERD. However, over the ten-year period under consideration, medium-high-tech industries continuously lost ground as inward BERD became increasingly more important in high-technology industries in the manufacturing sector and knowledge-intensive industries in the service sector: Starting in 2002, the share of inward BERD in medium-high-technology industries dropped from around 90 percent to only 73 percent in 2007. In contrast, the share of inward BERD in high-tech industries almost doubled from around 8.5 percent in 2002 to 16 percent in 2007. In the same vein, the share of inward BERD in knowledge-intensive industries more than tripled between 2002 and 2007, from around 9 percent to 24 percent.

In a sectoral perspective, a clear dominance of one particular sector becomes apparent: In 1998 and 2007, with about 77 percent and 40 percent of all inward BERD, respectively, motor vehicles was the major beneficiary of inward BERD among all industries. Far behind motor vehicles, rubber and plastic products and real estate, renting and business activities came in second and third in 1998. And while from 1998 to 2007 real estate, renting and business activities and financial intermediation advanced to the second and third rank, respectively, rubber and plastic products lost ground and relative attractiveness for inward BERD. Interestingly, also commercial research and development services lost relative attractiveness as the sector's share on total inward BERD halved from 5.5 percent in 1998 to only 2.6 percent in 2007.

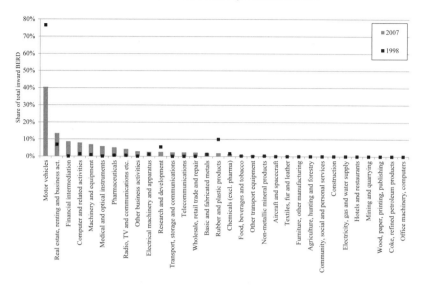

Source: Czech Statistical Office based on R&D survey and information from SBS, own calculations.

Figure 5.6 Share of inward BERD in different sectors on total inward BERD (Czech Republic, 1998 and 2007)

Figure 5.7 depicts inward R&D intensities by sector for 1998 and 2007, defined as the ratio of a sector's inward BERD to its total BERD which reflects a sector's degree of internationalisation. It highlights that in 2007 only 12 out of 32 industries had inward R&D intensities above 50 percent in the Czech Republic. Moreover, within this group, with inward R&D intensities above 90 percent, telecommunications, transport, storage and communications, motor vehicles and financial intermediation showed the highest degree of internationalisation. With 98.4 percent, the share of R&D activities performed by foreign-owned firms is highest in the telecommunications sector. In contrast, mining and quarrying, wood, paper, printing and publishing, coke and refined petroleum products and office machinery and computers reported no inward BERD at all.

In addition, Figure 5.7 also shows that with the exception of rubber and plastic products and the four aforementioned zero-inward BERD recipients, R&D activities of all industries became more internationalised between 1998 and 2007, reporting partly substantially higher inward BERD in 2007 than in 1998. Specifically, the involvement of foreign-owned firms in R&D activities of the telecommunications, the transport, storage and the communications sector increased dramatically during this period.

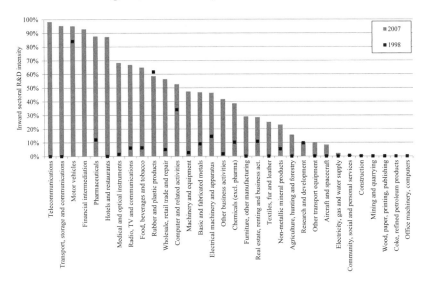

Source: Czech Statistical Office based on R&D survey and information from SBS, own calculations.

Figure 5.7 Inward sectoral R&D intensity (Czech Republic, 1998 and 2007)

The majority of total inward BERD in the Czech Republic originates from countries within the European Union. The largest country of origin is Germany, which provided between 53 percent in 2003 and 40 percent of total inward BERD in the Czech business sector in 2007 (Figure 5.8). Additionally, apart from Germany, the Netherlands and the UK were the second and third most important countries of origin, respectively.

Over the years, Germany – while maintaining its pivotal role – became relative less important while the Netherlands and all other EU countries become more vital sources of the country's inward BERD, together accounting for between 13 percent in 2003 and 36 percent of all inward BERD in 2007. As a result, the concentration of inward BERD in the Czech Republic decreased in this period.

In contrast to the composition of inward BERD in Belgium and Switzerland, firms from the United States and other non-EU countries contribute only very little to inward BERD in the Czech Republic. The share of US firms on inward BERD is only around 2 percent, which is less than the corresponding share of the Russian Federation. Even lower (less than 3 million EUR) is total inward BERD from Asian countries including Japan and Korea. Surprisingly low is also inward BERD from Slovakia with only 3 million EUR. Slovakia and the Czech Republic are neighbouring countries which together formed the state of Czechoslovakia until·1993, so economic linkages between the two countries should be strong.

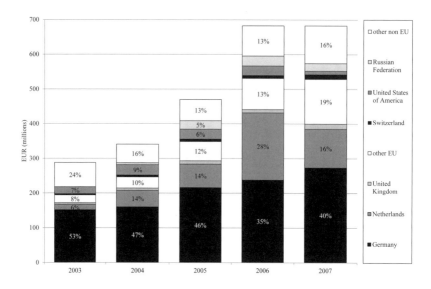

Source: Czech Statistical Office based on R&D survey and information from SBS, own calculations.

Figure 5.8 Inward BERD by country of origin (Czech Republic, 2003-2007)

A breakdown of inward BERD by country of origin and industry of destination highlights that Germany, the most important country of origin, strongly bundles its inward R&D expenditure and dominates the Czech motor vehicles industry with 215.2 million EUR or 74.3 percent of the industry's total BERD. Similarly, industries such as telecommunications and chemicals (including pharmaceuticals) predominantly fund their R&D activities by means of inward BERD, with the Netherlands providing more than 50 percent of all total industry-level BERD. With 25.3 million EUR (or 42.9 percent of total BERD), Italy, on the other hand, is the major country of origin for inward BERD in the Czech medical and optical instruments industry. R&D expenditure of Italian firms in this sector, however, only amount to a tenth of the corresponding expenditure of German firms in the Czech automotive industry.

A more diversified pattern emerges for industries such as wholesale, retail trade and vehicle repair, machinery and equipment, computer and related activities or other business activities. These industries source from different countries to different degrees. Interestingly, the US plays a non-negligible role in other business activities, contributing around 11 percent of the industries' overall BERD.

SWITZERLAND

Switzerland has some characteristics that makes it very interesting for a country case study: first, the Swiss business sector is among the most R&D intensive in the world. The GERD/GDP ratio of Switzerland reached nearly 3 percent in 2008 (OECD 2013, p. 21). Such an R&D intensive environment offers large potential spillovers to foreign-owned firms. Strengths of the Swiss economy are in pharmaceuticals, chemicals, machinery and electrical and electronic equipment. Second, Switzerland is home to a large number of multinational firms, and the country has a very large stock of outward FDI relative to GDP (OECD 2010, p. 85). We can thus expect a large volume of outward BERD as well. Third, Switzerland is in geographical proximity to three large EU countries, but not a member of the EU itself. This may have consequences for the structure of inward, but also outward BERD.

Data on inward and outward BERD for Switzerland is less complete than in other countries (Figure 5.9). Total BERD is only available for the years 2000, 2004 and 2008, and inward and domestic BERD only for the year 2008. Thus, only the year 2008 is included in the analysis.

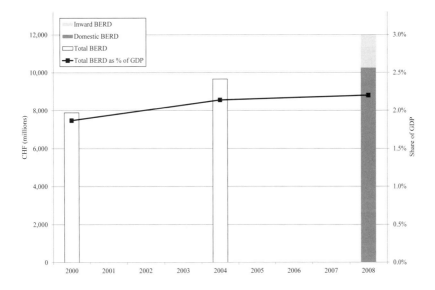

Source: Swiss Federal Statistical Office, own calculations.

Figure 5.9 Total BERD, inward BERD, domestic BERD and total BERD as % of GDP (Switzerland, 1998-2008)

Total BERD increased by more than 50 percent since 2000. In the year 2008, total BERD in Switzerland accounts for almost 12 billion CHF. 2,632 R&D active enterprises operated in Switzerland in 2008, 378 of them were foreign-owned (Swiss Federal Statistical Office 2011).

Inward BERD accounts for 14 percent of total BERD in 2008 (Figure 5.9). This is only a low share compared to other countries of similar size and R&D intensity. Hence, Switzerland demonstrates that a high aggregate R&D intensity, geographical proximity to main R&D performing countries, and openness does not necessarily correlate with high degrees of inward BERD. In this respect, Switzerland is more similar to Finland than to Austria, Israel or Belgium. The low share of inward BERD on total BERD, however, does not necessarily indicate a low attractiveness of the country; in absolute terms, Switzerland attracts roughly the same amount of inward BERD as Ireland or Finland. It may rather be a sign of the R&D intensity of domestically owned firms in Switzerland.

Like in Belgium and the Czech Republic, inward BERD in Switzerland is also concentrated in only few industries. High-technology manufacturing industries account for the largest share, followed by the medium-high-technology manufacturing industries and knowledge intensive services (Figure 5.10).

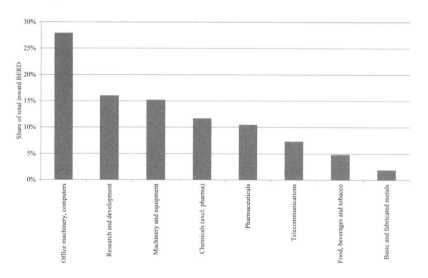

Source: Swiss Federal Statistical Office, own calculations.

Figure 5.10 Share of inward BERD in different sectors on total BERD (Switzerland, 2008)

Almost 30 percent of inward BERD in Switzerland is in the office machinery and computer sector. Second and third are commercial research and development services (16 percent), and machinery and equipment (15 percent). The prominent share of commercial R&D services in the sectoral composition of inward BERD points to the role of Switzerland as a location of corporate R&D centres. Firms in this sector are often affiliated to a multinational enterprise as their sole client.

Some readers may be surprised that the pharmaceutical and the chemical industry are not among the Top Three sectors according to inward BERD. However, the image of Switzerland being strong in chemicals and pharmaceuticals is not rejected by the figure. Both sectors together account for 22 percent of all inward BERD in Switzerland, Moreover, a considerable share R&D activities in commercial R&D services may consist pharmaceutical and chemical research. This sector also includes R&D centres of multinational firms organized as independent legal entities, which makes the assignment to the correct industry difficult.

Inward sectoral R&D intensity, the share of inward BERD on total sectoral BERD, is highest in chemicals (Figure 5.11). Foreign-owned firms account for 31 percent of total BERD in this sector. The chemical industry is followed by the telecommunications sector (28 percent), research and development services (24 percent) and the machinery sector (19 percent).

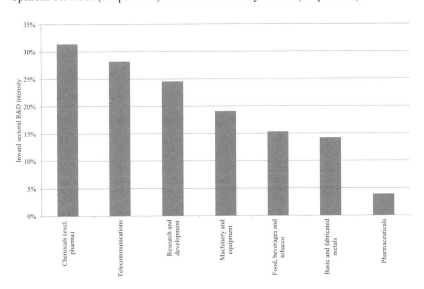

Source: Swiss Federal Statistical Office, own calculations.

Figure 5.11 Inward sectoral R&D intensity (Switzerland, 2008)

The pharmaceutical industry, which has inward sectoral R&D intensities of more than 70 percent in Belgium and the Czech Republic, reveals only a value of below 5 percent, which indicates that more than 95 percent of all R&D expenditure in this sector is raised by domestically owned firms. The low level of R&D internationalisation in Switzerland is a direct result of the dominance of domestically owned firms in the Swiss pharmaceuticals sector.

There are 378 R&D active foreign-owned firms from 23 different countries in Switzerland (Swiss Federal Statistical Office 2011). However, firms from only four countries account for almost 70 percent of inward BERD (Figure 5.12): Germany, the United States, France, and the UK. German and US firms are the biggest R&D spenders in Switzerland and raise 30 percent and 21 percent of total inward BERD respectively. France and the United Kingdom account for 9 percent of inward BERD each. Furthermore, firms from the Netherlands, Italy, Sweden, Austria and Japan are contributing substantial amounts to Swiss inward BERD. This distribution once again shows that R&D internationalisation is still mainly taking place between high-income countries.

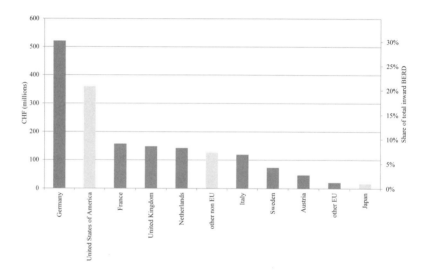

Source: Swiss Federal Statistical Office, own calculations.

Figure 5.12 Inward BERD by country of origin (Switzerland, 2008)

The importance of Switzerland in the internationalisation of R&D is mainly due to the role of the country as source of outward BERD. Figure 4.1 in Chapter 4 has already illustrated that Swiss firms invest much more in R&D abroad than the size of the country would suggest; in absolute terms, affiliates of Swiss MNEs spent 15.7 bn CHF (or around 10 bn EUR) on R&D outside Switzerland, compared to 12 bn CHF of BERD spent inside Switzerland. To our knowledge, Switzerland is the only country where firms spend more on R&D abroad than at home, and outward BERD exceeds total BERD. This makes Switzerland the second largest R&D performer abroad, ahead of Germany but behind the United States. This remarkable position can mainly be explained by the global R&D activities of Swiss pharmaceutical firms (Figure 5.13). 67 percent of total outward BERD originates from this industry. Chapter 6 discussed some reasons for the high levels of internationalisation in pharmaceutical R&D.

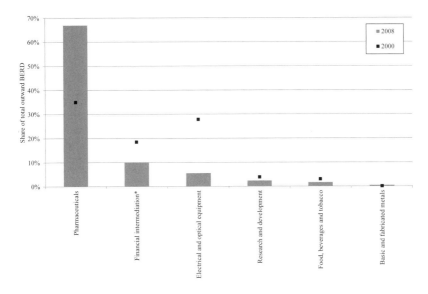

*2004 instead of 2008
Source: Swiss Federal Statistical Office, own calculations.

Figure 5.13 Share of various industries on total outward BERD (Switzerland, 2000 and 2008)

Outward BERD in pharmaceuticals has doubled since the year 2000, when the sector accounted for only 35 percent of total. In 2000, the pharmaceutical sector ranked just slightly above the electrical and optical instruments with a share of 27.8 percent (5.6 percent in 2008). In 2008, this sector was overtaken by the financial intermediation, now accounting for more than 10 percent of outward BERD. There is also some outward BERD in the food, beverages and tobacco industry and in commercial research and development services. These account for a share of 2.4 percent on total.

Another way to look at Swiss outward BERD is to relate outward BERD to the corresponding domestic R&D expenditure at the sectoral level. The ratio of outward BERD to domestic BERD (Figure 5.14) reveals the relative importance of R&D activities abroad. In this perspective, financial intermediation reach a value of almost 700 percent, which indicates that BERD of affiliates of Swiss banks and insurance companies located abroad is almost seven times the corresponding BERD at home. Swiss pharmaceutical firms reveal also a very high share of outward sectoral R&D intensity. Outward BERD accounts for almost 230 percent of domestic BERD in this sector. Other sectors with considerable R&D activities of Swiss firms abroad include the food, beverages and tobacco industry and commercial research and development services.

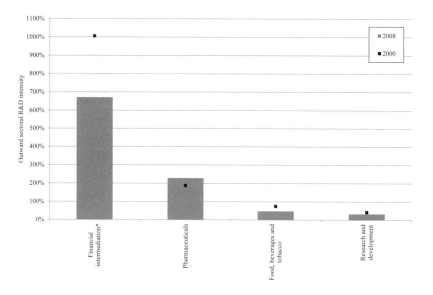

*2004 instead of 2008
Source: Swiss Federal Statistical Office, own calculations.

Figure 5.14 Ratio of outward BERD to domestic BERD at sectoral level (Switzerland, 2000 and 2008)

These very high shares again point to the highly internationalised character of the Swiss economy. Moreover, despite huge investments in R&D abroad, Swiss firms are still performing considerable R&D activities in Switzerland. Additional research on the motives and goals of innovation activities of Swiss firms abroad (Arvanitis and Hollenstein 2011) indicate that knowledge-oriented motives of foreign R&D indeed positively influence the innovation performance of domestic firms, whereas market- and resource-oriented strategies have a positive impact on labour productivity.

CROSS-COUNTRY OBSERVATIONS

This chapter presented an in-depth view of R&D internationalisation in three small European countries, Belgium, the Czech Republic and Switzerland. All three countries share some similarities with respect to R&D activities of foreign-owned firms:

First, R&D expenditure of foreign-owned firms is concentrated in a small number of medium high- and high technology sectors in all three countries. The pharmaceutical, the chemical and the automotive industry are among these most important sectors.

Second, the US and Germany are the main countries of origin for inward BERD. Moreover, the Netherlands and France have some importance in each country. Smaller countries and firms from 'other non-EU countries' – which also includes emerging economies – play no role as countries of origin so far.

Third, we can identify one single multinational firm as the main source of inward BERD in two of the three countries. In the Czech Republic, the high shares of Germany in the automotive sector can be traced back to the takeover of main national R&D player (Skoda) by a foreign company (VW). In Belgium, a considerable share of inward BERD can be attributed to Janssen Pharma, a subsidiary of US the pharmaceutical MNE Johnson and Johnson, which is the largest performer of R&D in the Belgium business sector. Hence, foreign takeovers of domestic firms do not necessarily lead to a decline of domestic R&D capabilities.

Finally, there are no signs of a substitution effect between inward BERD and domestic BERD in the two countries where time series are available. Increases in inward BERD in absolute terms are associated with rising R&D expenditure of domestically owned firms in both countries. There may be even some complementarities between inward and domestic BERD, as data for Belgium and the Czech Republic show, where inward and domestic BERD grew faster in the final years of the observation period. Compared to Belgium, and the Czech Republic, foreign-owned firms contribute in Switzerland only little to total business sector R&D in relative terms. This is, however, a result of the fact that domestic BERD is very high in Switzerland; in absolute terms, inward BERD in Switzerland corresponds to values of Ireland or Finland. Just like in Belgium, inward BERD in Switzerland is mainly concentrated in the chemical and pharmaceuticals industry. Almost 70 percent of inward BERD comes from four countries: Germany, the United States, France and the United Kingdom.

Switzerland has the second-largest stock of R&D activities abroad, just ahead of Germany. This high outward intensity is mainly driven by the activities of Swiss pharmaceutical companies. The Swiss example shows that considerable R&D activities abroad can go hand in hand with a high domestic R&D intensity, and that outward BERD is not necessarily displacing domestic R&D activities.

NOTES

1. http://en.janssenpharmaceutica.be/our-story/history. The case of the Janssen takeover is interesting case, because the company had also an affiliate in Germany, and a change in ownership of the Belgium parent company led to a subsequent ownership change of the German affiliate as well. After the takeover, Janssen further expanded its global presence with research centres in the US, Germany, the UK, Spain, and India. This type of company history may illustrate why it is sometimes difficult to identify the final controlling country of a firm.
2. R&D expenditure data for Belgium in a sectoral breakdown is only available by *product field* and not by the *main activity* of the firm. This means that R&D expenditure of one sector can be assigned to more than one product field. If a firm has R&D activities in machinery and in computer services, total R&D expenditure of the firm is divided between these two product fields. This makes service R&D of manufacturing firms more visible; it can, however, also reduce R&D expenditure of the service sector, when service firms perform a lot of R&D in manufacturing product fields. To facilitate the presentation of the data, product field will be used as a synonym for industrial sectors in this section.

REFERENCES

Arvanitis, S. and H. Hollenstein (2011), 'How do different drivers of R&D investment in foreign locations affect domestic firm performance? An analysis based on Swiss panel micro data', *Industrial and Corporate Change*, **20**(2), 605-40.

Belderbos, R., Leten, B. and S. Suzuki (2009), 'Does excellence in scientific research attract foreign R&D?', Maastricht: UNU-Merit Working Paper 2009-066.

CSC (2011), *Smart specialisation in Europe: European specialisation data by industry*, Stockholm: Center for Strategy and Competitiveness (CSC), Stockholm School of Economics.

Dachs, B. and A. Pyka (2010), 'What drives the internationalisation of innovation? Evidence from European patent data', Economics of Innovation and New Technology **19**(1), 71-86.

EPCA (2007), *A Paradigm Shift: Supply Chain Collaboration and Competition in and between Europe's Chemical Clusters*, Brussels: European Petrochemical Association (EPCA).

OECD (2010), *Measuring Globalisation: OECD Economic Globalisation Indicators 2010*, Paris: Organisation for Economic Co-operation and Development.

OECD (2013), *Main Science and Technology Indicators 2/2012*, Paris: Organisation for Economic Co-operation and Development.

Swiss Federal Statistical Office (2011), *International aspects of Swiss research and development in 2008. From the internationalisation of enterprises to international public cooperation*, Neuchâtel: FSO News.

Teirlinck, P. (2005), 'Location and Agglomeration of Foreign R&D Activities in a small open Economy', in A. Spithoven, A. and Teirlinck (eds.), *Beyond Borders. Internationalisation of R&D and Policy Implications for Small Open Economies*, Amsterdam, Elsevier, pp. 207-34.

6. The Sectoral Perspective

Georg Zahradnik

Innovation is highly sector-specific; it is well documented that innovation processes differ widely across technologies and industries (Marsili 2001; Malerba 2005a, b; Peneder 2007). Concepts such as 'high-technology' or 'low-technology' sectors (Hatzichronoglou 1997), sectoral systems of innovation (Malerba 2002, 2004, 2005b), or technological regimes (Malerba and Orsenigo 1996; Marsili 2001) have found wide recognition in the literature as well as in public discussions on technology policy. The sector is also a relevant category in international economics. There are large differences between industries in the share multinational firms have on aggregate production and employment (Barba Navaretti and Venables 2004). In the words of Markusen (1995, p. 172), 'multinationals tend to be important in industries and firms with four characteristics: high levels of R&D relative to sales; a large share of professional and technical workers in their workforces; products that are new and/or technically complex; and high levels of product differentiation and advertising. These characteristics appear in many studies, and I have never seen any of them contradicted by any study'.

The following chapter compares the internationalisation of business R&D across different sectors. Due to data constraints, the analysis is limited in two respects: first, the data only allow an analysis of inward BERD data but not of outward BERD data. Second, the countries with data available differ across sectors and over time.[1] As a result, only the analysis of the six largest sectors[2] – five manufacturing sectors and knowledge-intensive services – is feasible and the interpretation of the results has to be done carefully.

All five manufacturing sectors included are high technology or medium-high technology sectors: pharmaceuticals, machinery and equipment, electrical and optical equipment (including office, accounting and computing machinery; electrical machinery and apparatus; radio, TV and communications and medical, precision and optical instruments) motor vehicles and other transport equipment (including aircraft and spacecraft). The only non-manufacturing sector considered is real estate, renting and business activities. It includes most knowledge intensive services (KIS), and in most countries even a huge proportion of total services. As mentioned before, these six sectors are of outstanding absolute importance, each of them attracting between

5.2 billion PPS EUR (machinery and equipment) and 16.4 billion PPS EUR (pharmaceuticals) inward BERD in 2007 worldwide.

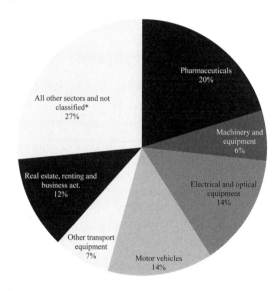

Note: Included countries see Note 1; * includes all other sectors but also all reported cross-border R&D which cannot be allocated to any specific industrial sector.
Source: OECD, Eurostat, national statistical offices, own calculations.

Figure 6.1 Sectoral distribution of cross-border BERD (2007)

As shown in figure 6.1, these six sectors account for at least 73 percent of total worldwide cross-border BERD. Out of the remaining 27 percent of total world-wide cross-border BERD, all other sectors account for a small fraction of these 27 percent, the larger part are expenditures which cannot be allocated to any industrial sector.

SECTORAL DIFFERENCES IN R&D INTERNATIONALISATION

Figure 6.2 compares the inward sectoral R&D intensities for these six sectors over time. This intensity is defined as the ratio of sectoral inward BERD to total sectoral BERD for all countries with inward data available in a given year. Pharmaceuticals are the sector with the highest inward R&D intensity and thus the most internationalised sector over the whole period. However, there is a sharp decline of inward intensity from 2003 (about 45 percent) to 2004 (about 30 percent). This decline is not caused by a reduction of inward

BERD but by a massive increase of the reported domestic BERD in the US from 6.2 billion PPS EUR in 2003 to 19.2 billion PPS EUR in 2004, an increase of 12.8 billion PPS EUR or 199 percent within one year. The result is an increase of the worldwide sectoral BERD in pharmaceuticals of almost exactly the same amount, 13.3 billion PPS EUR. Combined with a fairly stable worldwide inward BERD (11.9 billion PPS EUR in 2003 and 12.1 billion PPS EUR in 2004) this leads to the observed decrease of the sectoral R&D intensity.

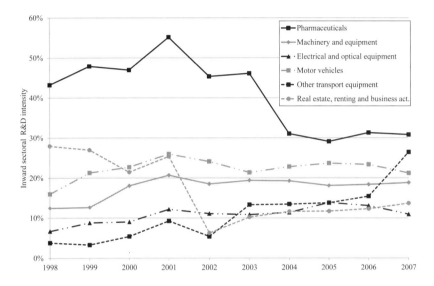

Note: Included countries see Note 1.
Source: OECD, Eurostat, national statistical offices, own calculations.

Figure 6.2 Inward sectoral R&D intensity (1998-2007)

The second massive drop in sectoral R&D intensities is in real estate, renting and business activities from 2001 to 2002. Again, it is not caused by a decrease in inward BERD but an increase in total BERD caused by an increase in domestic BERD. Data for this sector for the US is not available before 2002, and the inclusion of US data boosts total sectoral BERD from 7.4 billion to 45.7 billion PPS EUR while inward BERD only increases from 3.3 billion to 6.0 billion PPS EUR.

The third outstanding annual change in intensity levels, the increase of the intensity level of other transport equipment from 2006 to 2007, is again caused by a change in the largest economy, the US. However, in this case the movement is caused by a change in the inward BERD data, a massive increase of inward BERD in the aircraft and airspace sector in the US, which is included in other transport equipment. This may be due to a takeover of a US aircraft company. The three remaining sectors all have stable and comparable low intensity levels for the most recent years.

Figure 6.3 displays the concentration of inward BERD across destination countries for the six sectors considered measured by a Herfindahl Index. This concentration index tells us the skewness of the distribution of inward BERD by destination countries. A low Herfindahl value indicates that inward BERD in the sector is equally distributed across different countries. Four of the six sectors show decreasing and converging concentration levels, indicating a more even distribution and a larger number of host countries.

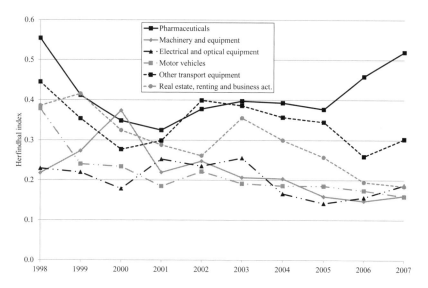

Note: Included countries see Note 1 Source: OECD, Eurostat, national statistical offices, own calculations.

Figure 6.3 Concentration of inward BERD (1998-2007)

Pharmaceuticals, and to a smaller extent other transport equipment, have sustained higher concentration levels. The concentration in the pharmaceutical industry even increased considerably over the last observation years. This is caused by the growing role of the US as a destination for inward BERD in the pharmaceutical industry, increasing from 7.3 billion PPS EUR in 2005 to 11.6 billion PPS EUR in 2007. At the same time, inward BERD in this sector in all other countries of the world together slightly decreased. As a result, more than 70 percent of worldwide inward BERD in this sector in 2007 is located in the US.

R&D INTERNATIONALISATION IN THE PHARMA-CEUTICAL INDUSTRY

The previous section pointed to the pharmaceutical industry as the most internationalised sector, both in terms of total inward BERD as well as in terms of the share of BERD controlled by multinational firms. This section investigates the reasons behind the high degree of R&D internationalisation in this sector.

A first striking feature of the pharmaceutical industry is a decreasing R&D productivity. Between 2000 and 2009, R&D expenditure in the US pharmaceutical industry more than doubled (OECD 2012). However, the number of new molecular entities (NMEs) approved by the Food and Drug Administration (FDA) and introduced into U.S. markets decreased to about 20 to 30 per year in the same period (Comanor and Scherer 2013). As a consequence, R&D productivity in the pharmaceutical industry decreased and development costs per new drug approval increased considerably. DiMasi and Grabowski (2007) estimate the total capitalised costs per approved NME to be 1.3 bn USD on average.

In addition, the pharmaceutical industry is characterised by strong regulations in all major functions, deriving from uncertainty about drug safety and efficacy (Danzon 2000, 2006). Effects of those regulations are twofold: the industry's cost structure as well as competition changes due to regulation of safety, efficacy and quality; whereas regulation of price, reimbursement and promotion affect demand and profitability (Danzon 2000, p. 1057). Therefore, requirements to pharmaceuticals further added to the intrinsically high cost of R&D and led to launch delays of new drugs.

As a result of cost increases and productivity decreases in R&D, the number of large, R&D active companies decreased over time and the sector became increasingly concentrated (Comanor and Scherer 2013). Firms tried to exploit potential economies of scale, scope and risk-pooling by horizontal mergers (Danzon 2000, p. 1083). Due to the high R&D costs, companies only perform in areas in which they excel themselves, and outsource the remaining products and processes to specialised suppliers. This concentration process is still on-going. In addition, small firms are gaining importance as providers of R&D services and new tools for enhancing R&D productivity. New drugs increasingly originate from small, often single-product firms, which frequently are start-up biotech firms (Comanor and Scherer 2013). These small biotechnology start-ups predominantly originate from academic research and emerge in clusters around universities and other research organisations. Hence, relevant knowledge and potential collaboration partners are also highly concentrated in a few regions around the world, such as Cambridge/UK, Boston/US, San Francisco/US, or Munich/DE. A mutual dependence between large and small firms emerged in the sector, where small firms specialise in discovery, and enjoy the advantages of a rapidly advancing scientific base, while large firms have the resources and expertise to do the detailed and highly expensive clinical testing and commercialisation. This in turn offers strong incentives for collaborations, alliances, and mergers and acquisitions (see inter alia Danzon 2000, 2006; Comanor and Scherer 2013).

All those factors favour national and international mergers and acquisitions, collaborations, partnerships, and joint ventures. In turn, cross-border mergers and acquisitions have led to a high degree of internationalisation in R&D activities of the pharmaceutical industry. In addition, the high R&D costs force firms to worldwide commercialisation (Danzon 2000, p. 1056). The pharmaceutical market is a global one and research-based pharmaceutical companies exploit products globally through licensing, exports and production in local subsidiaries.

GEOGRAPHICAL DISTRIBUTION OF INWARD BERD AT THE SECTORAL LEVEL

Figure 6.4 provides the share of total inward BERD by host country for each of the six sectors considered – pharmaceuticals, machinery and equipment, electrical and optical equipment (including office, accounting and computing machinery; electrical machinery and apparatus; radio, TV and communications and medical, precision and optical instruments) motor vehicles, other transport equipment (including aircraft and spacecraft) and real estate, renting and business activities – in 2007.

Besides the US, which play a dominant role as location for inward BERD in pharmaceuticals, only two more countries, Germany and Belgium, account for more than 5 percent of the total sectoral inward BERD. All other countries of the world together only account for about 15 percent of total sectoral inward BERD, explaining the before mentioned high concentration in that sector.

Machinery and equipment, one of the sectors with the lowest concentration by controlling country, is the sector with the highest cumulated share for all EU countries, attracting more than 2/3 thirds of total inward BERD in this sector. While the US plays a much smaller role, with more than 30 percent it still accounts for the lion share of the remaining inward BERD. Interestingly inward BERD in this sector is widely distributed across different EU countries. While two of the largest EU economies, Germany and the United Kingdom, are ranked two and three worldwide, also smaller economies, including Sweden (6.6 percent of total inward BERD) and Austria (5 percent) play a certain role. With seven countries each attracting more than 5 percent of total inward BERD, this sectors has the highest number of countries above this threshold.

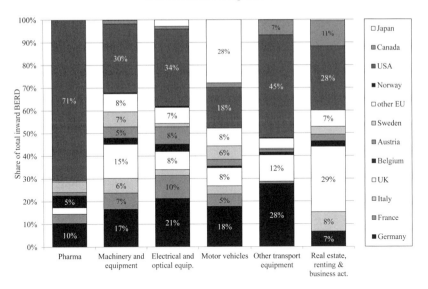

Note: Included countries see Note 1.
Source: OECD, Eurostat, national statistical offices, own calculations.

Figure 6.4 Share of total inward BERD by host country and sector (2007)

The overall picture is similar for the electrical and optical equipment sector. With more than 20 percent of total sectoral inward BERD Germany clearly leads the EU. In contrast, small and medium sized EU countries with large domestic MNCs, including the Netherlands, Finland and Sweden; attract significantly less inward BERD in this sector.

Motor vehicles differ in one important way from all other sectors. This is the only manufacturing sector where Japan, and not the US, is the largest attractor of inward BERD. However, the important role of Japan as a destination of inward BERD is mainly caused by the activity of a single French MNE in Japan.[3] Inward BERD in other transport, the sector with the second highest concentration of inward BERD, is again dominated by the US with a share of more than 45 percent in 2007. The second important country is Germany with another 28 percent. Two more countries, the United Kingdom (11.6 percent) and Canada (6.7 percent) are of some importance, all other countries of the world play with together only 8.7 percent share a limited role.

The only service sector, real estate, renting and business activities, is also the only sector with an EU country, the United Kingdom attracting most inward BERD. Germany and France, major attractors or inward BERD in most manufacturing sectors, play a comparable small role while Canada, of no global importance in all manufacturing sectors but other transport, is with 11.2 percent of total inward BERD ranked three worldwide. With the US ranked two, all top three countries are English speaking countries and share a similar cultural background. Unfortunately there is no data available for Ireland in 2007; in 2005, Ireland attracted another 3 percent of worldwide inward BERD.

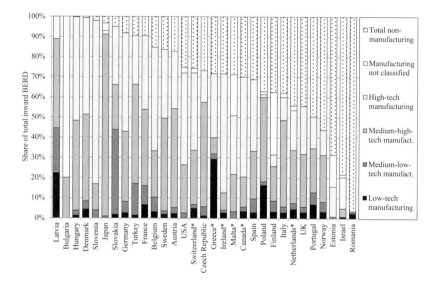

Note: * 1999 (Greece), 2001 (Canada, Netherlands), 2005 (Ireland) and 2008 (Malta, Switzerland) instead of 2007; Due to data constraints in the services sector, we only consider five industries: four manufacturing industries and total non-manufacturing (including KIS and LKIS but also all other non-manufacturing sectors).
Source: OECD, Eurostat, national statistical offices, own calculations.

Figure 6.5 Inward BERD by type of industry (2007)

Inward BERD by type of industry and country (Figure 6.5) reveals again that high and medium-high technology manufacturing industries play and outstanding role in almost all countries where data is available. Inward BERD from non-manufacturing sectors is only relevant in a few small and medium sized countries. Examples are Estonia and Israel, where foreign-owned firms in computer services have a considerable share on overall inward BERD. However, in most of these countries total inward BERD is comparable low and the results reflect the activities of a small number of actors. Also the countries with above average shares of low and medium-low technology industries have comparable small total inward BERD. It is important to note that the low importance of non-manufacturing in some countries may at least partly be caused by poor coverage of the services sector in some country's R&D surveys.

CONCLUSIONS

A cross-sectoral comparison of inward BERD reveals that inward BERD in various sectors is still concentrated in a small number of countries. However, we see a trend towards a wider variety of countries involved in the internationalisation of business R&D at the sectoral level. The sheer size of business R&D in the United States of America strongly influences the results. While the importance of KIBS increases over time also in the contest of business R&D internationalisation, high- and medium-high-tech manufacturing sectors are still of outstanding importance and account for at least 60 percent of global cross-border R&D.

NOTES

1. Includes **Belgium** (2000-2007), **Czech Republic** (1998-2007), **Germany** (2001-2007, pharmaceuticals only 2003-2007 and electrical and optical equip. only 2005-2007; inward values in 2002, 2004 and 2006 own calc.), **Estonia** (only machinery and equip. 2006-2007, electrical and optical equip. 2003-2007 and real estate, renting and business act. 2003-2007), **Spain** (2003-2007, excl. pharmaceuticals 2003-2005), **France** (1998-2007, electrical and optical equip. only 2001-2007 and excl. real estate, renting and business act.; inward values in 1999, 2000 and 2004 own calc.), **Ireland** (2003-2005, pharmaceuticals 1999-2001 and 2005, machinery and equip. 1999-2005 and real estate, renting and business act. 2005; inward values in 2000, 2002 and 2004 own calc.), **Italy** (2001-2007, excl. pharmaceuticals, other transport equip. included in motor vehicles; inward values in 2003 and 2004 for real estate, renting and business act. own calc.), **Hungary** (only machinery and equip. 1998-1999, electrical and optical equip. 2003-2007 and motor vehicles 1998-1999), **Netherlands** (1998-2001 and 2007, pharmaceuticals only 1999-2001, other transport equip. only 1998 and excl. real estate, renting and business act.), **Austria** (2003-2007, pharmaceuticals, electrical and optical equip. and real estate, renting and business act. only 2004-2007; inward values in 2005 and 2006 own calc.); **Poland** (1998-2007, pharmaceuticals, real estate, renting and business act. only 2005-2006; inward values in 2002 and 2002 for other transport equip. own calc.); **Portugal** (1999-2007, excl. pharmaceuticals; inward values in 2000, 2002, 2004 and 2006 own calc.), **Romania** (only machinery and equip. 2004-2005, motor vehicles 2004-2006, other transport equip. 2005 and real estate, renting and business act. 2005-2007), **Slovenia** (only machinery and equip. 1998-1999 and real estate, renting and business act. 1998 and 1999), **Slovakia** (only machinery and equip. 2003-2007, electrical and optical equip. 2004-2005, real estate, renting and business act. 2003-2004 and 2006-2007), **Finland** (pharmaceuticals 1998-2001 and 2005-2006, machinery and equip. 1998-2001 and 2005-2007, electrical and optical equip. 1998-2001 and 2007, motor vehicles 2000 and 2005-2006, other transport equip. 1998-2001 and 2007, real estate, renting and business act. no data), **Sweden** (1998-2007, inward values in 2004 and 2006 own calc.), **United Kingdom** (1998-2007, inward values in 2005 and 2006 own calc.), **Turkey** (1999-2000 and 2002 excl. other transport equip. and real estate, renting and business act.), **Norway** (2007, excl. pharmaceuticals), **Japan** (1998-2007, excl. pharmaceuticals, real estate, renting and business act. 2003-2007), **United States** (1998-2007, excl. real estate, renting and business act. 2002-2007; electrical and optical equip. only includes NACE sections 30 and 31 in 1998, 31 in 1999 and 2000, 30-32 in 2001, 31 and 33 in 2002, 30 and 33 in 2004, 33 in 2005, 31 and 33 in 2006, inward value in 1999 for motor vehicles and other transport equip. own calc.), **Canada** (1998-2001 and 2006-2007, excl. Pharmaceuticals 1998-2001).

2. The sectors included are the NACE 1.1 sections 24.4, pharmaceuticals; 29, machinery and equipment; 30-33 electrical and optical equipment (including office, accounting and com-

puting machinery; electrical machinery and apparatus; radio, TV and communications and medical, precision and optical instruments); 34, motor vehicles, trailers and semi-tailers; 35, other transport equipment (including aircraft and spacecraft) and 70-74, real estate, renting and business activities.

3.   The share of French companies on total inward BERD in Japan increased from only 1 percent in 1998 to 51 percent in 1999 due to a two way alliance between French Renault and Japanese Nissan.

REFERENCES

Barba Navaretti, G. and A.J. Venables (2004), *Multinational Firms in the World Economy*, Princeton and Oxford: Princeton University Press.

Comanor, W.S. and F.M. Scherer (2013), 'Mergers and innovation in the pharmaceutical industry', *Journal of Health Economics* **32**(1), 106-13.

Danzon, P.M. (2000), 'The pharmaceutical industry', in B. Bouckaert and G. de Gees (eds), *The encyclopedia of law and economics*, Cheltenham: Edward Elgar, pp. 1055-1091.

Danzon, P.M. (2006), 'Economics of the pharmaceutical industry', NBER Reporter: Research Summary Fall 2006, http://www.nber.org/reporter/fall06/danzon.html

DiMasi, J.A. and H.G. Grabowski (2007), 'The cost of biopharmaceutical R&D: is biotech different?', *Managerial and Decision Economics* **28**(4-5), 469-79.

Hatzichronoglou, T. (1997), *Revision of the high-technology sector and product classification*, Paris: OECD.

Malerba, F. (2002), 'Sectoral systems of innovation and production', *Research Policy* **31**(2), 247-64.

Malerba, F. (2004), *Sectoral Systems of Innovation. Concepts, Issues and Analyses of Six Major Sectors in Europe*, Cambridge: Cambridge University Press.

Malerba, F. (2005), 'Sectoral systems of innovation', in J. Fagerberg, D. Mowery and R.R. Nelson (eds), *The Oxford Handbook of Innovation*, Oxford: Oxford University Press, pp. 380-406.

Malerba, F. (2005b), 'Sectoral systems of innovation: A framework for linking innovation to the knowledge base, structure and dynamics of sectors', *Economics of Innovation and New Technology*, **14**(1-2), 63-82.

Malerba, F. and L. Orsenigo (1996), 'Schumpeterian patterns of innovation are technology-specific', *Research Policy* **25**(3), 451-78.

Markusen, J.R. (1995), 'The boundaries of multinational enterprises and the theory of international trade', *Journal of Economic Perspectives* **9**(2), 169-89.

Marsili, O. (2001), *The anatomy and evolution of industries: technological change and industrial dynamics*, Cheltenham: Edward Elgar.

OECD (2012), *Main Science and Technology Indicators 1/2012*, Paris: OECD.

Peneder, M. (2007), 'Sectoral taxonomies: Identifying competitive regimes by statistical cluster analysis', in H. Hanusch and A. Pyka (eds), *Elgar Companion to Neo-Schumpeterian Economics,* Cheltenham: Edward Elgar, pp. 525-43.

7.   The Relationship between the European Union and United States of America

Bernhard Dachs

The first R&D units abroad were established by multinational firms from the United States of America and the United Kingdom in the 1950s and 1960s (Cantwell 1995). Firms from some smaller European countries (in particular Switzerland and Sweden) started to internationalise R&D relatively early as well, while firms from France, Germany, Italy, or Japan started much later (UNCTAD 2005, p. 122). Since the beginning of the new millennium, new players from South America and from South-East Asia are entering the stage (Asakawa and Som 2008; Baskaran and Muchie 2008; Di Minin and Zhang 2010). R&D internationalisation can thus be described as a process of continuous de-concentration. The aim of this chapter is to study this process of de-concentration from the perspective of the two main host economies, the European Union[1] and the United States of America. I look at business R&D of EU firms performed in the United States and compare it with the business R&D expenditure of US firms in the European Union. Due to a lack of EU data[2] the chapter will mainly rely on US data provided by the Bureau for Economic Analysis, US Department of Commerce.

THE AGGREGATE PICTURE

The European Union and the United States are the two main players in the internationalisation of business R&D, both as home and host countries. The relationship between the US and the EU is thus the single most important bilateral relationship in the internationalisation of business R&D (see also Chapter 4 and 8).

Figure 7.1 illustrates the development of this relationship over time. The figure depicts inward BERD performed by US multinational enterprises in the EU and inward BERD by EU MNEs in the US from 1998 to 2010 in percent of the 1998 value. Both aggregates have grown substantially over time at a comparable speed. The proportion of the two aggregates remained fairly constant until 2007, the last year before the global financial crisis.

From 2008, R&D expenditure of EU firms in the US decreased, while R&D expenditure of US firms in the EU continued one more year, and then declined. As a consequence, a gap opened which indicates that the EU remained an attractive location for R&D of US firms, while the US lost attractiveness for EU multinationals.

However, one has also to consider that there is a break in the time series between the years 2006 and 2007. The US Bureau of Economic Analysis (BEA) which provides the data states that *'(...) statistics for 2007 and future years are not strictly comparable with statistics from 2006 and earlier'* (BEA 2012). Beginning with 2007, the BEA included data from both bank and nonbank affiliates. Until 2006, data only included data from nonbank affiliates. This change, however, can hardly explain the drop in R&D expenditure of EU firms in the US from 2007 to 2009 and why this drop was more severe than the reduction of R&D expenditure of US firms in the EU. It seems more likely that this development can be explained by changes in firm behaviour following the crisis. Here, a further analysis at the firm level seems appropriate.

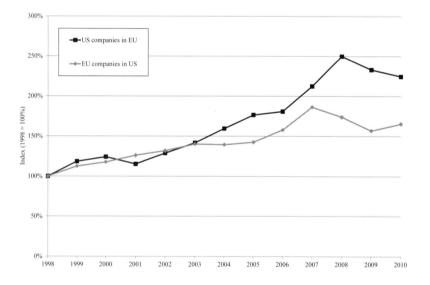

Note: US companies in EU only include activities in the EU-15 (1998-2003) and EU-25 (2004-2006). Only Nonbank affiliates are included up to 2006 (EU companies in the US) and 2008 (US companies in EU).

Source: Bureau for Economic Analysis, US Department of Commerce, own calculations.

Figure 7.1 BERD of US firms in the EU and EU firms in the US (1998-2010)

The relationship between the EU and the US has strengthened in terms of absolute BERD invested, but not in relative terms. EU firms are still – by far

– the most important source of inward BERD in the US with a share of 53 percent in the year 2010. At the same time, about 57 percent of total US outward BERD in 2010 is located in the EU. However, both the share of the EU on total US inward BERD, as well as the share of the EU on total US outward BERD is decreasing (Figure 7.2).

These decreases in relative shares are mainly due to the emergence of new R&D locations in Asia and in other non-European OECD countries. Athukorala and Kohpaiboon (2010) conclude that the distribution of US outward BERD reflects shifts in market size and in the R&D capabilities of host countries. China has indeed considerably increased both, aggregate R&D expenditure and GDP per capita. The last section of this chapter will discuss these changes in detail. There is no information on the share of US firms in total EU inward BERD; however, evidence from patent inventions presented in Chapter 13 suggests that the US is also losing ground as a location for R&D of EU firms.

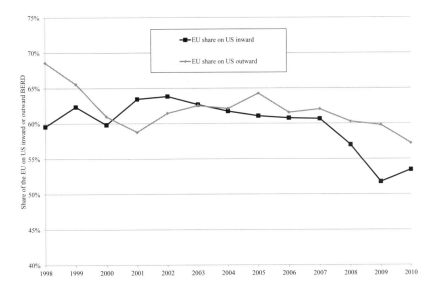

Note: EU share on US outward only include activities in the EU-15 (1998-2003) and EU-25 (2004-2006). Only Nonbank affiliates are included up to 2006 (EU share on US inward) and 2008 (EU share on US outward).

Source: Bureau for Economic Analysis, US Department of Commerce, own calculations.

Figure 7.2 Share of the EU on US inward and outward BERD (1998-2010)

INWARD BERD OF EU FIRMS IN THE US

Despite decreases in their relative share, the EU is still the most important investing economy in terms of inward BERD in the US. EU firms hold a share of 53 percent on total US inward BERD in 2010. Swiss companies add another 18 percent of inward BERD in the US, pushing the European share to more 70 percent of total US inward BERD.

In a next step, I take a closer look at the distribution of inward BERD of EU firms in the US by countries of origin. Such an analysis has to be done very carefully due to several data constraints. First, the analysis can only employ US inward data, since there is no outward BERD data available for most EU countries. Second, the US statistical office does not provide a value for the EU-27 as a whole. The only country aggregate available is total Europe and a few large economies in terms of business R&D expenditure. The EU total used for the analysis therefore includes total Europe, excluding Switzerland.

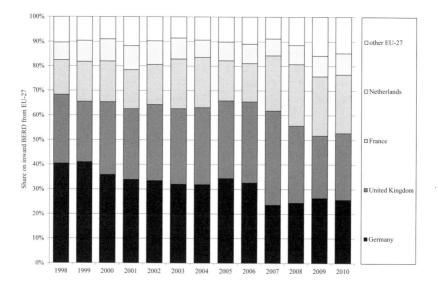

Source: Bureau for Economic Analysis, US Department of Commerce, own calculations.

Figure 7.3 Share of various EU member states on total EU inward BERD in the United States (1998-2010)

Figure 7.3 reveals that firms from three EU countries are of outstanding importance, Germany, France and the United Kingdom. These three countries together account for around 80 percent of total EU inward BERD in the US. Until 2006, Germany was the most important of these three countries. In

2006, the United Kingdom overtook Germany as the most important foreign investor country in business R&D in the US. It is difficult to say if this development was caused by changes in the structure of inward BERD in the US, or by changes in data collection which took place between 2006 and 2007 described above. Evidence at the sectoral level not reported here indicates that the growth between 2006 and 2007 occurred mainly in pharmaceuticals. 3 bn. of the 6 bn. USD increase between two years can be attributed to pharmaceuticals.

Altogether, the share of the big three EU member states went down while the share of inward BERD from other EU countries increased from 17.6 percent in 1998 to 23.4 percent in 2010. Thus, the same de-concentration trends as in many other variables can also be observed in US inward BERD.

OUTWARD BERD OF US FIRMS IN THE EU

I now turn to the opposite perspective, R&D expenditure of US firms in the European Union. Figure 7.1 has already indicated that R&D expenditure of US firms in the EU grew faster since 2000 than vice versa. The European share of is around 53 percent, which is considerably lower than the corresponding share of the EU on US inward BERD. Europe is nevertheless the most important host country of US overseas R&D activities by far.

In the following Figure 7.4, total outward BERD of US firms in the EU is divided between the shares of Germany, the United Kingdom, other large EU member states including France, Italy and Spain, a group of small and medium sized EU member states including Austria, Belgium, Denmark, Finland, Greece, Ireland, Luxembourg, the Netherlands, Portugal and Sweden, and all EU member states that joined the Union in 2004 or later (EU-12).

The most important development depicted in Figure 7.4 is the rise of small and medium sized EU member states as host countries for R&D activities in the EU. Their share increased by nearly 10 percentage points between 1994 and 2010 at the expense of all large EU member states. The rise of US outward BERD to Ireland is most remarkable. In 2007, outward BERD to Ireland is nearly five times the absolute value of 1998. In absolute numbers, Ireland has surpassed Italy and the Netherlands in terms of received outward BERD, even if one considers the drop in R&D expenditure during the global financial crisis. A similar growth of R&D expenditure of US firms can also be seen in Belgium (see Chapter 5 for an in-depth analysis). In 2010 US outward BERD to Belgium is larger than outward BERD to France or total Latin America.

There were also considerable increases of US outward BERD to the EU-12 between 1998 and 2010. Starting from a very low level of 68 million USD in 2004, R&D expenditure of US affiliates in the EU-12 rises to 254 million USD in 2007. Despite this gain, the EU-12 still accounts for only 0.7 percent of total US outward BERD and for 1.2 percent of US outward BERD to the

EU in 2010. This is only a fraction of the share of India (4.2 percent) or China (3.7 percent) in 2010. The largest recipients of US outward BERD in the EU-12 in 2010 are Poland (136 million USD), followed by the Czech Republic (68 million USD), and Hungary (65 million USD).

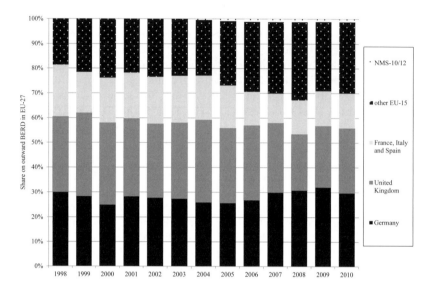

Note: NMS-10/12 includes from 2004-2007 the Czech Republic, Estonia, Cyprus, Latvia, Lithuania, Hungary, Malta, Poland, Slovenia and Slovakia and in 2007 additionally Bulgaria and Romania. Spain included in other EU-15 in 1999.
Source: Bureau for Economic Analysis, US Department of Commerce, own calculations.

Figure 7.4 Share of various EU member states on US outward BERD in the European Union (1999-2007)

NEW PLAYERS IN THE INTERNATIONALISATION OF R&D

The last years have seen the arrival of new players in the internationalisation of business R&D, including Brazil, China, India, Korea, Malaysia, Mexico, or Singapore. According to UNCTAD (2005, p. 139), 'the rise of developing Asia and Oceania has been the most dramatic development in the global landscape of R&D'.

How does the rapid development of these countries change the relationship between the US and the EU in R&D internationalisation? Figure 7.5 gives an answer to this question. It compares the distribution of US outward BERD in 1994 with the distribution in 2010. The total share of the EU corresponds to the white areas in both pie charts of the Figure and corresponds to the values reported in Figure 7.2.

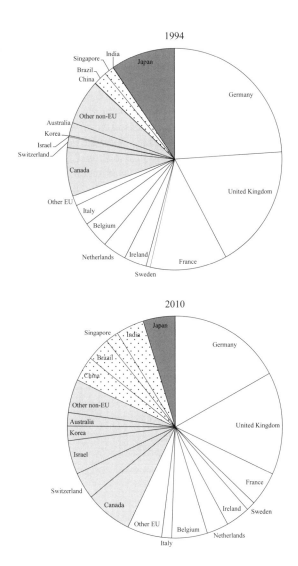

Source: Bureau for Economic Analysis, US Department of Commerce, own calculations.

Figure 7.5 Countries' shares on outward BERD of US firms (1994 and 2010)

There is indeed a significant decrease in the share of US outward BERD to developed countries and the to EU in particular, and rising shares of South-East Asian economies, especially of China, Singapore, India and Malaysia. The EU share on US outward BERD has decreased from 70 percent in

1994 to 57 percent in 2010. In turn, the shares of emerging economies (dotted area) grew considerably. But new players are not only emerging in South-East Asia. Israel, for example, grew from virtually no US outward BERD in 1994 to nearly 2 billion USD in 2010, and also other non-EU OECD countries such as Mexico, Canada and Australia (all marked in grey) could considerably increase their share on total US outward BERD in this period.

A comparison of relative shares, however, does only tell half the truth. In absolute terms, US outward BERD has increased *in all world regions* until 2008 (Figure 7.6). Between 1994 and 2008, outward BERD of US firms more than tripled in nominal terms from 11.8 billion USD to 41.7 billion USD. Growth of R&D expenditure, however, was much faster in emerging economies. The share of non-OECD Asia (China, India, and Singapore to name the most important countries of this group) increased more than ten-fold, from 391 Mio to 4,546 Mio USD. This was a very impressive growth in relative terms; however, in absolute terms, most of increases in US outward BERD have been spent in the EU, in particular in Germany, the UK, and France. Outward BERD of US firms to the EU grew from 8,271 Mio USD to 25,130 Mio USD in 2008. Outward BERD of US firms in Japan, in contrast, grew only moderately from 1,130 Mio USD 2 bn USD.

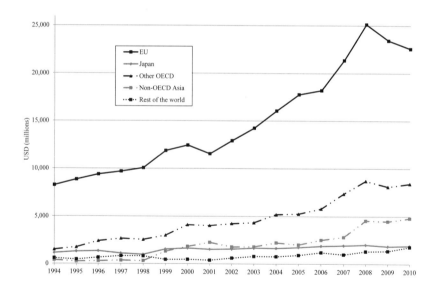

Source: Bureau for Economic Analysis, US Department of Commerce, own calculations.

Figure 7.6 Overseas R&D expenditure of US firms (1994-2008, million USD)

This clearly shows that the internationalisation of business R&D is not a zero-sum game, where gains of one location – the emerging economies – inevitably mean a loss for another location. In fact, as has been demonstrated by Thursby and Thursby (2006) and other contributions discussed Chapter 2, firms have different motives to do R&D at different places. So, each country has its own profile of attractors, which develop over time and endogenously create incentives for the enlargement of R&D activities.

CONCLUSIONS

Despite the emergence of new players, the United States and the European Union are still the two dominant economies in the internationalisation of R&D. EU firms (excluding Swiss firms) account for 53 percent of all R&D expenditure of foreign-owned firms in the US. At the same time, about 57 percent of the US overseas R&D expenditure is spent in the EU. Further decreases in relative shares of the EU and the US are likely in the future, as emerging economies will further gain attractiveness, and EU and US multinational firms will further increase their turnover and production in these countries.

Moreover, the development of inward BERD in the EU and the US clearly shows that R&D internationalisation is not a zero-sum game. The data provided evidence for relative shifts, but there is no absolute loss or substitution of inward BERD in the EU or the US by activities in Asia in absolute terms. US outward BERD has increased in all world regions until 2008, and reductions since 2008 may be due to the global financial crisis than to a fundamental shift in internationalisation strategies of firms. Therefore, there is no reason to fear that the EU-27 will lose its attractiveness in absolute terms – as long as the EU can preserve its growth prospects, locational advantages for R&D, and a favourable business environment.

NOTES

1. The European Union is regarded as one single entity in this chapter. Trans-border R&D activities between member states of the European Union (for example R&D activities of French firms in Germany) are excluded from the data presented in this chapter.
2. There is no aggregate data for the European Union as a whole, just data for each member country. Due to confidentiality and a lack of data for some countries, it is not possible to provide a comprehensive picture for the EU-27 based on this data.
3. More information is provided at http://www.bea.gov/iTable/index_MNC.cfm

REFERENCES

Asakawa, K. and A. Som (2008), 'Internationalization of R&D in China and India: Conventional wisdom versus reality', *Asia Pacific Journal of Management* **25**(3), 375-94.
Athukorala, P.-C. and A. Kohpaiboon (2010), 'Globalization of R&D by US-based

multinational enterprises', *Research Policy* **39**(10), 1335-347.

Baskaran, A. and M. Muchie (2008), 'Foreign direct investment and internationalization of R&D: the case of BRICS economies'. Aalborg: DIIPER & Department of History, International and Social Studies Working Paper.

BEA (2012). *Data on direct investment and MNC,* http://www.bea.gov/iTable/iTable.cfm?ReqID=2&step=1#reqid=2&step=1&isuri= 1&200=2&201=2

Cantwell, J. (1995), 'The globalisation of technology: What remains of the product cycle model?', *Cambridge Journal of Economics* **19**(1), 155-74.

Di Minin, A. and J. Zhang (2010), 'An Exploratory Study on International R&D Strategies of Chinese Companies in Europe', *Review of Policy Research* **27**(4), 433-55.

Thursby, J., and M. Thursby (2006), *Here or There? A survey of factors in multinational R&D location*, Washington DC: National Academies Press.

UNCTAD (2005), *World Investment Report 2005: Transnational Corporations and the Internationalization of R&D*, New York and Geneva: United Nations.

8. The Structure of Cross-Country R&D Expenditure: A Social Network Analysis Perspective

Thomas Scherngell

The analysis of the volume and magnitude of R&D internationalisation provides valuable insights into patterns of R&D internationalisation from a country-by-country centric view. However, the internationalisation of R&D generates multiple relationships between countries; analysing these relationships in the whole system of trans-border R&D activity is an important additional aspect. In this sense, it is necessary to move from a dyadic perspective – focusing on R&D by firms from country A in country B – to a network perspective that basically also takes the R&D activities of firms from a dyad in all other countries of the system into consideration.

Thus, this chapter moves one step further and analyses the structure of R&D internationalisation from a network perspective. In doing so, we look at the whole set of countries and relationships between these countries as measured by inward BERD. The aim of this approach is to make sense of the structure of this network, to identify the countries which are well connected with all other countries, or have no connection with parts of the network. In addition, we will identify the strongest links at the level of individual countries, as well as see if there are sub-groups of countries in the network which are well-connected with each other, but have only weak linkages with countries outside the sub-group. We consider the inward BERD linkages between countries as an indicator for international technology diffusion (Keller 2004). The chapter is organised as follows. The next subsection introduces the social network perspective on R&D internationalisation and defines the network under consideration in a formal manner. Afterwards, structural characteristics of the network are presented, mainly focusing on indicators for cohesion of the network. Then we present some actor characteristics highlighting the position of specific countries in the network in terms of different network analytics centrality measures, before the network is analysed and visualised with respect to its spatial configuration. The chapter closes with an analysis of the relative strengths of the network links in terms of a Jaccard Index and a short summary.

A SOCIAL NETWORK PERSPECTIVE ON INTERNATIONAL R&D FLOWS

Social network analysis (SNA) has come into fairly wide use for the analysis of social systems in the recent past. SNA offers a wide range of analytical tools disclosing the structure of large social systems. Central to network analysis is identifying, measuring, and testing hypotheses about the structural forms and substantive contents of relations among actors (Knoke and Young 2008), in our case firms aggregated to the country level. This distinctive structural-relational emphasis sets social network analysis apart from individualistic, variable-centric traditions in the social sciences. The main underlying assumption in this context is that structural relations are often more important for understanding observed behaviour than are attributes of the actors.

The network analysed in this chapter consists of countries and inward BERD linkages between them. All countries where sufficient data is available are included. We will describe the cross-country network of inward BERD as a whole, and shed light on the position and roles of different countries in this network. Further we will visualise the spatial structure of the network under consideration by means of spatial network maps. After that we will identify the relative most important country pairs in terms of their bilateral inward BERD relations, providing important insight into the geographical patterns of R&D internationalisation.

Initially, it is necessary to formally define the network so that respective network analytic measures can be derived. A network can be viewed in several ways. In our context, the most useful view is as a graph consisting of nodes (vertices) and edges (links). A familiar representation is obtained by letting V be a set of nodes representing countries participating in the inward BERD network, and E be a set of edges where elements of E are unordered pairs of distinct nodes v_i, v_j representing a link in the form of inward BERD between a pair $\{v_i, v_j\}$. The two sets together are called a simple graph $G_1=(V, E)$ where all pairs $\{v_i, v_j\}$ are distinct; the number of edges incident on a vertex $i=1, ..., n$ is called the degree k_i.

Note that G_1 represents an unweighted graph by definition. In our case, it is natural to consider the weighted form given by $G_2=(V, E, W)$ where $W=\{w_1, w_2, ..., w_n\}$ represent weights between two nodes v_i and v_j denoting the magnitude of inward BERD. In the current analysis, we will draw on both types of graphs for different kinds of indicators and descriptive statistics. Readers should further note that we symmetrise G_2 by taking the sum of inward BERD between two countries as weights between them, i.e. both G_1 and G_2 represent undirected graphs. This is more appropriate to handle in a social network analysis framework.

Though in our case interpretation of specific measures from network analysis is problematic, for instance with respect to traditional interpretations of network indicators in terms of information flows between nodes, the network analytic perspective is useful for identifying and describing the structure of cross-country inward BERD. By this, the chapter fits very well into the literature stream that investigates R&D networks from a network analytic perspective, using information on different forms of R&D interactions, such as joint research projects (see, for instance, Breschi and Cusmano 2004, Scherngell and Barber 2009 and 2011), joint publications (see, for instance, Hoekman et al. 2010, Scherngell and Hu 2011) joint assignment of patents (see, for instance, Maggioni et al. 2007) or – as in our case – inward BERD between countries.

STRUCTURAL CHARACTERISTICS OF THE NETWORK

In a first step, Figure 8.1 visualizes the inward BERD network using G_2. Countries that show a relatively higher intensity of bilateral inward BERD relationships are positioned nearer to each other. The node size corresponds to the weighted degree centrality of a country that is defined as the sum of a country's inward and outward BERD. Outward BERD is approximated by the corresponding inward BERD of the partner country.

The results clearly demonstrate that the United States represents the central hub in this network in terms of absolute size showing the highest interaction intensity with other countries. The most important partners in terms of absolute size are the UK, Germany, Switzerland and France. The graph visualisation further reveals that the UK shows striking higher interaction intensity with the US than with larger European countries, such as Germany or France. Germany has the highest interaction intensity with the US followed by the Netherlands, while France shows comparably high interactions with Japan. A surprising result is also that Switzerland is more connected with non-European countries, particularly the US and Japan, than embedded in the European sub-network.

We investigate the structure of the inward BERD network between the 27 countries with indicators that investigate the connectedness and cohesion of this network, or, in other words, how well-connected the countries in this network are (Figure 8.1). Table 8.1 comprises respective SNA measures also used in similar empirical works based on other forms of R&D interactions (see, for instance, Breschi and Cusmano 2004). Details on the mathematical definition of the indicators listed in Table 8.1 are given by Wasserman and Faust (1994). For comparison purposes we relate the SNA indicators calculated for the network of inward BERD with those calculated for a random Erdös-Renyi graph using the same number of nodes ($n = 27$) (see Wasserman and Faust 1994).

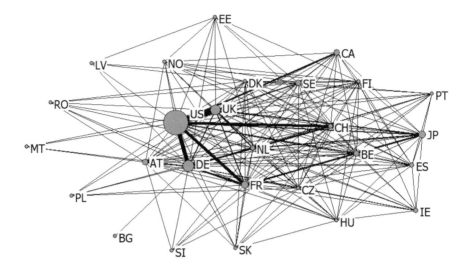

Note: Vertex positions were determined so that countries that are strongly interconnected are
          positioned nearer to each other. Node size corresponds to the weighted degree centrality
          of a country that is defined as the sum of a country's inward and outward BERD, the
          strength of the lines correspond to the sum of inward BERD between any two countries.
Source: OECD, Eurostat, national statistical offices, own calculations.

Figure 8.1 Inward BERD network between 27 countries[1] (2007)

The results from Table 8.1 indicate that the connectedness and cohesion of
the inward BERD network is comparably high. The density of the inward
BERD network shows a value of 0.554, i.e. more than 50 percent of all possible relationships between any two countries are established; a much higher
value than is usually found for real-world social networks as indicated by the
density for the random graph. The true density may be even higher, because
some data are not available due to confidentiality.

The high degree of connectedness and cohesion is also reflected by the
average path length – given by the average of the shortest paths between all
pairs of nodes – that is much smaller as for the random graph. This is con-
firmed by the clustering coefficient which measures the likelihood that two
associates of a country are associates themselves, for example country A and
country B are connected under the condition that country A is connected to a
country C to which also country B is connected. In our case, we can speak of
a very 'cliquish' network showing explicitly a so-called small world character (see Watts and Strogatz 1998).

Table 8.1 Indicators for cohesion in the inward BERD network (2007)

Indicator	Network of inward BERD	Random graph*
Number of nodes *n*	27	27
Number of edges *l*	202	54
Density	0.554	0.148
Clustering-coefficient	0.762	0.116
Diameter	2	5
Average path length	1.466	2.437
Mean degree	14.961	4.120
#*n* higher than mean degree (in %)	55.555	33.124

Note: We use the unweighted graph G1 for these indicators
* Erdös-Renyi conceptualisation of random graphs
Source: OECD, Eurostat, national statistical offices, own calculations.

Connectedness and cohesion of the network is also reflected by the diameter – referring to the highest path length observed in a network – showing a value of 2 for the inward BERD network as compared to a value of 5 for the random graph. The mean degree, i.e. the mean number of partner countries for any country, shows a value of 14.9, while for the random graph the mean degree is 4.1. The number of nodes that have a higher degree than the mean is more than 50 percent, indicating that most countries have many interaction partners while the minority of the countries has very few interaction partners.

ACTOR CHARACTERISTICS OF THE NETWORK

A central point in the context of the network analysis of inward BERD is the role that different countries take in this network. The concept of centrality is a useful approach to investigate this issue. We shortly introduce this concept; the mathematical specification of the indicators is given in Wasserman and Faust (1994). In this analysis we focus on four different types of centrality measures that are calculated for each country:

First, degree centrality is defined as the ratio of the degree of a node and the maximum degree in a network of the same size (i.e., the total number of edges connected to a node). Second, eigenvector centrality accords each vertex a centrality that depends both on the number and the quality of its connections by examining all vertices in parallel and assigning centrality weights that correspond to the average centrality of all neighbours. Third, closeness centrality of a vertex is defined as the inverse of the mean geodesic distance (i.e., the mean length of the shortest path) from this vertex to every other vertex in a connected graph. Fourth, betweenness centrality is measured by the frequency of one actor positioned on the shortest path between other groups of actors arranged in pairs. Those actors, who are located on the shortest paths between many actors, therefore hold a key position for controlling the flow of information within the network (gatekeeper function).

Table 8.2 presents the results on the centrality rankings of our 27 countries participating in the inward BERD network. The first column contains the calculated values for degree-based centrality. Germany shows the highest degree centrality among the countries under consideration, followed by the US. This means that Germany has the highest number of partner countries. The Netherlands has a higher number of partner countries than France or the UK. The Czech Republic shows more partner countries than Austria, Switzerland, Belgium, Finland and Sweden though it has a lower magnitude of inward BERD in total, pointing to a comparably spatially dispersed partner structure of the Czech Republic. The number of partner countries of Japan is just slightly higher than the average, i.e. the partner structure of Japan is more concentrated than, for instance, the one of France, Germany, the UK and the US. Readers, however, have to bear in mind that missing or confidential data is a challenge here, and some of the effects we see here may be due to the data quality rather than the propensities of the network.

If we turn to eigenvector-based centrality, the ranking changes significantly. The US shows the highest eigenvector centrality indicating that its partner structure is focused on countries that show a high centrality by themselves. Obviously the high eigenvector-based centrality of the US and the UK is also to a large extent related to the quite high interaction intensity between them. Further interesting changes in the ranking as compared to the degree-based centrality are subject to Switzerland, Japan and Canada. Switzerland changes from rank 8 to rank 5, i.e. though it has a lower number of partners than, for instance, Austria, but it is connected to more partners that also have a relatively higher centrality. The same is true for Canada that even changes from rank 17 for the degree-based centrality to rank 8 for the eigenvector-based centrality mainly related to its comparably strong inward BERD relationships with the US, and Japan changing from rank 14 to rank 6. In contrast, the Netherlands, Austria, the Czech Republic and Denmark that show a comparably high degree-based centrality take a lower ranking for the eigenvector-based centrality, indicating that on average these countries have more interactions with partner countries showing a low centrality, such as the Eastern European countries.

The results for closeness and the betweenness-based centrality are similar to those for the degree-based centrality ranking. This points to a low modularity of the network, or, in other words, there are no separated groups of countries in the network which are connected only via specific countries that take the role of 'gatekeepers'.

Table 8.2 Different centralities of countries[1] in the inward BERD network

degree		eigenvector		betweenness		closeness	
DE	1.00	US	92.04	DE	15.15	DE	100.00
US	0.92	UK	68.24	US	5.99	US	92.86
NL	0.88	DE	54.49	NL	3.74	NL	89.66
FR	0.85	FR	43.09	UK	3.73	FR	86.67
UK	0.85	CH	32.20	FR	2.96	UK	86.67
CZ	0.81	JP	18.58	AT	2.81	CZ	83.87
AT	0.77	NL	14.58	CZ	2.31	AT	81.25
CH	0.77	CA	11.64	DK	1.99	CH	81.25
BE	0.73	SE	11.55	CH	1.94	BE	78.79
DK	0.73	BE	8.80	FI	1.75	DK	78.79
FI	0.73	AT	7.60	SE	1.16	FI	78.79
SE	0.73	ES	5.11	BE	0.75	SE	78.79
ES	0.65	IE	3.51	ES	0.31	ES	74.29
JP	0.65	FI	2.28	JP	0.31	JP	74.29
HU	0.58	DK	1.41	EE	0.31	HU	70.27
NO	0.54	CZ	1.17	HU	0.27	CA	68.42
CA	0.54	NO	0.77	NO	0.25	NO	68.42
IE	0.46	HU	0.51	CA	0.05	IE	65.00
PT	0.46	PT	0.35	LV	0.03	PT	65.00
SK	0.38	RO	0.26	IE	0.02	SK	61.90
EE	0.35	PL	0.23	SK	0.02	EE	60.47
RO	0.31	SI	0.13	BG	0.00	RO	59.09
PL	0.23	EE	0.09	MT	0.00	PL	56.52
SI	0.23	SK	0.08	PL	0.00	SI	56.52
LV	0.19	MT	0.05	PT	0.00	LV	55.32
MT	0.15	LV	0.00	RO	0.00	MT	54.17
BG	0.04	BG	0.00	SI	0.00	BG	50.98

Source: OECD, Eurostat, national statistical offices, own calculations.

THE SPATIAL STRUCTURE OF THE NETWORK

Figure 8.2 complements the network visualisation of Figure 8.1 by focusing on the spatial structure of the inward BERD network in Europe. Here, we do not position the nodes according to methods from spectral graph theory, but according to their spatial location, i.e. nodes representing participating countries are positioned at the location of the capital city of the respective country. Again, node size corresponds to the weighted degree centrality of a country that is defined as the sum of a country's inward and outward BERD.

Note: Vertex positions were determined so that countries that are strongly interconnected are positioned nearer to each other. Node size corresponds to the weighted degree centrality of a country that is defined as the sum of a country's inward and outward BERD, the strength of the lines correspond to the sum of inward BERD between any two countries.
Source: OECD, Eurostat, national statistical offices, own calculations

Figure 8.2 Inward BERD relationships between European countries (2007)

The spatial network map presented in Figure 8.2 clearly reveals a clustering of inward BERD and a high degree of interaction in the centre of Europe. Germany now appears as the central hub showing high interaction intensity in particular with the direct spatial neighbours Netherlands, Switzerland and Austria. The UK has particular high interaction intensity with Sweden and France, while Spain shows the strongest connections with France and Belgium. Finland appears to have a diverse set of partner countries but in terms of absolute size the interactions are less intensive.

Eastern European countries are in general connected to the core of the inward BERD network in Europe, but with comparably low magnitudes. The Czech Republic shows the highest degree of embeddedness. EU-12 countries are mostly connected to Western Europe. Connections between the EU-12 countries are weak, despite the strong integration in the communist era. This can be explained by the fact that there are still only a few multinational companies originating from the EU-12 which have set-up R&D activities in neighbouring countries.

Further, the results show that integration of business R&D is far less developed than the integration of academic research, including universities and research organisations, as shown by a similar representation of a spatial network map based on international collaboration in the European Framework Programmes (FPs – see Scherngell and Barber 2011). In the FPs, EU-12 countries seem to be rather well integrated in pan-European research collaborations, while this is not the case for the inward BERD network.

THE RELATIVE STRENGTH OF INWARD BERD LINKS BETWEEN INDIVIDUAL COUNTRIES

The exploratory analyses from above shed some light on the structure of cross-country inward BERD from a social network perspective, in particular on the existence of links between countries and their size. However, from social network analysis we know that we should consider the relative strength of the links between individual nodes or countries in our case. One appropriate measure to capture the relative size of the cross-region collaborative links is the Jaccard index (see, for instance, Leydesdorff 2008).

The index is defined as

$$J_{ij} = \left(y_{i\bullet} + y_{\bullet j} - y_{ij} \right)^{-1} y_{ij} \qquad i,j = 1, ..., n \qquad (8.1)$$

where

$$y_{i\bullet} = \sum_{\substack{j=1 \\ j \neq i}}^{n} y_{ij} , \qquad y_{\bullet j} = \sum_{\substack{i=1 \\ i \neq j}}^{n} y_{ij} \qquad i,j = 1, ..., n \qquad (8.2)$$

where y_{ij} is the number of observed inward BERD relationships between countries i and j.

The Jaccard index relates the strength of the relationship between country A and B to the total number of relationships of countries A and B. The idea is that a certain amount of inward BERD, say 100 Mio EUR, between two small countries has a larger magnitude than between two large countries compared to overall inward BERD. The calculation of the J_{ij} coefficient for our (i, j)-country pairs leads to interesting results concerning the spatial structure of global inward BERD. Table 8.3 presents the top 20 links in terms of the Jaccard index.

Table 8.3 Top-15 country pairs in terms of their relative link size

Country[1] pair		Jaccard index
UK	US	0.266
DE	US	0.163
FR	JP	0.150
FR	US	0.118
CH	US	0.114
DE	NL	0.094
DE	AT	0.084
DE	CH	0.069
DE	FR	0.068
NL	JP	0.058
SE	UK	0.054
US	CA	0.049
SE	NO	0.045
ES	NL	0.044
FR	UK	0.042
NL	UK	0.040
ES	PT	0.038
JP	US	0.037
AT	CA	0.033
AT	CH	0.032

Source: OECD, Eurostat, national statistical offices, own calculations.

The table reveals that the strongest links in relative terms are different from the strongest links when taking absolute volumes of inward BERD between two countries. Second, the by far highest relative interaction intensity is identified for the country pair UK and US. Organisations that are located in the US relatively most often invest in R&D in the UK and receive R&D investments from the UK. The same is true for organisations located in the UK.

The second highest Jaccard index is observed for Germany and the US. Interestingly, France seems to have the relative highest interaction intensity with Japan which is quite surprising considering the inward BERD structure of all 27 countries. This can be explained by the activities of one single French multinational enterprise – Renault – in Japan. The same result is obtained for the Netherlands also showing the highest relative interaction intensity with Japan. Also Switzerland has the highest Jaccard index with an extra-European country, namely the US.

As mentioned above, the structure of the network of inward BERD points to some geographical logic in that we find high interaction intensities between countries that are located close to each other in geographical space. This is also reflected by the results obtained for the Jaccard index in Table 8.3. Fifty percent of the Top 20 country pairs in terms of their relative link size are direct spatial neighbours (10 country pairs). When we leave out the US and Japan, the results become even more striking as all non-direct-neighbour interactions of the Top-20 country pairs refer to pairs that consist of the US or Japan. This is a particularly interesting result and will be further evaluated by the econometric analysis of Chapter 9.

CLOSING COMMENTS

This chapter presented a social network analytic view on the network of inward BERD relationships between countries. In contrast to traditional, country centric views, the chapter complements the picture on R&D internationalisation patterns by shifting attention to structural relationships in the whole system of trans-border R&D activities, rather than the raw intensity of inward BERD two countries. Networks are defined to constitute a system of nodes and edges that interconnect these nodes. In this analysis nodes are represented by countries interconnected by edges representing inward BERD between these countries. Such a graph-theoretic representation of the network is useful for the analysis of patterns, structural features and the spatial distribution of the network of inward BERD relationships between 27 countries. Taking inward BERD as proxy for channels of international technology diffusion (Keller 2004), the network analytic perspective provides valuable insights into pathways of technology at a global scale, and how countries are connected to these pathways.

The results show that the US constitutes the central hub in the network of R&D internationalisation, showing the highest interaction intensity with other countries, with the UK, Germany, Switzerland and France being the most important partner countries. The UK shows higher interaction intensity with the US than with larger European countries, such as Germany or France. Germany has the highest interaction intensity with the US followed by the Netherlands, while France shows comparably high interactions with Japan.

Indicators measuring cohesion and density of the network point to a rather high connectedness of the inward BERD network. This points to the general importance of the internationalisation of R&D and the strategic orientation of firms to distribute their R&D in different countries and/or the ability of countries to provide framework conditions to attract foreign R&D investments. Important insights into the roles of single countries in this inward BERD network are provided by the analysis of different types of centralities of each country. Germany shows the highest degree centrality among the countries under consideration, i.e. it has the highest number of partner countries, followed by the US and the Netherlands. Concerning Eigenvector based centrality taking into account the centrality of partners of a country, the ranking changes significantly. The US shows the highest eigenvector centrality indicating that its partner structure is focused on countries that show a high centrality by themselves. Countries like Switzerland, Japan and Canada show comparably low degree based centralities (i.e. they show a comparably low number of partner countries) but comparably high eigenvector based centralities (i.e. they have a high number of partner countries with a high centrality). The opposite is the case for the Netherlands, Austria, the Czech Republic and Denmark.

Further, the analysis of the relative importance of cross-country inward BERD by means of the Jaccard index produces interesting results. The by far highest relative interaction intensity is identified for the country pair UK and US. However, one striking result is that high relative interaction intensities are in most cases subject to geographically nearby partner countries, even to direct spatial neighbours. This result points to some geographical logic in global inward BERD relationships, indicating that the relative intensity of inward BERD of a country seems to be still focused on countries located nearby in geographical space.

Finally, some ideas for a future research agenda come to mind. First, one weakness of the analysis presented in this section is that it is based on a sample of countries for which inward BERD data are available. Using a larger set of countries may change the results in some respect, in particular with respect to the inclusion of rapidly developing countries such as China. Second, a longitudinal analysis would provide a deeper understanding on the evolution and changing patterns of the network of R&D internationalisation.

NOTE

1. AT … Austria; BE … Belgium; BG … Bulgaria; CA … Canada; CH … Switzerland; CZ … Czech Republic; DE … Germany; DK … Denmark; EE … Estonia; ES … Spain; FI … Finland; FR … France; IE … Ireland; JP … Japan; LV … Latvia; HU … Hungary; MT … Malta; NL … Netherlands; NO … Norway; PL … Poland; PT … Portugal; RO … Romania; SI … Slovenia; SK … Slovakia; SE … Sweden; UK … United Kingdom; US … United States of America.

REFERENCES

Barber, M.J., M.M. Fischer and T. Scherngell (2011), 'The community structure of R&D co-operation in Europe: evidence from a social network perspective', *Geographical Analysis* **43**(4), 415-32.

Breschi, S. and L. Cusmano (2004), 'Unveiling the texture of a European research area: Emergence of oligarchic networks under EU Framework Programmes', *International Journal of Technology Management* **27**(8), 747-72.

European Commission (2008), *Council conclusions on the definition of a "2020 vision for the European Research Area"*, 16012/08 RECH 379 COMPET 502, Brussels: European Communities.

Erdős, P. and A. Rényi (1959), 'On Random Graphs I', *Publicationes Mathematicae* **6**, 290-97.

Heller-Schuh, B., M.J. Barber, L. Henriques, M. Paier, D. Pontikakis, T. Scherngell, G.A. Veltri and M. Weber (2011), *Analysis of Networks in European Framework Programmes (1984-2006)*, Sevilla: European Commission.

Higham, D.J. and M. Kibble (2004), *A unified view of spectral clustering*, Mathematics Research Report 02, University of Strathclyde.

Hoekman J., K. Frenken and R. Tijssen (2010), 'Research collaboration at a distance: Changing spatial patterns of scientific collaboration within Europe', *Research Policy* **39**(5), 662-73.

Keller, W. (2004), 'International Technology Diffusion', *Journal of Economic Literature* **42**(3), 752-58.

Knoke, D. and S. Young (2008), *Social network analysis*, Los Angeles, London, New Delhi and Singapore: Sage Publications.

Leydesdorff, L. (2008) 'On the normalization and visualization of author co-citation data: Salton's cosine versus the Jaccard index', *Journal of the American Society for Information Science and Technology* **59**, 77-85.

Maggioni, M.A., M. Nosvelli and T.A. Uberti (2007), 'Space versus networks in the geography of innovation: a European analysis', *Papers in Regional Science* **86**(3), 471-93.

Newman, M. (2010), *Networks: An Introduction*, Oxford: Oxford University Press.

OECD (2008), *The internationalisation of Business R&D: Evidence, Impacts and Implications*, Paris: OECD.

Scherngell, T. and M.J. Barber (2011), 'Distinct spatial characteristics of industrial and public research collaborations: Evidence from the 5th EU Framework Programme', *The Annals of Regional Science* **46**(2), 247-66.

Scherngell, T. and M.J. Barber (2009), 'Spatial interaction modelling of cross-region R&D collaborations. Empirical evidence from the 5th EU Framework Programme', *Papers in Regional Science* **88**(3), 531-46.

Scherngell, T. and Y. Hu (2011), 'Collaborative knowledge production in China. Regional evidence from a gravity model approach', *Regional Studies* **45**(6), 755-72.

Wasserman, S. and K. Faust (1994), *Social Network Analysis: Methods and Applications*, Cambridge: Cambridge University Press.

Watts, D.J and S.H. Strogatz (1998), 'Collective dynamics of 'small-world' networks', *Nature* **393**, 409-10.

9. Host Country Determinants of R&D Internationalisation

Sandra Leitner and Robert Stehrer

The previous chapters drew a detailed picture of the current status of business R&D internationalisation at the level of countries and sectors. The aim of this chapter is to explain the sectoral and cross-country patterns identified above therefore seeking to identify the key drivers of R&D internationalisation. First, a descriptive analysis will look at the relationship between R&D internationalisation and the internationalisation of production and compare the relative R&D intensities of domestic and foreign-owned firms across countries and sectors. Additionally, econometric analyses are conducted to provide a broader and more general picture of the drivers of R&D internationalisation as identified in the literature. The analysis aims to identify a set of variables that determine the internationalisation decision of firms in R&D. Specifically, this analysis identifies host country characteristics that drive business R&D expenditure of foreign-owned firms.

INTERNATIONALISATION OF PRODUCTION AND R&D

In order to throw light on the relationship between production and R&D of foreign-owned firms across sectors and countries, the shares of inward R&D expenditure (defined as the share of business R&D of foreign-owned affiliates in total R&D of all firms in a sector) are compared with the shares of value added of foreign-owned firms (defined as the share of value added generated by foreign-owned firms to total value added generated by all firms in a sector). The analysis uses value added (instead of e.g. turnover) as a proxy for production since it more appropriately and precisely captures the value of firms' production activities. Specifically, the concept of value added explicitly excludes all inputs sourced from other sectors or from other countries and therefore captures the true value of production. In contrast, turnover clearly overrates the value of firms' production activities, particularly if foreign affiliates predominantly assemble parts and components obtained from other sectors or from abroad.

Specifically, we look at the following relation:

$$\frac{R \& D_{inward}}{R \& D_{total}} \stackrel{45°}{=} \frac{VA_{inward}}{VA_{total}} \tag{9.1}$$

Equation (9.1) emphasises that if the share of foreign-owned firms on R&D expenditure is equal or close to equal to their share of value added, host countries will align along or close to a 45 degree line. However, if the share of foreign-owned affiliates on R&D expenditure is larger than the value added share of foreign-owned affiliates, host countries are located to the north-west of the 45 degree line. A larger share of value added of foreign-owned firms (relative to the share of R&D expenditure of foreign-owned firms) will push host countries to the south-east. The analysis concentrates on the latter two cases and seeks to identify host countries off the 45 degree line as interesting cases to study. In particular, host countries positioned to the north-west of the 45 degree demarcation line mark countries or sectors with a high degree of internationalisation of R&D activities while the opposite corner (the area to the south-east of the 45 degree demarcation line) identifies host countries or sectors where production activities are more internationalised than R&D.

Data on R&D expenditure of foreign-owned firms ($R\&D_{inward}$) as well as total R&D expenditure ($R\&D_{total}$) were collected by the Austrian Institute of Technology and the Vienna Institute for International Economic Studies (wiiw) from national contact points (national statistical offices, science policy offices etc.) as described in Chapter 3. The OECD Activities of Foreign Affiliates statistics (OECD AFA) provides information on value added of foreign-owned affiliates in a host country (VA_{inward}), while data on total value added (VA_{total}) stem from the OECD Structural Analysis Database (OECD STAN).

In order to draw the most comprehensive picture and to provide a meaningful cross-country comparison, data points are identified by means of a backward-looking procedure. Specifically, the analysis predominantly focuses on the year 2007 as the last year covered in all datasets. However, if for a specific sector, no information on the R&D and value added shares are available for the year 2007; these shares are taken for the year 2006 instead. And in case a sector is not fully covered in 2006 (or 2005) either, shares are taken for the year 2005 (or 2004) instead. Moreover, due to lacking data for the service sector, the ensuing analysis focuses on the manufacturing sector only.[1]

Figure 9.1 depicts the shares of business R&D and value added of foreign affiliates in the overall manufacturing sector. It points at a broad variation in the share of business R&D of foreign affiliates across countries which range between only 6 percent in Japan and 85 percent in the Slovak Republic. Specifically, the degree of internationalisation of R&D in manufacturing is highest in the Slovak Republic, Austria and Portugal. The opposite holds true for the Irish manufacturing sector whose production activities are comparatively more internationalised. Generally, with a few exceptions only, Figure 9.1 highlights that the share of R&D of foreign affiliates is consistently higher than the share of value added which suggests that, research and development expenditure is more internationalised than production in the manufacturing sector in the majority of countries considered, a finding that is in line with those of the OECD (2009) for a comparable set of countries. Furthermore, Figure 9.1 reveals that R&D shares and value added shares of foreign-owned affiliates are positively related.

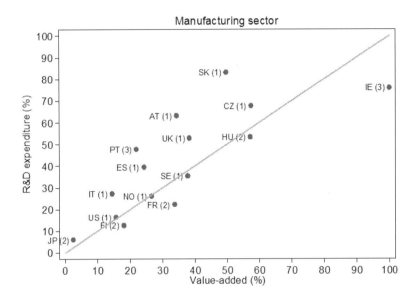

Notes: the share of value added for IE was rescaled to 100.
(1) refers to the year 2007, (2) to 2006, (3) to 2005 and (4) to 2004.
Source: Data collected from national contact points, OECD AFA, OECD STAN.

Figure 9.1 Share of R&D and value added of foreign-owned affiliates in manufacturing (2004-2007)

A similar analysis at the sectoral level reveals that in none of the sectors considered are all countries located either above or below the 45 degree line suggesting a substantial within-sector heterogeneity across countries for the sample of countries considered.[2] Table 9.1 provides an overview of the relationship between the internationalisation of R&D and production for total manufacturing and for individual manufacturing industries. It highlights that, for the sample of countries considered, production (still) appears to be more internationalised than R&D in the majority of sectors.

Table 9.1 Summary of emerging patterns – share of inward business R&D and value added of foreign-owned affiliates (2004-2007)

Sectors	Tech-intensity[3]	No. of observ.	General pattern: **Higher internationalisation in:**	Outliers above 45° line	below 45° line	Missing observations for:
Total manufacturing		15	R&D	SK, AT, PT	IE	
Food, beverages and tobacco	LT	14	R&D	SK, PT	IE	AT
Textiles, fur and leather	LT	11	similar	IT, UK	IE	PT, JP, SK, FI
Wood, paper etc.	LT	12	production	AT	IE, HU, CZ	PT, JP, SK
Coke, refined petroleum etc.	MLT	6	data issues	IT, UK	SE, FR	PT, SK, IE, CZ, AT, HU, ES, NO, US
Chemicals		13	R&D	SK, UK, AT, ES	FR, FI	NO, PT
Chemicals (excl. pharma)	MHT	8	similar		FR, IE	NO, IT, PT, HU, AT, CZ, SK
Pharmaceuticals	HT	8	production		FR, FI	NO, IT, PT, HU, AT, CZ, SK
Rubber and plastic products	MLT	14	production	SK	HU, FR, SE	PT
Non-metallic mineral products	MLT	15	production	PT, SK, FI	CZ, HU	
Basic and fabricated metals	MLT	14	R&D	PT, UK, FR, IE		AT
Machinery and equipment	MHT	15	similar		NO	
Office machinery, computer	HT	9	production	IT		HU, IE, JP
Electrical machinery and apparatus	MHT	12	production		IE, SE	AT, FI, IT
Radio, TV and communications	HT	10	similar	NO		IE, AT, IT, FI, US
Medical and optical instruments	HT	10	production	CZ	US	IE, AT, IT, FI, PT
Motor vehicles	MHT	12	similar	None	IE, AT, SK	
Other transport equipment	MHT	10	production	ES	SK, CZ, FR, SE	IE, AT, PT, IT, FI
Furniture, other manufacturing	LT	13	similar	IT, UK	IE, HU, SE	SK, US

Note: Areas highlighted in grey represent sectors with severe data issues, in which between 30 percent and more than 50 percent of all observations are missing; the last column captures the names of countries that are absent in the analysis.

In contrast, R&D is more internationalised than production in total manufacturing as well as in the food, beverages and tobacco sector, the chemicals and chemical products sector and the basic and fabricated metals sectors only.

However, this emerging picture must be interpreted with care as it is plagued by missing-data issues. Specifically, due to stringent confidentiality conditions, information on R&D and/or value added of foreign affiliates is not available for all manufacturing sub-sectors and missing in most service sectors. This missing-data problem is particularly true for medium-high-technology and high-technology sectors, which, by definition, are highly R&D intensive and whose research is expected to be more internationalised than production. In particular, with almost 50 percent of all country points missing, the missing-data problem is most severe in the coke, refined petroleum and nuclear fuel sector, followed by the chemicals and chemical products sector (less pharmaceuticals), the pharmaceuticals sector, the office, accounting and computing machinery sector and the radio, TV and communications sector, the medical precision and optical instruments sector as well as the other transport equipment sector for which 30 percent of all country points are absent. Moreover, this missing-data problem is also responsible for the apparent discrepancy in internationalisation patterns between the total manufacturing sector and all its sub-sectors. In particular, with mainly production as the more internationalised activity, manufacturing sub-sectors are unable to explain the higher degree of internationalisation of research in the total manufacturing sector. However, there is valid reason to believe that if all data were available, research would emerge as more internationalised (compared to production) in some or all of the above-mentioned medium-high-tech and high-tech sub-sectors.

THE RELATIONSHIP BETWEEN R&D INTENSITIES OF DOMESTIC AND FOREIGN-OWNED FIRMS

A comparison of R&D expenditure and value added shares of foreign-owned affiliates helps identify some characteristics of the process of R&D internationalisation; however it does not allow for a direct comparison of the R&D efforts of foreign-owned and domestically owned firms. Hence, a direct comparison of R&D intensities (as the share of R&D expenditure in value added) of foreign-owned and of domestic firms is drawn to identify and compare the relative size of R&D efforts undertaken by both types of firms.

Methodologically, we draw the following comparison:

$$\frac{R\&D_{foreign}}{VA_{foreign}} \overset{45°}{=} \frac{R\&D_{domestic}}{VA_{domestic}} \tag{9.2}$$

Equation (9.2) emphasises that if R&D intensities of foreign-owned affiliates correspond to the R&D intensities of domestic firms, countries will align along or close to a 45 degree line. However, if R&D intensities of foreign-owned firms are higher than R&D intensities of domestic firms, countries will be located to the north-west of the 45 degree line. Larger R&D intensities of domestic firms (relative to R&D intensities of foreign-owned firms) push host countries to the south-east. The ensuing analysis again predominantly focuses on the latter two cases. Again, data points are identified by means of a backward-looking procedure as outlined above.

Figure 9.2 shows results for the manufacturing sector and highlights that R&D intensities of both foreign-owned and domestic firms range between 0 and 15 percent. Moreover, R&D intensities of foreign-owned and domestic firms are pretty similar across countries considered. The Japanese and the Austrian manufacturing sectors are the only exceptions as the R&D intensities of foreign affiliates is close to 30 percent in Japan and 12 percent in Austria and as such, almost three times as high as R&D intensities of domestic firms (10 and 4 percent respectively). This strong disparity in R&D intensities of foreign-owned and Japanese firms can be attributed to the strong concentration of foreign-owned affiliates in the motor vehicles sector and their extensive investments in research and development.

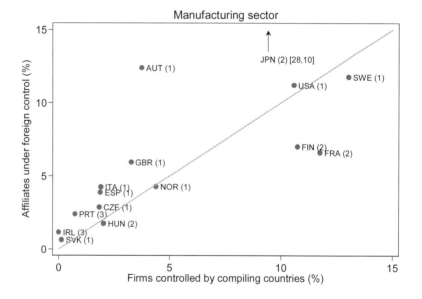

Notes: R&D intensity of domestically owned firms in IE was rescaled to 0.
(1) refers to the year 2007, (2) to 2006, (3) to 2005 and (4) to 2004.
Source: Data collected from national contact points, OECD AFA, OECD STAN.

Figure 9.2 R&D intensities in the manufacturing sector (2004-2007)

Table 9.2 provides an overview of findings for total manufacturing as well as all its sub-sectors. We find that, for the sample of countries considered, R&D intensities of both foreign-owned and domestically owned firms are similar in the majority of manufacturing sub-sectors.

Table 9.2 Summary of emerging patterns – domestic and foreign R&D intensities (2004-2007)

Sectors	Tech-intensity³	No. of observ.	General pattern: Higher R&D intensity in	Outliers above 45° line	Outliers below 45° line	Missing observations for:
Total manufacturing		15	similar	JP		
Food, beverages and tobacco	LT	14	similar	FR	NO, JP	AT
Textiles, fur and leather	LT	11	foreign firms	IT, AT, ES	SE	PT, JP, SK, FI
Wood, paper etc.	LT	13	foreign firms	AT		PT, JP
Coke, refined petroleum etc.	MLT	5	similar	JP		PT, SK, FI, IE, CZ, AT, HU, ES, NO, US
Chemicals		13	similar		FR, SE, FI	NO, PT
Chemicals (excl. pharma)	MHT	8	similar	SE	JP, FR	NO, IT, PT, HU, AT, CZ, SK
Pharmaceuticals	HT	8	domestic firms	UK	FI, FR, SE	NO, IT, PT, HU, AT, CZ, SK
Rubber and plastic products	MLT	14	domestic firms		FI, FR, SE	PT
Non-metallic mineral products	MLT	15	domestic firms	FI, ES	CZ, JP	
Basic and fabricated metals	MLT	14	foreign firms	FR, IE	SE	AT
Machinery and equipment	MHT	15	foreign firms		NO	
Office machinery, computer	HT	9	similar	DATA ISSUES		AT, FI, PT, ES, NO, SK
Electrical machinery and apparatus	MHT	12	domestic firms		SE	AT, FI, IT
Radio, TV and communications	HT	10	similar	NO	FR, SE	IE, AT, IT, FI, US
Medical and optical instruments	HT	10	domestic firms	CZ	JP, US	IE, AT, IT, FI, PT
Motor vehicles	MHT	12	similar	JP	FR	IE, AT, SK
Other transport equipment	MHT	10	domestic firms	ES	CZ, FR, SE	IE, AT, PT, IT, FI
Furniture, other manufacturing	LT	14	similar	IT, UK	IE, JP, SE	US

Note: Areas highlighted in grey represent sectors with severe data issues, in which between 30 percent and more than 50 percent of all observations are missing; the last column captures the names of countries that are absent in the analysis.

Again, due to prevailing missing-data issues, emerging patterns must be interpreted with care. In particular, in some of the medium-high technology and high-technology sectors considered (the coke, refined petroleum and nuclear fuel sector, the chemical industry, the pharmaceutical sector, the office, accounting and computing machinery sector, the radio, TV and communications sector, the medical precision and optical instruments sector and the other transport equipment sector), between 30 to 50 percent of all data points are missing, potentially providing a biased picture of the relative scale of R&D intensities of both domestic and foreign-owned firms.

All in all, the graphical analysis of R&D intensities offers important lessons for the econometric analyses of drivers of R&D internationalisation. Specifically, it points out, first, that except for a few outliers per industry, countries locate along the 45 degree line. This highlights that R&D intensities of both domestically owned and foreign-owned firms are strongly related. High R&D intensities of domestically owned firms are (closely) matched by high R&D intensities of foreign-owned firms. Or, put differently, the scale of R&D intensities of domestically owned firms is an important driver of R&D expenditure of foreign-owned firms. This latter observation is substantiated by results of econometric analyses (which control for additional crucial characteristics) which point at robust complementarities between R&D intensities of domestic and foreign-owned firms. Second, in none of the sectors considered are all countries located either above or below the 45 degree line. Hence, for the sample of countries considered, in none of the sectors are R&D intensities of foreign-owned affiliates consistently higher or lower than R&D intensities of domestic firms suggesting evidence of non-negligible within-sector cross-country heterogeneity.

HOST COUNTRY DETERMINANTS OF R&D INTERNATIONALISATION

The ensuing analysis sheds light on and identifies potential drivers of business R&D expenditure of foreign-owned firms at both, country and industry levels. For that purpose the following model is estimated:

$$\ln RDinflow_{ikt} = \alpha_0 + \beta_z X_{zikt} + \varepsilon_{ikt} , \qquad (9.3)$$

where $\ln RDinflow_{ikt}$ is the log of inward BERD for sector i in country k at time t and X_{zikt} is a matrix of z explanatory variables. The selection of variables is motivated by the literature review presented earlier in this report and comprises the following variables at both the country as well as sectoral level: country-specific variables include the log of total real national GDP to capture the size of the host economy, or equivalently, the host market. Since firms may have to adapt their products and production processes to local demand patterns, consumer preferences or to comply with legal regulations and laws, they may find it easier to cover their cost of adaptive R&D in larger markets with higher demand for their goods and services and consequently larger revenues.

Moreover, empirical studies have pointed at the pivotal role a skilled labour force has in successfully conducting R&D and in generating product and process innovations, rendering cross-country differences in the quality and size of a skilled workforce an important driver of cross-border R&D flows. Specifically, the shortage of highly skilled science and engineering talent explains the relocation of product development to other parts of the world (Lewin et al. 2009) while the abundance of graduates in science and technology and strong scientific and engineering capabilities in a host country account for the inflow of business R&D into a host country (e.g. Hedge and Hicks 2008). Hence, a highly qualified and skilled workforce in the host country with strong scientific and engineering capabilities is expected to increase inward BERD. This link between the quality and size of a skilled workforce and inward BERD is accounted for by the share of tertiary graduates in the fields of science, mathematics, computing, engineering, manufacturing and construction in the total labour force.

Finally, the attractiveness of countries for overseas R&D activities is shaped by public policy. Specifically, science, technology and innovation (STI) policy measures like public subsidies for R&D performing firms or measures to foster co-operation among firms or between firms and universities and other research organisations determine locational advantages and influence internationalisation decisions of firms in R&D (Steinmueller 2010). Hence, the share of government budgetary appropriations or outlays for R&D (GBAORD) in real GDP is included to capture the role STI policies play in driving R&D expenditure of foreign-owned firms.

Inward business R&D expenditure is also shaped by very specific characteristics of sectors in host countries which render them more or less attractive for inward R&D expenditure. In that respect, labour costs as percentage of value added is included as a proxy for unit labour costs (ULC) which captures the relative cost and productivity of labour of a sector in a host country. Since high ULC render both production and R&D relatively expensive activities, sectors with high ULC are expected to attract less inward business R&D.

Moreover, the extent of inward R&D expenditure crucially depends on a sector's attractiveness to foreign-owned investors in terms of FDI. In that respect, the sectoral FDI intensity, as the share of the inward FDI stock in total gross sectoral output, is included to capture the pivotal role FDI plays for R&D activities.

Furthermore, as pointed out by Athukorala and Kohpaiboon (2010), both the R&D intensity of production processes and the need to adapt products and production processes to local conditions and preferences differ widely across sectors. Hence, a sector's domestic R&D intensity defined as total sectoral domestic R&D expenditure as percentage of sectoral value added is included to capture that some host country sectors inherently require higher R&D expenditure which renders higher inward business R&D expenditure a necessary prerequisite for any successful adaptive or innovative R&D activities or production activities of foreign-owned affiliates. This hypothesis is also supported by findings of the graphical analysis which highlights that, on average, business R&D expenditure of foreign-owned affiliates are positively related to business R&D expenditure of domestic firms.

Additionally, sectors differ with regard to their size, as proxied by sectoral employment as percentage of the total labour force. Specifically, current sector size is the result of past employment expansions by successful and profitable firms. And since firm profitability crucially depends on its ability to continuously generate marketable innovations, sizeable resources are allotted to research activities and the development of new products and/or productivity-enhancing processes by both domestically owned as well as foreign-owned firms. Hence, inward BERD is expected to be higher in larger sectors. Account is also taken of the differences in the ability to attract inward business R&D across EU-15 and EU-12 member countries by including dummy variables for both groups (with non-EU member countries as reference). Finally, ε_{ikt} is the error term.

The data for the analysis are drawn from various sources. The dependent variable (i.e. inward BERD) stems from the dataset as described in Chapter 3. Moreover, country-level variables like real GDP or information on the number of tertiary graduates in the fields of science, mathematics, computing, engineering, manufacturing and construction come from different OECD sources. Furthermore, data on labour costs, value added and size originate from the OECD Structural Analysis Database (OECD STAN), while information on government budgetary appropriations or outlays for R&D stem from the OECD Main Science and Technology Indicators. The OECD AFA statistics is the source for value added of foreign-owned firms, while inward stocks on foreign direct investments (FDI) are taken from the OECD International Direct Investment Statistics (OECD IDI). Due to missing data for the service sector in many countries, services are excluded.

Given data quality and availability, the econometric analysis uses the short unbalanced panel from 2004 to 2007 and analyses the overall sample comprising a set of OECD and non-OECD countries (OVERALL) on the one hand and three sub-samples on the other.[4] Methodologically, a pooled OLS approach without time fixed effects is taken as the Hausman test is not rejected while the Breusch-Pagan Lagrange multiplier test is rejected.

Table 9.3 presents results and highlights that the set of relevant drivers differs considerably between EU-15 and EU-12 countries. Specifically, with the exception of the EU-12 country sample, larger host markets that promise larger revenues to foreign-owned firms induce higher business R&D expenditure of foreign-owned affiliates. In particular, a 1 percent increase in the host country's real GDP is found to increase business R&D expenditure of foreign-owned affiliates by between 0.5 percent and around 1 percent.

Table 9.3 Results for host country determinants of R&D internationalisation (2004-2007)

Dep.Var.: log inward BERD	OVERALL	EU	EU-15	EU-12
Variables	(1)	(2)	(3)	(4)
Constant	-10.724***	-10.303***	-6.942**	-11.091
	(5.97)	(4.32)	(2.50)	(0.93)
Country level				
Log real GDP	0.913***	1.005***	0.712***	0.528
	(7.94)	(5.72)	(3.79)	(0.40)
Share of tertiary graduates	1.070	0.576	-0.493	10.895**
	(0.72)	(0.39)	(0.29)	(2.59)
Share of GBAORD in real GDP	1.606***	0.627	-0.783	4.424*
	(2.84)	(1.02)	(0.86)	(1.84)
Sector level				
Labour cost over value added	-0.007	-0.011	0.023*	-0.031**
	(0.85)	(1.11)	(1.83)	(2.13)
FDI intensity	0.023***	0.019***	0.015***	0.096***
	(4.26)	(3.35)	(2.69)	(4.69)
Domestic R&D intensity	0.030***	0.034***	0.035***	0.035
	(3.23)	(3.06)	(3.07)	(1.26)
Size	0.098	0.218*	0.230	0.023
	(0.86)	(1.84)	(1.31)	(0.16)
Dummy: EU15	0.605*			
	(1.66)			
Dummy: EU12	0.459	0.051		
	(0.83)	(0.11)		
No of observations	229	181	106	75
Adj. R²	0.570	0.499	0.272	0.525

Note: t-statistics in parentheses, *** p<0.01, ** p<0.05, * p<0.1
Methodologically, a pooled OLS approach without time fixed effects is applied. Column (1) uses the overall sample, column (2) is based on the overall EU sample; column (3) uses the EU-15 sub-sample only, while column (4) uses the EU-12 sub-sample only.

Moreover, human capital, as proxied by the share of tertiary graduates in technology-related fields in the total labour force, is an important determinant of inward BERD only for the group of EU-12 countries (column (4)). Hence, for the group of EU-12 countries only, there is sound evidence that strong prevailing scientific and engineering capabilities attract inward business R&D

expenditure. In contrast, no such role can be attributed to human capital in the group of EU-15 countries (column (3)).

As advocated by Steinmueller (2010), science, technology and innovation policy measures determine locational advantages and may therefore influence internationalisation decisions of firms in R&D. The analysis demonstrates that STI policies, as proxied by the share of government budgetary appropriations or outlays for R&D (GBAORD) in total national real GDP, is essential, but for the overall sample and the EU-12 sub-sample only. Hence, in EU-12 countries, STI policies are important drivers of inward R&D expenditure.

Furthermore, some sectoral characteristics of host countries are of importance. Specifically, labour costs as percentage of value added have a significant positive effect on inward R&D expenditure in the group of EU-15 countries (column (3)) but a significant negative effect in the group of EU-12 countries (column (4)). Hence, high labour costs (relative to value added) are associated with higher R&D expenditure of foreign-owned affiliates located in EU-15 countries but with lower R&D expenditure of foreign-owned affiliates located in EU-12 countries. This might reflect the very specific R&D activities that are conducted in different country groups. The EU-12 is an attractive region for more routine and less demanding or sophisticated R&D activities of foreign firms. Hence, R&D expenditure tends to be lower if labour costs increase as routine R&D activities may be conducted more cheaply elsewhere. In contrast, the EU-15 is an attractive region for less routine but more sophisticated and novel R&D activities, activities which tend to be more expensive also.

Empirical results also consistently demonstrate that inward FDI and inward R&D expenditure are strategic complements. By comparison, the effect is considerably stronger among EU-12 countries (column (4)) than among EU-15 countries (column (3)).

Furthermore, a sector's domestic R&D intensity (as the share of R&D expenditure of domestic firms in value added of domestic firms) is positively associated with business R&D expenditure of foreign-owned affiliates, for all but the EU-12 sample. Specifically, industries that are inherently more R&D intensive are also found to experience significantly higher inward business R&D expenditure. The coefficient, however, is quite small, so huge changes in domestic R&D intensity are associated with only minor changes in the level of inward BERD.

In addition, sector size is an important driver of business R&D expenditure of foreign-owned affiliates in the overall EU sample only (column (1)).

Finally, some country-group dummies were included to capture in how far business R&D expenditure of foreign-owned affiliates are significantly higher (or lower) for the group of EU-15 or EU-12 countries (compared to non-EU countries). Column (1) highlights that – compared to non-EU member countries – EU-15 countries experience significantly higher inward business R&D expenditure. Furthermore, column (2) stresses that EU-15 and EU-12 countries receive similar amounts of inward business R&D expenditure.

SUMMARY

This chapter provides a descriptive analysis of the relationship between R&D internationalisation and the internationalisation of production by comparing the relative R&D intensities of domestic and foreign-owned firms across countries and sectors. A simple graphical analysis points towards significant differences across countries with respect to the importance of foreign R&D and reveals that R&D shares and value added shares of foreign-owned affiliates are positively related. Furthermore it highlights that research and development is more internationalised than production in the manufacturing sector in the majority of countries considered as in most cases the share of R&D of foreign affiliates is consistently higher than the share of value added. A further graphical inspection shows that R&D intensities of foreign-owned and domestic firms are pretty similar across the countries considered with a few exceptions like Japan and Austria. This latter observation is substantiated by results of econometric analyses (which control for additional crucial characteristics) which point at robust complementarities between R&D intensities of domestic and foreign-owned firms. At a more detailed sectoral level there is however evidence for non-negligible within-sector cross-country heterogeneity. The econometric analysis underpins these results, particularly showing that inward FDI and inward R&D expenditure are strategic complements and that the domestic R&D intensity is positively associated with business R&D expenditure of foreign-owned affiliates for advanced countries. Other control variables show that size, human capital and STI policies are conducive for attracting foreign R&D. These results are in line with findings from a gravity model including both home and host country determinants (see Leitner et al., 2013).

NOTES

1. Belgium, Bulgaria, Canada, Denmark, Estonia, Germany, Israel, Latvia, Malta, the Netherlands, Poland, Romania, Slovenia had to be excluded due to insufficient data on value added of foreign-owned affiliates Moreover, lacking data on both value added and business R&D expenditure of foreign-owned affiliates led to the exclusion of Australia, Greece, Iceland, Korea, Malta, Luxembourg, Switzerland and Turkey. As a result, 15 countries are included in the analysis: Austria (AT), the Czech Republic (CZ), France (FR), Finland (FI), Hungary (HU), Ireland (IE), Italy (IT), Japan (JP), Norway (NO), Portugal (PT), Spain (ES), Sweden (SE), Slovakia (SK), the UK and the US.
2. Graphs are available upon request.
3. We distinguish between high- (HT), medium-high- (MHT), medium-low- (MLT) and low-technology (LT) manufacturing sectors.
4. The three sub-samples consist of 22 EU member countries (EU), 13 of the EU-15 member countries (EU-15) (Austria, Belgium, Denmark, Finland, France, Germany, Ireland, Italy, the Netherlands, Portugal, Spain, Sweden and the UK) and 9 EU-12 member countries (EU-12) (Bulgaria, the Czech Republic, Estonia, Hungary, Latvia, Poland, Romania, Slovakia and Slovenia) to identify differences in drivers across sub-groups.

REFERENCES

Athukorala, P.-C. and A. Kohpaiboon (2010), 'Globalization of R&D by US-based multinational enterprises', *Research Policy* **39**(10), 1335-347.

Hedge, D. and D. Hicks (2008), 'The maturation of global corporate R&D: Evidence from the activity of U.S. foreign subsidiaries', *Research Policy* **37**(3), 390–406.

Leitner, S., R. Stehrer and B. Dachs (2013), 'Determinants of international R&D activities – Evidence from a gravity model', in T. Scherngell (ed.), *The geography of networks and R&D collaborations*, Berlin: Springer Verlag, forthcoming.

Lewin, A. Y., S. Massini and C. Peeters (2009), 'Why are companies offshoring innovation? The emerging global race for talent', *Journal of International Business Studies* **40**(6), 901-25.

OECD (2009), *The Impact of the Crisis on ICTs and their Role in the Recovery*, DSTI/ICCP/IE(2009)1/FINAL, Paris: OECD.

Steinmueller, W. E. (2010), 'Economics of Technology Policy', n: B.A. Hall and N. Rosenberg (eds), *Handbook of Economics and Innovation*. Vol. 2, Amsterdam: Elsevier, pp. 1182-1218.

10. Drivers of R&D Internationalisation in the Automotive Industry and in Knowledge-intensive Business Services

Bernhard Dachs and Doris Hanzl-Weiss

The previous chapter has identified various drivers of R&D internationalisation at the country level. Internationalisation processes in R&D, however, are highly sector- and firm-specific, and there exists a considerable degree of heterogeneity with respect to drivers and motives below the country level. Motives to locate R&D abroad can be even more differentiated when we look at the sectoral level (Hedge and Hicks 2008).

Thus, this chapter will complement the econometric analysis of drivers presented in the previous chapter with an in-depth view on the drivers of R&D internationalisation in the automotive industry and in knowledge-intensive business services. Both industries have been identified in Chapter 7 as key sectors in R&D internationalisation. The case study will focus on the automotive sector in Czech Republic, Slovakia, Hungary and Romania, and at knowledge-intensive business services in Estonia, Israel, and in the United Kingdom.

INTERNATIONALISATION OF R&D IN THE AUTOMOTIVE SECTOR

The automotive industry is classified as a medium-high technology industry based on its R&D intensity, thus accounting for a large share of total business R&D. In addition, the sector is highly internationalised. In the EU-12 the automotive industry benefited from a strong inflow of FDI which provided a strong impetus for inward BERD. Looking more deeply at the Czech Republic, Slovakia, Hungary and Romania, this section will examine the importance of the automotive sector for FDI and R&D internationalisation in these four countries: What factors determine the extent of R&D undertaken by foreign affiliates? Did the growth of R&D activities by foreign affiliates simply follow the pattern of FDI flows? Why are some countries more attractive than others?

R&D internationalisation patterns in the automotive sector in the EU-12

The automotive sector, defined according to the NACE rev.1. classification as NACE 34 'motor vehicles, trailers and semi-trailers', is the most important manufacturing sector in the Czech Republic, Hungary and Slovakia where it accounts for production shares of 19 percent, 18 percent and 21 percent respectively. In Romania the automotive sector is comparably smaller and has only a share of 6 percent (see Table 10.1). Here the food, coke and basic metals industries are relatively more important. Overall, the inflow of FDI has considerably shaped the automotive industry in the EU-12. Today, the automotive sector accounts for 25 percent of total manufacturing inward FDI stock in the Czech Republic, 23 percent in Hungary and Slovakia and 11 percent in Romania. In the first three countries, the automotive industry is the major recipient of foreign investment, while in Romania it is on the fourth place (see Table 10.1).

Table 10.1 Share of the automotive industry on total manufacturing (2008)

	CZ	HU	RO	SK
Production	19.3[1)]	17.6	6.3[2)]	21
FDI inward stock	24.9	23.1[1)]	10.6[1)]	23.4
BERD	39.1	13.8[2)]	25.2[2)]	0[2)]

Notes: 1) NACE 34+35.- 2) 2007.
Source: wiiw Industrial Database, wiiw FDI Database, EUROSTAT BERD statistics.

Since the collapse of communism in 1989, FDI inflows transformed the automotive industry in the EU-12 into a competitive, export-oriented industry. The first foreign company to arrive was Volkswagen in the Czech and Slovak Republics in 1991 (still Czechoslovakia then). Volkswagen formed joint-ventures with already existing companies which became Škoda Auto and VW Bratislava respectively (Hanzl 1999). However, foreign investment climate was unfavourable in these first years in the Czech Republic and Slovakia, other than in Hungary. Hungary opened its economy to foreign investors soon after 1989 and automotive investors arrived quickly in the country: Opel (engines) and Suzuki came in 1992, Audi (engines) in 1993, all by means of green-field investments. Suppliers followed soon. In Romania, Daewoo from South Korea formed a joint-venture in 1994, Renault acquired 51 percent of Automobile Dacia Pitești in 1999 with whom it had a long-time licence agreement (see Hanzl 1999).

After this first wave of privatisation and investments in the 1990s, the automotive industry continued to attract FDI in the 2000s as well: Choosing Slovakia, PSA Peugeot Citröen announced to build a green-field plant in 2003; Kia Motors in 2004. Production started in both plants in 2006. Locating in the Czech Republic, Toyota Peugeot Citröen made an investment decision in 2002 and started production in early 2005. Hyundai announced to invest in the Czech Republic in 2005, following its sister company KIA, and the plant was completed in 2008. Finally in Hungary, Mercedes decided to build an assembly plant in Kecskemét in 2008. Only in Romania, the investment path was not that smooth: Due to the collapse of the main parent company Daewoo, the Romanian company got into troubles and the state took over shares from the Automobile Craiova company in 2006. Stakes of the company were sold step-by-step to Ford between 2007 and 2009.

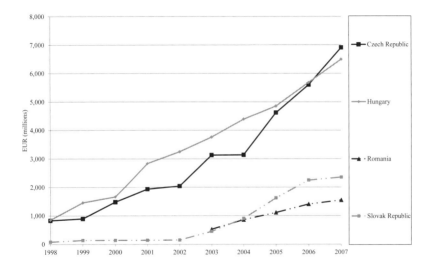

Notes: 35+45 for Hungary and Romania.
Source: wiiw FDI Database.

Figure 10.1 FDI inward stock in the automotive sector (1998-2007, million EUR)

Thus the stock of FDI in the automotive sector in the Czech Republic and Hungary climbed from 800 million EUR in 1998 to 6.9 billion EUR and 6.4 billion EUR in 2007 respectively (see Figure 10.1). In Slovakia, the FDI stock was quite low until 2002 (around 140 million EUR) but started to rise afterwards. In 2007, it already reached 2.3 billion EUR. For Romania, data are only available from 2003 onwards. Here, we observe a slight increase and a stock of 1.5 billion EUR in 2007.

The automotive industry accounts for a large share of business R&D expenditure in manufacturing (see Table 10.1): it is highest in the Czech Republic with 39 percent, 25 percent in Romania and 14 percent in Hungary. For Slovakia, data was zero for the year 2007. Internationalisation of R&D is strong in the EU-12 as well: the automotive industry's share in total inward BERD (see Table 10.2) stood at 40 percent in the Czech Republic in 2007, at 26 percent in Hungary but was lower in Slovakia and Romania.

Table 10.2 Inward BERD in the automotive sector (2003 and 2007)

	Inward BERD (million EUR)		Inward sectoral R&D intensity, %		Share of total inward BERD
	2007	2003	2007	2003	2007
CZ	275.7	95.5	95.1	56.0	40.4
HU	53.5	81.6 [1)2)]	100.0	16.3 [1)]	25.7
RO	0.3	7.6 [1)]	0.9	11.6 [1)]	0.4
SK	(c)	.	.	0 [1)]	3.9 [3)]

Notes: 1) 2004; 2) Total BERD includes only manufacturing; 3) 2006.
Source: EUROSTAT BERD statistics, Czech Statistical Office, EUROSTAT FATS statistics.

It is interesting to compare R&D expenditure with the FDI figures stated above: Although the stock of FDI is nearly the same in the Czech Republic and Hungary, R&D expenditure is six times higher in the Czech Republic, positioning the country as the hub of automotive R&D in the region. R&D is dominated by foreign investors, as the figures for the inward sectoral R&D intensity in Table 10.2 suggest (nearly 100 percent in the Czech Republic and Hungary). Inward BERD in Romania, in contrast, is small and fluctuating over years. For Slovakia, data for BERD as well as for inward BERD are confidential in some years, but zero for others. This is striking as the motor vehicles industry is a major recipient of FDI in the Slovak Republic which is not reflected in the data on inward BERD. This suggests that large automotive companies do not perform R&D activities in the Slovak Republic but rather transfer technology from their home countries.

Common motives and drivers of R&D internationalisation in the EU-12

Chapter 2 has discussed various motives and drivers for R&D internationalisation, including the adaptation of products and processes to local market characteristics (demand-side, asset-exploiting behaviour), and the availability and costs of local knowledge (supply-side, asset-seeking behaviour). Often, policy-factors are mentioned as well (e.g. tax breaks or subsidies). In order to investigate the importance of these motives and drivers for the automotive industry in the EU-12, we use a range of sources: scientific literature, the fDi Markets database, information from inward investment agencies and company case studies. In this section we will provide some general remarks on motives and drivers, followed by an analysis based on fDi Markets database, while the next section goes into detail per country.

Generally one has to acknowledge the specific history of the EU-12, starting with the heritage of the communist regime, its collapse in 1989 and the transition period following thereafter which results in a number of drivers common to all EU-12 countries. Transformation encompassed the change to market systems, the opening up of trade and privatisation. Prospects for EU-accession shaped the economy and policy thereafter including e.g. the adoption of the EU acquis. With accession to the EU on 1st May 2004 for the Czech Republic, Hungary, and Slovakia and on 1st January 2007 for Romania, framework conditions changed again. A variety of European funds and programmes became accessibly for these countries, and support for R&D increased. Regarding these factors – which themselves can be seen as motives and drivers – general motives and drivers for R&D internationalisation were subject to change during this long time period.

Kubeczko et al. (2006) stress the importance of 'R&D histories' as a result of path dependencies. Thus, recent patterns of R&D in the automotive sector can partly be explained by specialisation patterns already existing during the communist regime. We can broadly group motives and drivers into three groups: (1) heritage from communism, (2) historical motives, mainly encompassing the 1990s and (3) recent motives, encompassing the period from 2000 until today.

Under the Council for Mutual Economic Assistance (CMEA) division of labour, the Czech Republic specialised on cars (Škoda), Hungary on buses and on components, Slovakia on lights trucks. Romania was not integrated in the CMEA system and tried to produce everything (companies Dacia and Oltcit, see Hanzl 1999). During the 1980s, only Czechoslovakia and East Germany were developing passenger cars, other car manufacturers in the region were producing under licences from West European firms.

Based on sectoral case studies in the automotive and pharmaceutical industries, Kubeczko et al. (2006) conclude that foreign investment in R&D in the EU-12 was driven by three main factors (thus relating to historical reasons): the quality on human resources, the labour costs and the access to local markets. Especially the long-run tradition of the automotive industry in the Czech Republic is highlighted, as well as the availability of highly qualified R&D personnel. On the other hand, favourable framework conditions including tax incentives were found to be overestimated.

Overall, historical reasons can change, e.g. the abundance of qualified labour which can turn into a shortage of qualified personnel today. Overall, the FDI analysis in the next section provides a picture on recent motives and drivers.

Recent motives and drivers

An overview of investment projects in the automotive R&D sector based of the fDi Markets database provides additional evidence on recent motives and drivers. This database lists recent FDI projects by country and by business activities. Business activities 'research and development' as well as 'design, development and testing' seem most appropriate for the questions of this chapter. The automotive sector was defined as automotive OEM plus automotive components.

Table 10.3 Destination country analysis: projects per year (2003-2011)

Country	HU	CZ	RO	SK	Total
2003		2			2
2004		3		1	4
2005	1				1
2006	3	2	2		7
2007	1	1	1		3
2008	4		1	1	6
2009			1		1
2010	1	1	2		4
2011			1		1
Sum	10	9	8	2	29
Total in %	34.5	31	27.6	6.9	100

Note: Only projects with the activities 'research and development' and/or 'Design, development and testing'.
Source: FDI Intelligence from Financial Times Ltd (fDi Markets database), September 2011.

Overall, in the period between January 2003 and September 2011, fDI Markets recorded 29 investment projects from 16 companies in the automotive sector for these 2 business activities in the Czech Republic, Hungary, Romania and Slovakia. The main results are:

- The leading activity was 'design, development and testing' accounting for 79 percent of all investment projects, only 21 percent were 'research and development' projects. These latter projects were announced only by automotive components suppliers and *not* by OEMs and were mainly registered for Hungary (67 percent), 17 percent for the Czech Republic and 17 percent for Slovakia and none for Romania.
- Within the automotive industry, automotive suppliers account for the majority (72 percent) of all investment projects. Only 28 percent were

done by OEMs with a strong focus on Romania (Renault, also Ford), less on the Czech Republic (Volkswagen, Daimler).

- Regarding the source country of investment, Germany accounted for the highest number of investment projects (55 percent), followed by France (21 percent), the United States (14 percent), the UK (7 percent) and Sweden (3 percent).
- Looking at the country attracting the greatest number of projects, 34 percent of all projects were registered in Hungary (Robert Bosch with 4 projects), 31 percent in the Czech Republic, 28 percent in Romania and 7 percent in Slovakia (only 2 investment projects, see Table 10.3).
- Referring to companies, Robert Bosch was the most active in the region (with 4 projects is Hungary and 2 in the Czech Republic), followed by Renault with 5 projects in Romania (see Table 10.4).

Table 10.4 Company analysis: projects per year per country (2003-2011)

Company	Origin	2003	2004	2005	2006	2007	2008	2009	2010	2011	Total
Robert Bosch	DE		CZ	HU	CZ, HU		HU		HU		6
Renault	FR				RO	RO	RO		RO	RO	5
Continental	DE						HU	RO			2
ZF Friedrichshafen	DE				HU	CZ					2
Visteon	US		CZ				SK				2
Knorr Bremse	DE						HU, HU				2
Ricardo	UK		CZ								1
Volkswagen	DE				CZ						1
Ford	US								RO		1
Valeo	FR	CZ									1
Other			CZ	SK	RO, HU	HU			CZ		6
Overall Total		2	4	1	7	3	6	1	4	1	29

Note: Only projects with the activities 'research and development' and/or 'Design, development and testing'.
Source: FDI Intelligence from Financial Times Ltd (fDi Markets database), September 2011.

The fDi Markets database provides also limited information on the motives for investing. In the sample, reasons for five investment projects were available. In four cases (representing all four countries!), the availability of skilled workforce was mentioned. Infrastructure and logistics, the presence of suppliers or joint venture partners, the proximity to markets or customers and lower costs were each mentioned two times. The domestic market growth was only referred to in Romania, financial incentives were also mentioned only once (also in Romania). Apart from motives and drivers common to all EU-12 countries, there are also more specific drivers which will be discussed below by country.

Czech Republic

During the 1980s, only the former Czechoslovakia and East Germany were developing their own passenger cars. With the collapse of communism, privatisation decided over the future of R&D departments, with some companies closing or scaling down their R&D activities. According to Pavlínek et al. (2010), the majority of R&D centres in the Czech automotive industry survived.

Today, there are more than thirty R&D active companies in the Czech automotive sector including Porsche Engineering Services, Mercedes-Benz Technology, Ricardo, Idiada, Swell, Valeo, Visteon, Aufeer Design, Valeo, Visteon, Bosch, Continental, Honeywell, Siemens, TRW, or ZF Automotive (Czech Invest 2011). The Czech investment agency CzechInvest identifies the following factors for R&D establishment: the well-established automotive market, high-level technical education, local industrial tradition and highly skilled engineers. There is one automotive cluster in the Czech Republic, the Moravian-Silesian Automotive Cluster (Janosec 2010).

The most successful privatisation was that of Škoda Auto, where R&D was maintained and later further extended. In fact, Pavlínek et al. (2010) stress the concentration of Czech automotive R&D on Škoda Auto, which holds more than 75 percent of total R&D in the sector (see company case study below). In 1998, the government introduced a system of investment incentives for foreign and domestic investors. In 2004, a number of companies decided to build R&D centres (Siemens Automotive Systems, Robert Bosch, Behr Czech Ltd.). Since 2005, R&D is supported indirectly through a new tax credit on R&D (Kubeczko et al. 2006). Overall, Pavlínek et al. (2010) state that between 1995 and 2007, the number of larger automotive R&D centres with 100 and more employees increased from 4 to 5 only, that of small R&D facilities with less than 20 employees, however, increased from 35 to 88 during this period. Thus, Škoda Auto retained its dominant position but the importance of large foreign-owned first-tier suppliers grew. Pavlínek et al. (2010) conclude that suppliers concentrate R&D on technical support, adaptation, testing and development of vehicle part and not on applied and basic research.

Čadil et al. (2007) distinguish between historical motives and still present motives for setting up R&D activities in the Czech Republic: Historical motives include the start of the privatisation process as a main milestone for R&D investment, second the high quality and low cost of human resources due to long industrial tradition, and third, the strategic location of the Czech

Republic with its proximity to Germany together with good infrastructure. Čadil et al. (2007) also see a shift of localisation motives from low cost strategy to sophisticated intensive strategies, based on the quality of domestic R&D infrastructure including universities and research institutions today. In addition, investment incentive schemes are 'now considered as one of the most important factors for establishment of R&D activities' (Čadil et al. 2007, p. 27). From the historical motives, skilled labour force, industrial tradition and geographical position are still relevant. However, also certain drawbacks are mentioned. These are the lack of qualified labour today, low quality of R&D management, low level of corporation (research institutes and multinationals), as well as low support of R&D activities in large multinationals (see Čadil et al. 2007). Pavlinek et al. (2010) mention a number of factors prevailing recently for foreign companies to develop automotive R&D in the Czech Republic. These include the well-developed supplier sector, industrial tradition, level of technical education, government investment incentives and the need for first-tier suppliers to cooperate closely with assemblers on R&D (Pavlinek et al. 2010, p. 486).

Key to understanding the development of the Czech automotive industry is the history of Škoda Auto: Taken over by Volkswagen at the beginning of the 1990s, Škoda Auto maintained its brand and its pre-1989 R&D facilities. Later on, further functions were developed and some routine R&D operations were transferred to the company e.g. computer aided design in 1999. Motives for these steps included the cheaper and skilled R&D labour force as well as its abundance. 'The basic goal is to adapt VW technologies for Škoda models and to design Škoda models based on VW Group's platforms' (Pavlinek et al. 2010). Besides opening a design centre, Škoda Auto established a technology centre in Mladá Boleslav in 2008 that delivers R&D solutions for the entire Volkswagen Group (Czech Invest 2011). Thus, the number of R&D employees rose from 600 in 1991 to 1420 in 2005 and 1563 in 2008 (see also Kubeczko et al. 2006, p.53). Overall, the Czech Republic has become the hub of automotive R&D expenditure in the region, thanks to Škoda Auto. Pavlinek et al. (2010), state that Škoda Auto accounts for more than 75 percent of Czech automotive R&D. 'Without Škoda Auto, the Czech automotive R&D expenditures would be only slightly higher than those of Hungary' (see Pavlinek et al. 2010).

Hungary

Several multinationals have set up R&D centres in Hungary e.g. Audi, Bosch, Knorr-Bremse, Magna, ThyssenKrupp, Arvin Meritor, Denso, Continental, Visteon, WET, Draxlmaier, Edag, Temic Telefunken, DENSO and ZF. The Hungarian Investment and Trade Development Agency (ITDH 2010) considers the following factors favourable for locating automotive R&D in Hungary today: (a) Hungary's strategic position, together with developed logistics and infrastructure (four trans-European motorways running through Hungary). Proximity to the Balkans, Ukraine and Russia are also mentioned. (b) Membership in the EU implies taking over the EU-acquis (concerning safety and quality regulations, data security or intellectual property rights) but also a market of 483 million people. (c) A pool of already present suppliers, with 'fourteen of the world's top 20 Tier-1 suppliers already being in Hungary' (ITDH 2010). In addition, 'Hungary is the regional leader in the production of petrol engines' (ITDH 2010). (d) Highly skilled and cheap labour force together with academic and university infrastructure carrying out automotive-related R&D. (e) And finally a supportive government policy (ITDH 2010). Overall, ITDH also stresses the history of automotive inventors in Hungary. In addition, several clusters were established, i.e. the Pannon Automotive Cluster (PANAC), the North Hungarian Automotive Cluster (NOHAC), and the Hungarian Vehicle Development Cluster (MAJÁK).

During the last 20 years, foreign investors have faced different environments in Hungary leading to different behaviour. Inzelt (2000) distinguishes two periods for FDI in R&D: The first period, from late socialism in 1988 to 1996/1997, as a phase of 'acquaintance and adjustment' and a second period from 1996/1997 onwards as a phase of 'feeling at home'. The environment during the first period was characterised by opening up the economy, mass privatisation and building of a market economy. 'The acquisition of an R&D laboratory was usually an accident. The laboratory was part of the privatized company's package' (Inzelt 2000, p. 250). Foreign investors were reluctant to set up new laboratories and the 'role of host countries was technology adoption' (Inzelt 2000, p.248). At the beginning of the second period, the Hungarian government encouraged FDI in R&D by launching of direct measures including tax concessions, co-financing schemes for setting up competence centres, and university-industry cooperative research laboratories. Motivated by this incentive programme, in addition to cheap and skilled labour, Audi and Knorr-Bremse established R&D units in Hungary (OECD 2000). Hence, Inzelt (2000) sees a new trend in this second period with a new behaviour of investors and an increase in investment in R&D. Also Kubeczko et al. (2006) state that, 'some foreign investors have also realized the world-class knowledge of Hungarian scientists and engineers, and setting up either in-house R&D units or joint research groups with universities' (Kubeczko et al. 2006, p. 30). In addition to cost advantages, a new R&D scheme launched in 2006 encouraged R&D.

Knorr-Bremse: Knorr-Bremse already established contacts to Hungary in 1969 when it had a licence contract for brake systems for the Hungarian IKARUS bus producer. In 1989, it formed a joint venture called KB-SZIM but became the whole owner in 1993. In 1995, the R&D centre was established in Budapest for electronic development and a R&D group in Kecskemét. In 1999, a new R&D centre was built (Palkovics 2010). Knorr-Bremse had a good cooperation with Budapest Technical University from the beginning (Biegelbauer et al. 2001). The main motivations of Knorr-Bremse to found R&D in Hungary were (Palkovics 2010): a high level university system with world-wide accepted schools for vehicle system dynamics in Hungary; original ideas leading to innovate products; a proper attitude of engineers and high efficiency; lower development costs; long term scientific cooperation between Knorr-Bremse and research place in Hungary; availability of highly qualified personal (in contrary to Western Europe at that time); active personal contacts in the past; cultural issues not forming a barrier and government level support. R&D investment schemes approved by the government in 1997 also contributed to the new investment in 1999 (Business Eastern Europe August 24, 1998).

Romania

R&D in the Romanian automotive industry has particularly developed since 2005. Selected foreign companies have invested in Romania such as Continental, Siemens, Ina Schaeffer etc. The establishment of Renault Technology Romania significantly increased R&D expenditure in Romania (ACEA 2011). Factors speaking in favour for investing in the Romanian automotive industry in general include its strategic position with great development potential, engineering tradition, technical education and built domestic R&D network, presence of car manufacturers and suppliers, cheap and relatively high qualified labour force and a positive attitude of the government to foreign investments in the automotive industry (see Švač et al. 2010). There is one automotive-cluster in the country. Selected automotive R&D investments include:

- Renault Technology Romania (RTR): The engineering centre was set up in 2006 by Renault (France). Main fields of RTR's activity are designing and improving vehicles and adapting engines and powertrains. It is located at three sites: Bucharest (design offices), Piteşti (engineering services at body assembly and powertrain plants) and Titu, where a testing centre was opened in 2010. According to Renault, 'to be competitive, Renault needs to be close to local customers and to fast-changing consumer tastes on the new markets' (Renault 2011). In 2009, RTR employed about 2,200 people, with the announcement of an additional 800 to be added (Autoevolution 2011).
- Continental Automotive (Germany): Overall, Continental has three R&D centres in Romania (Timişoara, Sibiu and Iaşi). In 2000, Continental Automotive Timisoara (former Siemens VDO, acquired by the Continental corporation in 2007) started its activities in Timisoara with an R&D centre. The Continental Automotive Divisions added in 2006 an electronic unit plant in Timisoara and an R&D centre in Iaşi. The Automotive divisions in Sibiu inaugurated the same year a new R&D centre (Continental 2011).

- Ford: US car maker Ford planned to build a technical centre in Craiova, Romania, in November 2010, where it will develop new models. The company will invest several hundred million Euros into the facility, which will create a brand new concept and feature a technological and innovation centre. Ford hopes that its new facility will rival that of Renault Technologie Roumanie's centre located in Titu (*FDI Intelligence* from Financial Times Ltd, September 2011).

Slovak Republic

Today, main R&D centres in Slovakia are Johnson Controls Engineering Centre Trenčin, R&D LEONI Autokabel Slowakia Trenčin, Continental Automotive Systems R&D Centre Zvolen, ON Semiconductor Bratislava Development Centre, Technolgy Lab Siemens Žilina or ZKW Slovakia R&D centre Krušovice (SARIO 2011). The Slovak Investment and Trade Development Agency (SARIO 2011) presents the following key facts that speak in favour of Slovakia as a location for R&D: highly qualified human resources at affordable costs; presence of production plant operation in high-tech and medium high-tech industries; presence of foreign R&D centres and technology clusters; a broad domestic R&D and innovation network; established cooperation between industries and domestic universities and R&D incentives. There is one automotive cluster in Slovakia, the Automotive Cluster-West Slovakia. Selected automotive R&D investments include:

- Johnson Controls (United States) runs one of the biggest technology centres in Slovakia for design of automotive components, system and modules. It opened in 2004 and now employs 500 employees, in order to 'extend the engineering network to include the Eastern European growth markets and to respond to customers' growing presence there' (Johnson Controls 2011). Reasons for investing include: infrastructure and logistics, proximity to markets or customers, regulations or business climate, as well as skilled workforce availability (*FDI Intelligence* from Financial Times Ltd September 2011).
- Continental Automotive Systems R&D centre Slovakia (Germany): Gerhad Baucke, the plant manager, states the following reason to invest in Slovakia (SARIO 2011): 'The main reason why we decided to establish R&D in Slovakia is the fact that Slovakia is still considered to be a Best-Cost-Country; secondly the region of Banska Bystrica we chose offers well educated and qualified young engineers and furthermore our plant in Zvolen is in the closed proximity to the Technical University of Zvolen.'
- ZKW Slovakia, affiliate of the Austrian ZIZALA Lichtsysteme GmbH, planned to build a technology centre in 2010 for EUR 2.3 million, creating 32 new jobs (WKO 2010).

INTERNATIONALISATION OF R&D IN KNOWLEDGE-INTENSIVE BUSINESS SERVICES

Knowledge-intensive services and knowledge-intensive business services (KIBS) in particular came into focus of policy in recent years. One reason for this attention is the growth performance of these services. KIBS grow faster than most other sectors. According to data from EUKLEMS (Timmer et al. 2008), employment in KIBS (defined here as renting, computer services, R&D services and business activities, NACE 71-74) in the EU-25 increased from 14.4 Mio persons in 1995 to more than 24.6 Mio persons in 2007. In contrast, employment in manufacturing decreased from 36.8 Mio persons to 33.8 Mio persons in the same period.

Before we discuss the drivers of inward BERD in KIBS, it is important define KIBS exactly. KIBS can be divided into three sub-groups:

- The first sub-group are computer services (NACE 72), which include software development (NACE 72.2), as well as hardware-related consulting (NACE 72.1); data processing and database activities (NACE 72.3-72.4) such as the provision of internet-based services and also the maintenance and repair of office and computer machinery (NACE 72.5).
- A second sub-group is research and development (NACE 73). This includes organisations that provide R&D services to third parties on a commercial basis, such as contract research organisations, but also R&D units affiliated to a multinational company group which are organized as independent firms. Examples for this type of organisation are the Novartis Institutes for BioMedical Research, Shell Research Ltd, Procter & Gamble Technical Centers, or Microsoft Research Ltd. The activities of these corporate R&D centres are assigned to NACE 73, and not to the industry of the parent company group, even if the centre only performs R&D only for one single client, its company group. This makes it sometimes difficult to reveal the nature of activity on NACE 73.
- The third sub-group of KIBS, other business services (NACE 74.1-74.4), consists of two broad sub-categories. They include, on the one hand, legal and economic consulting activities (NACE 74.1) and advertising (NACE 74.4). Moreover, NACE 74.1 also includes the activities of holding companies, for example regional headquarters of multinational firms. On the other hand, the third sub-group includes technical consultancy such as architectural and engineering activities (NACE 74.2) and technical testing and analysis (NACE 74.3). Since it is often not possible to split up NACE 74, labour recruitment (NACE 74.5), security services (NACE 74.6) and industrial cleaning (NACE 74.7) are also included in KIBS.

The boundaries between the three sub-sectors are often fluid. Large IT consulting firms usually also provide computer services, and software firms increasingly provide also consultancy services in the implementation process of a new software. Boundaries between IT consultancy and management consultancy, and between advertising and 'new media' firms are blurred as well. Moreover, there are also close links between computer services and other KIS industries, such as finance, communication and the media industries.

The internationalisation of KIBS in general and the internationalisation of R&D in KIBS were driven by both general and country-specific factors in recent years.

A general driver of internationalisation in KIBS is the usage of information and communication technologies (ICT) in services provision. Services are often characterised by intensive relations between client and service provider, which often requires that both parties stay in the same place and have face-to-face conversation (Hauknes 1998). Hence, many KIBS have been traditionally geographically bound, and service provision over distance was only possible if client or service provider moves to the place of the other party.

ICT opened new ways of service provision over distance to many KIBS firms (Van Welsum and Reif 2006). As a consequence, the use of ICT has increased the tradability of services, in particular of services dealing with the exchange, storage, processing and retrieval of standardised, digitised and codified information (UNCTAD 2004, p. 148f). This has opened new ways for service providers to meet the growing demand for services due to offshoring and to serve clients outside their town or region. As a consequence, foreign direct investment and trade in knowledge-intensive services have flourished since the 1980s. ICT also opened new ways for decentralised R&D in KIBS firms. New technological opportunities have been met by growing demand. The growth of KIBS is largely fuelled by intermediate demand – the use of KIBS by other firms for the production of goods (Peneder et al. 2003; Savona and Lorentz 2006).

These two general drivers, however, do not explain the considerable differences in the share of KIBS firms on inward BERD between countries illustrated by the figure above. Hence, there must be other, country-specific drivers. One of these country specific drivers is industrial specialisation. We measure specialisation by the share of KIBS in total BERD (Figure 10.2). The figure suggests a positive relationship between the share of KIBS on total BERD and on inward BERD; foreign-owned KIBS firms invest in R&D predominantly in countries which also have a high share of their total BERD in KIBS. In Estonia and the United Kingdom, KIBS account for more than 40 percent of total BERD, while the share of KIBS on total BERD even exceeds 60 percent in Israel.

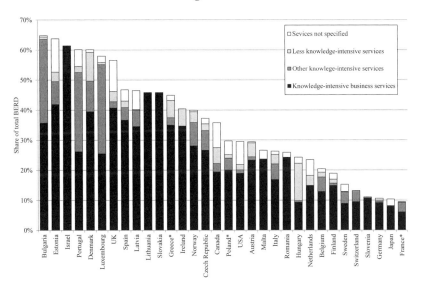

Note: KIBS includes NACE 70-74, other KIS 64.2 and 65-67, LKIS 50-52 and 55, other services the service sector (50-99) except KIBS, other KIS and LKIS. KIBS only includes 73 in Switzerland, 72, 73, 74.1 and 74.3 in the United States and 72 and 73 in Israel; * 2005 (Greece) and 2006 (Canada, France, Poland) instead of 2007.
Source: OECD, Eurostat, National statistical offices, own calculations.

Figure 10.2 Share of service industries on total BERD, 2007

KIBS have a pivotal role in the internationalisation of R&D. KIBS account for the bulk of inward BERD in the service sector. In some countries, inward BERD in KIBS is even higher than inward BERD in manufacturing (see Figure 10.3 below).

Two countries stand out in the internationalisation of R&D in KIBS. First, the United Kingdom (together with the US) attracts the largest amount of inward BERD in KIBS (see also chapter 6 of this book). In 2007, inward BERD in KIBS in the UK was 3.1 billion EUR. In contrast, Germany, the largest host country in terms of total inward BERD, only attracts 0.6 billion EUR of inward BERD in KIBS. Most of the inward BERD in the UK goes into NACE 73, research and development services (65 percent), with smaller shares in computer services (20 percent), and other business services (13 percent).

Second, Israel has the largest share of KIBS on inward BERD of all countries (Figure 10.3). KIBS account for more than 75 percent of total inward BERD in the country. In Israel, the share of computer services is about 40 percent. The remaining 60 percent are in research and development services (NACE 73).

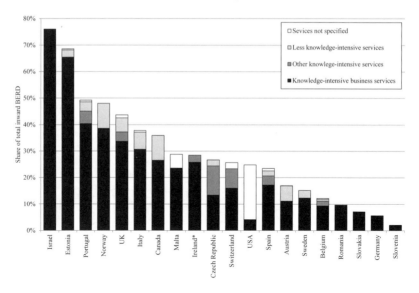

Note: KIBS includes NACE 1.1 sections 70-74; other KIS 64.2 and 65-67; LKIS 50-52 and 55; other services the service sector (50-99) except KIBS, other KIS and LKIS. Due to data constraints 65-67 is included in KIBS and not other KIS in Germany, Sweden and Canada. KIBS only includes 73 in Switzerland, 72, 73, 74.1 and 74.3 in the United States and 72 and 73 in Israel; * 2005 instead of 2007.
Source: OECD, Eurostat, National statistical offices, own calculations.

Figure 10.3 Share of various service industries on total inward BERD, 2007

In addition, Estonia is the third country to be included in this case study. Estonia has also a very high share (65 percent) of KIBS on inward BERD. In Estonia, inward BERD in KIBS is almost completely found in computer services (NACE 72). Moreover, it is the only EU-12 member state where inward BERD in services is higher than in manufacturing industries. This pattern of internationalisation is fundamentally different from that of the Czech Republic, Hungary or Slovakia.

Estonia

With a share of more than 40 percent of KIBS on total inward BERD, Estonia ranks among the countries where KIBS are of relative largest importance. However, it should be noted that this share of 40 percent corresponds to an absolute R&D expenditure of only 14.6 million EUR in 2007, which is small compared to the countries discussed before. Nevertheless, Estonia has the highest share of inward BERD in KIBS among all EU-12 countries, and only the Czech Republic receives more inward BERD in KIBS in absolute terms.

The high share of inward BERD in KIBS in software services in particular is even more remarkable if we look at the size of the ICT sector in Estonia.

Even if the whole ICT sector is considered, which includes also the manufacturing components, ICT only accounts for 3.8 percent of all Estonian companies and 4.1 percent of the employment. While the share of the sector on profits (6.4 percent) and value added (6.8 percent) is already significantly larger than the employment, the sector accounts for almost half (44.4 percent) of the total R&D expenditure in the country. Computer related and financial intermediation activities account for 49 percent of the private sector research personnel in Estonia in 2009. Software and computer services are the sector with by far the highest R&D intensity in the Estonian economy (Kalvet and Tiits 2009).

According to the WEF Global Competitiveness Report 2011 (WEF 2011), Estonia is the most competitive country out of the EU-12 countries and ranked as the 33rd best performer worldwide. Estonia performs particularly well regarding various indicators measuring the quality of higher education, the efficiency of labour markets, technological readiness and innovation, especially compared to other EU-12 countries. Estonia performs best of all EU-12 concerning the availability of latest technologies (rank 34 worldwide) and extent of firm level technology absorption (rank 36 worldwide). The quality of math and science education is considered to be the 20th best worldwide. Wage determination is the most flexible in the EU-27 and pay and productivity are closest related of all EU-27 countries. However, brain drain is considered to be an issue as Estonia is only ranked number 56th worldwide in the ability to retain and attract talented people (WEF 2011). The intensified utilisation of the widely available skills is therefore a focus of the Estonian Research and Development and Innovation strategy (Rannala and Männik 2010).

However, even more important than locational factors are in the case of Estonia the R&D strategies of one single company, Skype. Skype has been founded in Estonia, and the first version of the Skype software was developed in 2003 by three Estonian programmers. Skype was bought by eBay in 2005. After eBay's retreat in 2007 Microsoft bought Skype in 2011.

Today, Skype is by far the most important multinational software company active in Estonia, with the global development headquarter being located in the country. Almost 400 people work for Skype in Estonia, about half of Skype's total workforce (Kalvet and Tiits 2009).

Given that there were just 1,313 researchers (full-time equivalent) in the Estonian business sector in 2009 (OECD 2012), and foreign-owned firms account for a quarter of Estonia's total BERD, it is easy to recognise that Skype is responsible for the bulk of inward BERD in KIBS in Estonia.

The fDi Markets database lists for Estonia only five R&D investment projects in the software and IT services sector and none in business services. Three of these projects are by the UK online gaming software supplier Playtech, the world's largest publicity traded company active in this field (Kalvet and Tiits 2009). The other two projects are by US software producer Microsoft and Australian Seven Networks. Skype is not included in the fDi

Markets database. As a true global company, Skype is headquartered in Luxembourg, while the main sales office is located in the United Kingdom. The company develops the products in Estonia while the Irish affiliate of Skype is responsible for the copyright protection (Kalvet and Tiits 2009). This may explain which why Skype is not included in the database.

Israel

R&D in KIBS is in Israel of outstanding importance for the country's gross domestic R&D expenditure. KIBS account for about three quarters of inward BERD and about two thirds of total BERD in Israel. Besides this high importance of R&D in KIBS, Israel is also the country with the highest R&D intensity in the OECD (OECD 2011). According to the Global Competitiveness Report of the World Economic Forum (WEF 2011), the quality of Israel's research organisations is the highest worldwide, and a particular specialisation of these organisations is on ICT. Breznitz (2005) discusses reasons for the rise of the Israeli software and computer industry. He points out the industry's ability to focus on R&D intensive activities, and close ties to university and governmental research in the field.

In addition, Israel has one of the most developed entrepreneurial cultures in the world and produces more start-up companies per inhabitant than any other country in the world (Senor and Singer 2009). The availability of venture capital is the second best in the world, only outperformed by Quatar (WEF 2011).

These three factors account for the high attractiveness of Israel as a location of ICT-related R&D activities of multinational firms. The high levels of internationalisation of KIBS are driven by MNEs establishing subsidiaries and research laboratories in Israel by the acquisition of Israeli ICT firms.

US MNEs are of outstanding importance, as can be seen in the fDi Markets database. The database includes a total of 38 investment projects in Israel since 2003, most of them (36) in software and IT services. 28 projects have been established by US firms and another four by German firms. The estimated total volume of these projects is more than 600 million USD.

Within Israel, Tel Aviv is attracting one quarter of all projects. The vast majority of the projects can be classified as new projects (32). Only six are expansions of existing projects. This is an important difference to inward investments in other countries, for example Ireland, where most R&D-related investment projects are extensions of existing production activities.

While the single largest investor is Indian Tata Group (one project worth 62 million USD) and the third largest investor SAP from Germany (three projects with a total of 60 million USD) all other top 10 companies are US companies, including most major player in the software and IT industry with Google, IBM, Hewlett-Packard EMC Corporation, Microsoft, Juniper Networks each investing between 20 and 61 Mio USD on R&D projects in Israel since 2003.

United Kingdom

It has been argued in the literature that R&D activities of foreign-owned firms are attracted by agglomeration advantages, which may explain the uneven distribution of inward BERD across regions (Cantwell and Iammarino 2000; Teirlinck 2005; De Backer and Hatem 2010). These agglomeration advantages include, for example, the availability of a large pool of experts in ICT, the existence of universities specialised in ICT, which can provide skilled personnel and expertise in co-operations, or the existence of key users of KIBS and ICT such as financial services or corporate headquarters.

Agglomeration advantages play also a decisive role in attracting inward BERD in KIBS in the United Kingdom. The UK is a huge market for KIBS, and one of the world-wide centres of R&D in KIBS. As mentioned before, the UK is the most important location for R&D in KIBS in the EU-27, both in terms of inward investment but also in terms of total R&D expenditure in KIBS. This also includes R&D expenditure by formerly public R&D labs, which have been privatised. Worldwide, the UK is only second behind the by far larger United States. KIBS firms in the UK have spent about nine billion EUR on R&D in 2007, foreign-owned firms account for about one third or 3 bn EUR.

A considerable share of these activities is located in London. KIBS are attracted by urban regions in particular, since they rely on proximity to key clients (Wood 2002). The City of London is one of the largest agglomerations of financial services and KIBS in the world, and has a strong market position in the UK and world-wide (Wood and Wojcik 2010). This London KIBS and financial services cluster offers an extraordinary pool of skilled personnel, a large potential for the development of specialised services and a high number of potential clients among financial services as well as corporate headquarters.

In addition to market size and a critical mass of R&D in KIBS, the UK also offers a large pool of technological expertise and specialized scientific staff. Based on the results of the WEF Global Competitiveness Report (WEF 2011), the United Kingdom is ranked number seven worldwide in terms of the availability of latest technologies, ranked number three worldwide in the quality of scientific research institutions and on the second place in terms of university-industry collaboration in R&D. The United Kingdom is also able to attract talented people as the best performing EU-27 country in this respect and worldwide only outperformed by Switzerland, Singapore and the United States (WEF 2011).

A second driver that helps to understand the high share of KIBS in inward BERD in the UK is the role of the country as the preferred location for the European headquarters for non-European firms. The UK has the advantage of English being the dominant international language of business, and English law being the most used contract law in international business (Wood and

Wojcik 2010). The country can also build on its special relationship with the United States and its close historical relationships with many countries in Asia, Africa and the Middle East.

Regional headquarters of non-European multinational firms in the UK may also induce the location of headquarter functions, such as marketing, product development and R&D in the UK. This can explain the high share of inward BERD in NACE 73, research and development services, which also includes corporate R&D centres if they are organised as independent legal entities.

The fDi Markets database allows a closer look at inward investment in the UK. It includes a total of 120 R&D investment projects in the UK with a total volume of almost two bn USD since 2003. Only eight are in business services. The vast majority (112) is in software and IT services. Unfortunately the largest sub segment of KIBS in the UK, R&D services, is not included in the database. However, although only roughly on third of the KIBS sector is included, the overall picture is still similar to the results based on inward BERD data. US companies are of outstanding importance accounting for 69 out of the 120 projects. Other important countries are on the one hand other large EU countries including Germany (10 projects) and France (8 projects) but also India (8) Japan (6) and Canada (4). In particular the engagement of Indian companies in KIBS R&D projects in the UK is interesting. Close historical and cultural ties and the above-mentioned function of the UK as a gateway to the European market may be main reasons.

Surprisingly, the single most important UK metropolitan area for the projects included in the fDi Markets database is Belfast with 38 projects by 25 different companies. In contrast, only 10 companies performed 11 R&D projects in London. However, this might be caused by the fact the mostly R&D in software and IT services are included in the sample and also that only investment flows since 2003 are covered and not investment stocks.

FINAL REMARKS

This chapter investigated the drivers of R&D internationalisation for automotive and knowledge-intensive business services. Both sectors have been important performers of R&D as well as majors recipients of inward FDI in recent years. The analysis confirms some of the drivers identified in the econometric analysis of Chapter 9, and adds some new drivers which point to heterogeneous, highly sector- and firm specific character of R&D internationalisation.

In both industries, historical specialisation trajectories turn out to be essential in explaining recent internationalisation patterns. The Czech Republic was specialised in automotive industry already in the pre-transformation area, and could preserve its specialisation advantages – such as a skilled workforce in this sector – over time. Low labour costs as well as government incentives helped to keep the industry alive in the 1990s. A shift of strategies of foreign investors towards more technology-creating activities took place at the end of the 2000s. Historical specialisation patterns play also an important role in the evolution of inward BERD in KIBS in the UK.

Moreover, in all cases there are agglomeration effects at the industry level in place which further increase specialisation and raise attractiveness for foreign multinational firms. Examples are the large number of small, specialised R&D performers in the automotive industry of the Czech Republic, or the highly diversified KIBS industry in the City of London, which benefits from a large number of potential clients and the demand for highly specialised services. These agglomeration effects point also to the fact that inward BERD is usually highly concentrated in a few areas of a country.

In addition, the analysis also found some peculiar advantages which explain above-average attractiveness of single countries for inward BERD. The strong presence of foreign MNE in Israel, for example, can be explained by a series of takeovers of domestic start-ups by MNEs. The United Kingdom acts as a gateway to the European Single Market for non-European companies, which also implies that corporate R&D centres for the European market are located in the UK.

Finally, the case studies also highlight the importance of single firms for the understanding of overall R&D internationalisation patterns. The Czech Republic has positioned itself as the hub for automotive R&D in the region thanks to one single foreign-owned firm, Škoda Auto. In retrospect, the survival of Škoda was pivotal for the further development of inward BERD in the Czech automotive industry after the 1990s. Similarly, Estonia's high share of inward BERD in KIBS is mainly due to Microsoft's take-over of Skype. Similar examples that highlight how decisions of single firms determine overall internationalisation patterns can also found in other small countries.

REFERENCES

ACEA (2011), *Country Profile Romania*, European Automobile Manufacturers' Association, download November 21, 2011, http://www.acea.be/index.php/country_profiles/detail/romania

Autoevolution (2011), *Renault to launch 200 new Logan trim versions*, download November 21, 2011, http://www.autoevolution.com/news/renault-to-launch-200-new-logan-trim-versions-4258.html

Biegelbauer, P., E. Grießler and M. Leuthold (2001), *The Impact of Foreign Direct Investment on the knowledge base of Central and Eastern European Countries*, Vienna: Institute for Higher Studies, Reihe Politikwissenschaft.

Breznitz, D. (2005), 'The Israeli software industry', in A. Arora and A. Gambardella (eds), *From underdogs to tigers. The rise and growth of the software industry in Brazil, China, India, Ireland, and Israel*, Oxford: Oxford University Press, pp. 72-98.

Business Eastern Europe, various issues.

Čadil, V., Z. Kučera and M. Pazour (2007), *Localisation motives for research and development investment of multinational enterprises*, Prague: Technology Centre AS CR.

Cantwell, J. and S. Iammarino (2000), 'Multinational corporations and the location of technological innovation in the UK regions', *Regional Studies* **34**(4), 317-32.

Continental (2011), *Ten Years Continental Automotive business in Romania*, download November 21, 2011. http://www.conti-online.com/generator/www/com/en/continental/pressportal/themes/press_releases/2_corporation/locations/pr_2010_06_11_10years_automotive_romania_en.html

Czech Invest (2011), *Automotive industry*, Prague: Czech Invest.

De Backer, K., and F. Hatem (2010), *Attractiveness for innovation. Location factors for international investment*, Paris: OECD.

Financial Times (2011), *FDI Intelligence*, http://www.fdimarkets.com (accessed November 11, 2011).

Hanzl, D. (1999), *Development and prospects of the transport equipment sector in Central and Eastern European countries*, Vienna: wiiw Industry Studies 1999/4.

Hauknes, J. (1998), Services in innovation – innovation in services. Oslo: STEP.

Hedge, D. and D. Hicks (2008). 'The maturation of global corporate R&D: Evidence from the activity of U.S. foreign subsidiaries', *Research Policy* **37**(3), 390-406.

Inzelt, A. (2000), 'Foreign direct investment in R&D: skin-deep and soul-deep cooperation', *Science and Public Policy* **27**(4), 245-51.

ITDH (2010), *The automotive industry in Hungary: Engine of growth*, Budapest: Hungarian Investment and Trade Development Agency.

Janosec, J. (2010), 'Automotive sector in the Czech Republic', paper presented at the 2010 UNIDO Technology Foresight Training Programme, Gebze, Turkey.

Johnson Controls (2011), *Company information*, http://www. jci.com.

Kalvet, T. and M. Tiits (2009), *ICT Sector in Estonia. WP 9 Country Sector Report*, INGINEUS Impact of Networks, Globalisation and their Interaction with EU Strategies, Tallin.

Kubeczko, K., V. Baláz, T. Baczko, T. Damvakeraki, A. Havas, K.-H. Leitner, S. Leitner, T. Kalvet, M. Kriaucioniene, Z. Kuzera, J. Kucinski, J. P. Sammut, A. Vanags and M. Weber (2006), *Private sector R&D in the New Member States*. Vienna: ETEPS Research Report.

OECD (2000), *Regulatory reforms in Hungary*, Paris: OECD.

OECD (2011), *OECD Science, Technology and Industry Scoreboard 2011. Innovation and Growth in Knowledge Economies*, Paris: OECD.

OECD (2012), *Main Science and Technology Indicators Volume 2012/1*, Paris: OECD.

Palkovics, L. (2010), 'How companies and university can work together in order to prepare better engineers for industry', paper presented at the second Educators Seminar in Budapest organised by FISITA, Budapest.

Pavlínek, P., J. Ženka and P. Žižalová (2010), 'Functional upgrading thorough research and development in the Czech automotive industry', http://konference.osu.cz/cgsostrava2010/dok/Sbornik_CGS/Socioekonomicka_geog rafie/Functional_upgrading_through_research.pdf

Peneder, M., S. Kaniovski and B. Dachs (2003), 'What follows tertiarisation? structural change and the role of knowledge-based services', *The Service Industries Journal*, **23**(2), 47-67.

Rannala, R. and K. Männik (2010), *ERAWATCH Country Report 2010: Estonia*, Tallin: Erawatch Network.

Renault (2011), *Renault in Romania*, http://www.renault.com/en/groupe/renault-dans-le-monde/pages/renault-en-roumanie.aspx

SARIO (2011), *The automotive industry in Slovakia*, Bratislava: Slovak Investment and Trade Development Agency.
http://www.sario.sk/userfiles/file/podujatia/SARIO_Frankfurt_IAA.pdf

Savona, M. and A. Lorentz (2006), 'Demand and technology determinants of structural change and tertiarisation: An Input-Output structural decomposition analysis for four OECD Countries', Strasbourg: BETA Working Paper 2006–01.

Senor, D. and S. Singer (2009), *Start-up Nation: The Story of Israel's Economic Miracle*, New York, Boston: Twelve.

Švač, V., Chudoba, Š. et al. (2010), *Innovation trends and challenges and cooperation possibilities with R&D in automotive industry*, Trnava: Automotive Cluster West Slovakia.

Teirlinck, P. (2005), 'Location and agglomeration of foreign R&D activities in a small open economy', in A. Spithoven and P. Teirlinck (eds), *Beyond borders. internationalisation of R&D and policy implications for small open economies*, Amsterdam: Elsevier: pp. 207-234.

Timmer, M. P., M. O'Mahony and B. Van Ark (2008), *EU KLEMS Database, Edition March 2008*, http://www.euklems.net/.

UNCTAD (2004), *World investment report 2004: The shift towards services*. New York and Geneva: United Nations.

Van Welsum, D. and X. Reif (2006), *Potential Impact of International Sourcing on Different Occupations*, Paris: OECD.

WEF (2011), *The Global Competitiveness Report 2011-2012*, Geneva: World Economic Forum.

WKO (2010), *ZKW Slovakia will Technolgiezentrum um 2,3 Mio. Euro bauen*.
http://portal.wko.at/wk/format_detail.wk?AngID=1&StID=554266&DstID=0&titel =Slowakei:,ZKW,Slovakia,will,Technologiezentrum,um,2,3,Mio.,Euro bauen

Wood, P. (2002), 'Knowledge-intensive services and urban innovativeness', *Urban Studies*, **39**(5-6), 993-1002.

Wood, P. and D. Wojcik (2010), 'A dominant node of service innovation: London's financial, professional and consultancy services', in F. Gallouj and F. Djellal (eds.), *The handbook of innovation and services: a multi-disciplinary perspective* , Cheltenham: Edward Elgar, pp. 589-618.

11. Impacts of R&D Internationalisation on domestic R&D Activities

Sandra Leitner and Robert Stehrer

Host countries can benefit considerably from R&D activities of foreign-owned firms. The literature reviewed in Chapter 2 lists different types of benefits: first, R&D expenditure of foreign-owned firms may increase aggregate R&D and innovation expenditure of the country; second, inward R&D expenditure may give rise to substantial information and knowledge spillovers; third, foreign-owned firms may boost the demand for skilled personnel including R&D staff; finally, inward R&D and the presence of foreign-owned firms may lead to structural change and agglomeration effects. On the contrary, inward R&D may also entail negative effects for the host country. First, host countries may lose the control over their indigenous innovation capacity; second, if foreign-owned affiliates predominantly pursue adaptive innovation, this may lead to fewer radical innovations; third, multinational firms may separate research and production and their R&D may yield fewer jobs in the host country than in the case of a domestic firm; finally, the increased presence of foreign-owned firms may increase competition with domestic firms for skilled personnel, which may lead to a crowding-out of R&D activities of domestically owned firms.

Against that backdrop, the ensuing analysis attempts to identify impacts and consequences of the internationalisation of R&D and the presence of foreign-owned firms on the host country. First, the effects on the level of domestic R&D expenditure and domestic R&D intensities (defined as the share of R&D expenditure of domestically owned firms in their value added) are investigated. In a second step the analysis throws light on the effects on domestic patenting activities.

THE IMPACT OF INWARD BERD ON DOMESTIC R&D EXPENDITURE

As a first step, the analysis throws light on whether R&D activities of foreign affiliates crowd-in (complement) or crowd-out (substitute) domestic R&D spending. Particularly, the analysis examines if foreign and domestic R&D

expenditure is positively or negatively associated, without shedding light on the underlying causality. For that purpose, the following specification is analysed:

$$\ln DOMRD_{ikt} = \alpha + \beta \ln FORRD_{ikt} + \delta_{zikt} + \varepsilon_{ikt} \qquad (11.1)$$

where $\ln DOMRD_{ikt}$ is the log of domestic R&D expenditure in sector k of country i in time t, while $\ln FORRD_{ikt}$ is the corresponding log of R&D expenditure of foreign affiliates in sector k of country i in time t. Moreover X_{zikt} is a matrix of Z additional variables that capture both sector and country level characteristics of host countries. At the sectoral level, the size of a host country's sector as the share of a sector's employment in total labour force is included to account for potential size effects. In particular, large sectors not only act as major employers but may also be very dynamic and innovative sectors characterised by non-negligible R&D efforts and sizeable R&D expenditure.

Related to that, sectors which host successful and thriving firms also grow rapidly and expand employment very quickly. And in order to stay competitive and profitable, firms in rapidly expanding sectors may have to increase their R&D efforts and R&D expenditure. Hence, sectoral growth, captured by the annual sectoral employment growth rate, is included to capture whether R&D expenditure are higher in fast growing sectors.

Moreover, a sector's openness to international trade may affect the scale of domestic R&D expenditure. Basically, innovative activities are inherently risky, uncertain and resource-intensive but if successful, give rise to temporary monopoly positions characterised by above-normal rents which help guarantee firm survival and growth. However, faced with intense competition, firms may have to intensify their R&D efforts to keep pace with competition and their competitors' efforts. Hence, sectors that are more open and exposed to international trade, both in terms of imports and exports, tend to face fiercer competition and, as a consequence, also tend to be characterised by stronger R&D efforts and higher R&D expenditure. Openness is included as the share of the sum of a sector's exports and imports in total sectoral output.

Additionally, the analysis also accounts for characteristics of host countries at the country level. Specifically, the annual growth rate of a host country's real GDP per capita is included to account for improvements in host countries' standard of living. In particular, extensive R&D efforts in the past may have improved a country's standard of living, a trend that is however sustainable only if additional resources are allotted to R&D activities and the development of new product and/or process technologies. Moreover, the scale of domestic R&D activities may also crucially depend on the host country's specialisation in high-intensive technology products and exports, captured in terms of the contribution of medium-high-technology industries to the manufacturing trade balance (see OECD 2005). Generally, since medium-high-technology products are technically more sophisticated, they also tend to be more R&D intensive in their development. Hence, countries which specialise in the production and export of medium-high-technology products are also characterised by, on average, higher R&D efforts and R&D expenditure. Finally, public STI policies may be pivotal to the level of R&D expenditure of domestic firms – potentially facilitating access to funding or fostering R&D cooperation – encouraging resource-intensive and risky innovative activities of firms. Hence, the share of government budgetary appropriations or outlays for R&D (GBAORD) in real GDP is included to capture the role STI policies play for R&D expenditure of domestic firms.

The data for the analysis is drawn from various different sources. The dependent variable is calculated as the difference between total R&D expenditure of a country i in sector k and inward R&D expenditure in country i and sector k using the data as described in Chapter 3. Furthermore, all sector level control variables (size, growth rate of size and openness) originate from the *OECD Structural Analysis Database* (OECD STAN). The growth rate of real GDP per capita is calculated from official OECD data on real GDP per capita. The contribution of medium-high-technology industries (to the manufacturing trade balance) is calculated from data stemming from the *OECD STAN Bilateral Trade Database* while information on government budgetary appropriations or outlays for R&D stem from the *OECD Main Science and Technology Indicators*.

Generally, given data quality and availability, the ensuing econometric analysis focuses on the short unbalanced panel from 2004 to 2007. Moreover, due to scarce or altogether lacking data for the service sector, the analysis focuses on the manufacturing sector only. Additionally, given the panel nature of the data, both random and fixed effects models were estimated to account for unobserved country-sector heterogeneity. However, since the Hausman test rejected the null hypothesis that the difference in coefficients is not systematic, a fixed effects approach was taken with time fixed effects to account for common time effects. Finally, analyses are conducted for four different samples, the overall sample comprising a set of OECD and non-OECD countries on the one hand[1] as well as three sub-samples on the other. The three sub-samples consist of 21 EU member countries, 12 EU-15 member countries (Austria (AUT), Belgium (BEL), Denmark (DNK), Finland (FIN), France (FRA), Germany (GER), Ireland (IRL), Italy (ITA), the Netherlands (NLD), Spain (ESP), Sweden (SWE) and the UK (GBR)) and 9 EU-12 member countries (Bulgaria (BUL), the Czech Republic (CZE), Estonia (EST), Hungary (HUN), Latvia (LVA), Poland (POL), Romania (ROM), Slovakia (SVK) and Slovenia (SVN)).

Regression results presented in Table 11.1 demonstrate that except for the overall sample considered (column (1)), the level of foreign R&D expenditure is not significantly associated with the level of R&D expenditure of domestic firms. Hence, there is hardly evidence that R&D expenditure of foreign affiliates complement or substitute (crowd-in or crowd-out, respectively) domestic R&D expenditure.

Table 11.1 Impact of R&D internationalisation on the scale of domestic R&D expenditures in the host country (2004-2007)

Dep.Var.: log domestic R&D expenditure	OVERALL	EU	EU-15	EU-12
Variables	(1)	(2)	(3)	(4)
Constant	3.197***	2.747***	3.794***	-0.937
	(8.01)	(6.19)	(5.58)	(0.75)
Sector level				
Log R&D expenditure of foreign affiliates	-0.067*	-0.073	-0.072	-0.044
	(1.74)	(1.58)	(1.42)	(0.41)
Size	0.548**	0.566**	0.438	0.583
	(2.08)	(1.97)	(0.77)	(1.47)
Size growth rate	-0.004	-0.004	-0.002	-0.005
	(0.79)	(0.74)	(0.37)	(0.56)
Openness	0.000	0.000	0.000	0.004**
	(0.62)	(0.58)	(0.01)	(2.59)
Country level				
Real GDP per capita growth rate	0.010	0.008	0.111***	-0.008
	(1.53)	(0.96)	(3.20)	(-0.63)
Contribution of MHT sectors to manufacturing trade balance	0.159***	0.162***	0.115**	0.207**
	(4.05)	(3.78)	(2.22)	(2.14)
Share of GBAORD in real GDP	0.020	0.028	0.063	0.631
	(0.07)	(0.09)	(0.21)	(0.48)
No of observations	614	523	368	155
R^2	0.0318	0.0087	0.0352	0.0900
Number of i	274	231	170	61

Note: t-statistics in parentheses, *** $p<0.01$, ** $p<0.05$, * $p<0.1$
All regressions are based on FE estimation procedures and include time fixed effects. Column
(1) uses the overall sample, column (2) is based on the overall EU sample; column (3) uses the EU-15 sub-sample only, while column (4) uses the EU-12 sub-sample only.

Generally, significant positive effects are found for four variables only, for different sub-samples though. The level of domestic R&D expenditure tends to be higher in larger sectors in the overall sample and the EU sample only. For the group of EU-12 countries only, a sector's openness to international trade is associated with higher domestic R&D expenditure which indicates that probably due to keep pace with intense international competition, domestic firms in very open and internationally closely interweaved sectors tend to spend significantly higher resources on research. For the group of EU-15 countries only, R&D expenditure of domestically owned firms is also found to be significantly higher in countries whose standard of living has been improving. Finally, as expected, the contribution of medium-high-technology sectors to the manufacturing trade balance is positively associated with the level of domestic R&D expenditure. Hence, irrespective of sample considered, domestic R&D expenditure is significantly higher in countries which specialise in the production and export of medium-high-technology products. In contrast, no effects emerge for sector size growth or the share of government budgetary appropriations or outlays for R&D (GBAORD).

THE IMPACT OF INWARD BERD ON DOMESTIC R&D INTENSITY

Alternatively, the analysis looks at R&D intensities instead of absolute R&D expenditure, and identifies whether sectoral domestic and foreign R&D intensities represent complements or substitutes. It analyses the following specification:

$$\text{DOMRDint}_{ikt} = \alpha + \beta \, \text{FORRDint}_{ikt} + \delta_z X_{zikt} + \varepsilon_{ikt} \qquad (11.2)$$

where DOMRDint$_{ikt}$ is the share of domestic R&D expenditure in value added in sector k of country i in time t, while FORRDint$_{ikt}$ is the corresponding share of R&D expenditure in value added of foreign affiliates in sector k of country i in time t. Again, X$_{zikt}$ is a matrix of Z additional variables that capture both sector and country level characteristics of host countries only. Like before, the size of a host country's sector, the growth rate of the sector and the sector's openness are included at the sectoral level. In contrast to above, the log of real GDP as a proxy for the size of the economy or market and the contribution of medium-high-technology sectors (to the manufacturing trade balance (see OECD 2005)) are included at the country level.

Again, both random and fixed effects models were estimated to account for unobserved country-sector heterogeneity. However, the Hausman test did not reject the null hypothesis that the difference in coefficients is not systematic while the Breusch-Pagan Lagrange multiplier test rejected the presence of any random effects so that a pooled OLS approach was chosen with both time and country fixed effects to account for both common time effects and unobservable time-invariant country characteristics. Analyses are again conducted for various samples.

Results are presented in Table 11.2 below which highlights that – with the exception of the overall OECD sample (column (1)) – significant complementarities prevail between R&D intensities of foreign-owned and domestically-owned firms. Specifically, for the EU as a whole as well as for the group of EU-15 and of EU-12 countries, R&D intensities of domestic firms are high if R&D intensities of foreign affiliates are high too.

Table 11.2 Impact of R&D internationalisation on the domestic R&D intensity (2004-2007)

Dep.Var.: domestic R&D intensity	OVERALL	EU	EU-15	EU-12
Variables	(1)	(2)	(3)	(4)
Constant	30.538 (0.29)	10.270 (1.13)	33.984 (1.42)	9.406** (2.12)
Sector level				
R&D intensity of foreign affiliates	0.010 (0.04)	0.726*** (9.56)	0.765*** (8.07)	0.267** (1.99)
Size	-5.770** (2.45)	-1.593*** (3.12)	-2.113** (2.55)	-1.409*** (3.14)
Size growth rate	-0.117 (0.33)	0.097 (1.24)	0.178 (0.96)	0.073 (1.38)
Openness	0.019 (1.00)	0.007 (1.56)	0.007 (1.30)	0.003 (0.46)
Country level				
Log real GDP	-1.444 (0.52)	-0.047 (0.08)	-0.210 (0.08)	-0.294 (0.68)
Contribution of MHT sectors to manufacturing trade balance	1.227 (0.17)	0.767 (0.51)	4.925 (1.37)	-0.753 (0.68)
No of observations	429	346	221	125
Adj. R^2	0.0708	0.482	0.486	0.168

Note: t-statistics in parentheses, *** $p<0.01$, ** $p<0.05$, * $p<0.1$
All regressions are based on pooled OLS estimation procedures and include time fixed effects and country fixed effects. Column (1) uses the overall sample, column (2) is based on the overall EU sample; column (3) uses the EU-15 sub-sample only, while column (4) uses the EU-12 sub-sample only.

Moreover, Table 11.2 also highlights that complementarities between domestic and foreign R&D intensities are stronger in the EU-15 sample (column (3)). However, the underlying causality is still an open issue: did domestic firms increase their R&D intensities to match higher R&D intensities of foreign firms (as a measure to keep pace with foreign affiliates' R&D efforts) or did foreign affiliates increase their R&D intensities to match inherently higher R&D intensities of domestically owned firms in a sector (as a measure to keep pace with R&D efforts of domestic firms)? A test of the direction of this causality would require a longer time series on both inward and domestic R&D expenditure. Furthermore, the analysis shows that larger sectors tend to be characterised by significantly lower R&D intensities of domestic firms. This effect is stronger in the sample of EU-15 countries (column (3)) (compared to the group of EU-12 countries (column (4)).

In contrast, no effect is found for either sectoral growth or openness to international trade and competition. Finally, none of the country level control variables exhibits any significant effect on sectoral R&D intensities of domestic firms. These effects are entirely absorbed by the country fixed effects.

To sum up, the analysis of absolute R&D expenditure of foreign and domestic firms reveals (almost) no significant relationship between inward and domestic R&D expenditure. In contrast, however, a significant positive relationship emerges between R&D intensities of domestic and foreign firms which highlights that foreign firms do not crowd out domestic R&D activities. Rather, it supports the hypothesis that both, R&D expenditure of domestic and foreign firms complement each other. Both, foreign and domestic firms may react to the same incentives in their planning of R&D and may benefit from the same framework conditions. There may be cross-fertilisation by transfers of knowledge between the two groups. In addition, there may also be competitive pressures from one group that forces the other group to modify R&D efforts in order to remain competitive. In this respect, foreign R&D activities in a country contribute to the competitiveness of domestic firms and of the host country.

THE IMPACT OF INWARD BERD ON DOMESTIC PATENTING ACTIVITIES

Finally, the analysis also sheds light on the effects R&D activities of foreign affiliates have on host country patenting activities. In particular, it analyses whether higher R&D efforts of foreign affiliates spur domestic patent activities by increasing domestic firms' inventiveness and innovativeness: either through knowledge spillovers which help domestic firms to develop technological capabilities essential for any successful R&D activities, or through intensified R&D efforts of domestically owned firms so as to keep pace with and defy strong competition from foreign affiliates. For that purpose, the following specification is analysed:

$$\ln \text{DOMPAT}_{ikt} = \alpha + \beta_1 \text{FORRDint}_{ikt} + \beta_2 \text{DOMRDint}_{ikt} + \delta_z X_{zikt} + \varepsilon_{ikt} \quad (11.3)$$

where $\ln \text{DOMPAT}_{ikt}$ is the log of patent applications to the European Patent Office (EPO) of domestic firms in sector k of country i in time t while FORRDint_{ikt} and DOMRDint_{ikt} are the R&D intensities of foreign affiliates and domestic firms, respectively (as the share of R&D expenditure in value added) in sector k of country i in time t. Moreover, X_{zikt} is a matrix of Z additional variables that captures both sector and country level characteristics of host countries only. At the sectoral level, a sector's size (as the share of a sector's employment in total labour force), its growth rate as well as its degree of openness to international trade are included as potential determinants of domestic firms' patenting activities. In particular, larger sectors may also be very dynamic and innovative, hosting numerous firms that allot sizeable R&D expenditure to the development of new products or processes, which, for protective purposes, may be registered at the patent office. Furthermore, R&D efforts (and success) may be higher in quickly expanding sectors, resulting in higher patent applications.

A sector's openness to international trade as the share of the sum of exports and imports in total gross output is included to capture that faced with tougher international competition, firms may see the need to intensify their own R&D efforts in order to keep up with competition, to survive and thrive. As a consequence, new innovations may materialise which, for protective purposes, may be registered.

Furthermore, some host country characteristics are included. In particular, a host country's real GDP per capita growth rate is included to capture the role a growing standard of living plays for sector level domestic patenting activities. As such, innovative and patenting activities may be higher in economies characterised by swiftly improving standards of living, as consumers' 'love of variety' induces firms to continuously invest in R&D activities so as to develop new products and/or processes that match consumers' tastes and preferences and help firms expand profits and defend or expand market shares.

Account is also taken of the share of government R&D expenditure (for R&D activities conducted in the tertiary education sector) in total GDP as a proxy for public science, technology and innovation policies. In particular, countries with governments that are committed to funding tertiary sector research activities may also be more innovative, as crucial resources are provided for the highly resource-intensive but risky innovative activities, rendering successful innovations potentially more likely.

Finally, account is also taken of the contribution of medium-high-technology industries to the manufacturing trade balance (see OECD 2005) since a country's industry specialisation towards medium-high-technology products and medium-high-technology exports may be pivotal to the quality and effectiveness of domestic technological capabilities. Specifically, firms located in countries which strongly specialise in medium-high-technology products may possess superior technological capabilities to continuously develop technological novelties which, for protective reasons, may be patented.

The analysis uses different data sources. The dependent variable stems from the *OECD Patent Database*, R&D expenditure of foreign affiliates have been collected for the analysis of this book, while R&D expenditure of domestic firms is calculated as the difference between total R&D expenditure (see Chapter 3) and R&D expenditure of foreign affiliates. Furthermore, information on value added of foreign affiliates is taken from the *OECD Activities of Foreign Affiliates statistic* (OECD AFA) while information on value added of domestic firms is calculated as the difference between total sectoral value added (as included in the *OECD Structural Analysis Database* (OECD STAN) and value added of foreign affiliates. Additionally, data on sector size, growth and openness are calculated from data included in the *OECD Structural Analysis Database* (OECD STAN). Finally, the real GDP per capita growth rate and the contribution of medium-high-technology industries to the manufacturing trade balance are calculated from data taken from the *OECD STAN Bilateral Trade Database*.

Methodologically, both random and fixed effects models were estimated to account for the presence of unobserved country-sector heterogeneity. However, the Hausman test rejected the null hypothesis that the difference in coefficients is not systematic. Hence, a fixed-effects approach was chosen without time fixed effects. In line with above analyses, results are presented and discussed for various samples: the overall sample comprising a set of OECD countries, an overall sample of EU countries and two EU sub-samples comprising EU-15 and EU-12 countries, respectively.

Results are presented in Table 11.3 which stresses that host country patenting activities appear unrelated to both foreign affiliates' as well as domestic firms' R&D intensities. Hence, there is lacking evidence of either any knowledge spillover effect (that might spur domestic firms' inventiveness or innovativeness) or of any competition-driven effect (that induces domestic firms to intensify their R&D efforts and innovativeness to defy competition from abroad). Likewise, empirical evidence also stresses that host country patenting activities are unrelated to domestic firms' R&D intensities. The only exception is the group of EU-15 countries for which a positive and significant relationship emerges: hence, only for the group of EU-15 countries are higher R&D intensities of domestic firms associated with higher EPO patent applications. Generally, however, the absence of a significant relationship between (foreign and domestic) R&D intensities (as inputs in the highly resource intensive and uncertain innovative process) and host country patenting activities (capturing the output-side of an innovative process) is not much of a surprise. For one, patents represent imperfect proxies for the output of research activities: First, not all innovations are patented. Specifically, firms may consider the financial and/or administrative burden associated with any application procedure as too high or innovators may opt for other forms to maintain their competitive edge, like the exploitation of any first-mover advantage. And second, patents do not capture innovations of imitators. Hence, official patent statistics strongly underestimate a country's true innovativeness. Moreover, innovative processes are highly complex, resource intensive and highly uncertain, characterised by a continuous trial-and-error process without any guarantee that all research efforts will eventually materialise in marketable product or process innovations. Hence, higher R&D expenditure is no guarantee for any innovative success. Finally, there is a tendency that complex relationships vanish or become obstructed once higher levels of aggregation are analysed.

Table 11.3 Impact of R&D internationalisation on the domestic patenting activity in the host country (2004-2007)

	OVERALL	EU	EU-15	EU-12
Variables	(1)	(2)	(3)	(4)
Constant	2.361***	1.794***	4.910***	-0.760
	(7.58)	(5.08)	(27.86)	(1.20)
Sector level				
R&D intensity of foreign affiliates	0.005	0.006	0.003	0.009
	(0.76)	(0.83)	(1.09)	(0.60)
R&D intensity of domestic firms	-0.001	-0.001	0.003**	-0.003
	(0.23)	(0.19)	(2.20)	(0.38)
Size	1.298***	1.325***	0.199	1.649***
	(5.76)	(5.41)	(1.47)	(4.19)
Size growth	0.003	0.003	0.003	0.002
	(0.98)	(0.95)	(1.04)	(0.53)
Inward FDI intensity	0.003	0.003	-0.001	0.004
	(1.07)	(0.99)	(0.41)	(0.67)
Openness	0.000	0.000	0.000	0.000
	(0.01)	(0.04)	(0.95)	(0.11)
Country level				
Real GDP per capita growth	-0.002	-0.005	-0.008	-0.006
	(0.49)	(0.77)	(1.08)	(0.63)
Contribution of MHT sectors to manufacturing trade balance	0.030	0.027	0.054**	0.004
	(0.88)	(0.73)	(2.44)	(0.07)
No of observations	251	208	116	92
R^2	0.0395	0.0274	0.0409	0.00654
Number of i	107	84	54	30

Note: t-statistics in parentheses, *** $p<0.01$, ** $p<0.05$, * $p<0.1$
All regressions are based on fixed effects estimation procedures. Column (1) uses the overall sample, column (2) is based on the overall EU sample; column (3) uses the EU-15 sub-sample only, while column (4) uses the EU-12 sub-sample only.

As for the remaining sector level control variables, only the size of the sector appears to matter. In particular, empirical findings suggest that for all but the group of EU-12 countries, patenting activities are significantly higher in larger sectors.

Furthermore, no evidence is found that patenting activities are significantly higher in economies characterised by improving standards of living.

Finally, findings suggest that for the group of EU-15 countries only, a strong specialisation towards the production (and export) of medium-high-technology products is conducive to host country patenting activities.

THE IMPACT OF OUTWARD BERD ON DOMESTIC R&D ACTIVITIES

A main concern brought forward by critics of globalisation is that R&D activities of domestically owned firms abroad may substitute domestic R&D activities. Internationalisation of R&D may lead to a 'hollowing-out' of national R&D capacities and, as a consequence, to a continuous loss of domestic capabilities to develop and implement new technologies. Empirical evidence that could either confirm or reject this claim, however, is scarce (exceptions are Castellani and Pieri 2011 or D'Agostino et al. 2013). A case study on R&D activities of German firms in India in Chapter 12 of this book suggests that R&D activities in India complement similar activities in Germany. Data limitations are probably the main reason for this lack of empirical evidence since sufficient outward BERD is available for very few countries only. This is why all existing studies of the home country effect of R&D internationalisation (for example D'Agostin et al. 2013) rely on patent data instead of R&D data. Patent data, however, has some critical limitations (see Patel and Pavitt 1995 or Smith 2005): information on the location of patent inventors and patent applicants may be misleading since it reflects intellectual property right strategies rather than the location of R&D activity.

This section breaks with the established patent-data based tradition and follows an alternative expenditure-based approach: Outward BERD data of a particular country is proxied by the corresponding bilateral inward BERD data. Specifically, total outward BERD is calculated as the sum of all inward BERD data from a particular country of origin available from statistical offices (as described in Chapter 3). There are, however, limitations to this approach: huge differences appear when inward BERD and the corresponding outward BERD data is compared bilaterally (see Colecchia 2006). Moreover, a bias towards large countries may exist, since inward BERD data by firms from small countries is often unavailable due to issues of data confidentiality. However, even an analysis based on this imperfect data seems superior to the alternative – to leave the home country effects of R&D internationalisation unaddressed altogether.

This data is then complemented by additional data from different sources (like *OECD Structural Analysis Database* (OECD STAN), *World Development Indicators* (WDI), *OECD STAN Bilateral Trade Database* or *OECD Main Science and Technology Indicators*) to estimate the following model:

$$\ln RDd_{it} = \alpha + \beta \ln RDoutward_{it} + \delta_z X_{zit} + \varepsilon_{it} \tag{11.4}$$

where $\ln RDd_{it}$ is the log of domestic R&D expenditure in the manufacturing sector in country i at time t, $\ln RDoutward_{it}$ is the proxy for outward R&D and X_{zit} is a matrix of Z additional explanatory variables. At the sectoral level, X_{zit} includes: the growth rate of size of the manufacturing sector (in terms of employment), labour cost over value added and openness to trade (as the share of the sum of exports and imports in total output). At the country level, X_{zit} includes the growth rate of real GDP per capita, the share of graduates in the labour force (as a human capital proxy), the share of R&D personnel in labour force (as proxy for the host country's research potential), the share of total patents (per 1000 labour force), the contribution of medium-high-tech sectors to the manufacturing trade balance, the share of government budgetary appropriations or outlays for R&D and a dummy for EU-membership.

The analysis focuses on the manufacturing sector only for the period between 2003 and 2007. Different estimation techniques are used to account for the panel nature of the data. And since the Hausman test does not reject the null hypothesis that the difference in coefficients is not systematic but the Breusch-Pagan-Test rejects the existence of random effects, a pooled OLS approach is used. Three different specifications are estimated: basic pooled OLS without time or country fixed effects (1), pooled OLS with time fixed effects but no country fixed effects (2), and pooled OLS with both time and country fixed effects (3). Test statistics suggest that specification (3) is the preferred set-up for this regression.

The regressions considerably suffer from the low number of observations and data restrictions. It can, however, be noted that in none of the three specifications are domestic and outward BERD related negatively. Hence, there is no empirical support for the hollowing-out hypothesis which implies that outward BERD may substitute (or crowd-out) domestic R&D activities. On the contrary, columns (1) and (2) even suggest a complementary relationship between domestic and outward BERD – which is in line with other studies based on patents, FDI or export data (D'Agostino et al. 2013; BarbaNavaretti and Falzoni 2004). However, the preferred specification in column (3), does not find a positive and significant relationship between domestic and outward BERD.

Table 11.4 Impact of R&D internationalisation on the home country R&D expenditures (2004-2007)

Dep.Var.: log domestic R&D expenditure	(1)	(2)	(3)
Variables	pooledOLS_RDd	level_RDd	level_RDd
Constant	-1.494	-1.252	8.736***
	(1.12)	(1.00)	(3.20)
Sector level			
Log outward R&D expenditure	0.278***	0.326***	-0.056
	(4.46)	(5.23)	(1.23)
Size growth	0.012	0.065	-0.005
	(0.25)	(1.29)	(0.14)
Labour cost over VA	0.043***	0.038**	-0.001
	(2.83)	(2.61)	(0.04)
Openness to trade	-0.005*	-0.004	-0.013
	(1.85)	(1.44)	(1.01)
Country level			
Real GDP pc growth rate	-0.058**	-0.052*	-0.006
	(2.10)	(1.85)	(0.51)
Share graduates in labour force	0.629**	0.615**	-0.284
	(2.11)	(2.19)	(0.86)
Share R&D personnel	0.001***	0.001***	0.000
	(3.57)	(3.75)	(0.37)
Share total patents	0.218	0.113	0.006
	(0.70)	(0.38)	(0.02)
Contribution MHT sectors to manuf TB	0.224***	0.235***	0.022
	(3.45)	(3.76)	(0.34)
Share GBAORD in RGDP	1.524**	1.802**	-0.040
	(2.27)	(2.66)	(0.07)
Dummy: EU-member	1.271	0.935	
	(1.38)	(1.07)	
Country dummies	No	No	Yes
Year dummies	No	Yes	Yes
Observations	56	56	56
Adj. R²	0.94	0.948	0.994

Note: t-statistics in parentheses, *** p<0.01, ** p<0.05, * p<0.1
All regressions are based on pooled OLS. Column (1) uses pooled OLS without time or country
    fixed effects, column (2) uses pooled OLS with time but without country fixed effects;
    column (3 uses pooled OLS with time and country fixed effects).

SUMMARY

The literature has identified several channels through which host countries can profit from the presence of R&D intensive foreign-owned firms: i) financially better endowed foreign firms may induce domestic firms to intensify own R&D activities to keep pace with growing competition from abroad, ii) inward R&D expenditure may give rise to non-negligible knowledge spillovers, iii) inward R&D expenditure may increase the demand for skilled employees, and iv) inward R&D expenditure and the presence of foreign firms may result in structural change and agglomeration effects. Hence, wooing these firms has been high on the political agenda of many economies. Against that backdrop, the analysis seeks to shed light on whether and to what extent host countries profit from the presence of foreign affiliates and the extent of their R&D expenditure. For that purpose, it used a short unbalanced panel (2004-2007) covering the manufacturing sector only.

Empirical results highlight that domestic firms profit in various ways: while R&D expenditure of domestic firms are independent of the level of R&D expenditure of foreign affiliates, a positive and significant relationship emerges between R&D intensities of domestic and foreign firms (as the share of R&D expenditure in value added). Hence, R&D intensities of both domestic and foreign-owned firms are found to complement each other. Moreover, these complementarities differ across sub-samples considered and tend to be strongest in the sample of EU-15 countries. The analysis also explores the roles of both foreign and domestic R&D intensities in fostering host country patenting activities and shows that host country patenting activities appear unrelated to both foreign affiliates' and domestic firms' R&D intensities. The only exception is the group of EU-15 countries for which a positive but small effect can be detected suggesting that R&D intensities of domestic firms matter for host country patenting activities. Finally, the relationship between outward BERD and domestic R&D activity is analysed to address the potential hollowing-out effect of the internationalisation of R&D. However, the analysis is unable to find any evidence of substitution of domestic R&D expenditure by outward BERD. The result, however, is considerably limited by data restrictions.

NOTE

1. The overall sample comprises the following 27 countries: Austria (AUT), Belgium (BEL), Bulgaria (BUL), Canada (CAN), the Czech Republic (CZE), Denmark (DNK), Estonia (EST), Finland (FIN), France (FRA), Germany (GER), Hungary (HUN), Ireland (IRL), Israel (ISR), Italy (ITA), Japan (JPN), Latvia (LVA), the Netherlands (NLD), Norway (NOR), Poland (POL), Portugal (PRT), Romania (ROM), Slovakia (SVK), Slovenia (SVN), Spain (ESP), Sweden (SWE), the UK (GBR) and the US (USA).

REFERENCES

Athukorala, P.-C. and A. Kohpaiboon (2010), 'Globalization of R&D by US-based multinational enterprises', *Research Policy* **39**(10), 1335-347.

Barba Navaretti, G. and A.M. Falzoni (2004), 'Home country effects of foreign direct investment', in G. Barba Navaretti and A.J. Venables (eds), *Multinational firms in the world economy*, Princeton and Oxford: Princeton University Press, pp. 217-39.

Castellani, D. and F. Pieri (2011), 'R&D offshoring and the productivity growth of European regions', Valencia: Working Papers in Applied Economics WPAE-2011-20.

Colecchia, A. (2006), 'Note on internationalisation of R&D: A pilot study undertaken by the NESTI task force', Paris: OECD Working Party of National Experts on Science and Technology Indicators.

D'Agostino, L. M., K. Laursen and G. D. Santangelo (2013), 'The impact of R&D offshoring on the home knowledge production of OECD investing regions', *Journal of Economic Geography* **13**(1), 145-75.

OECD (2005), *OECD science, technology and industry scoreboard*, Paris: OECD.

Patel, P., and K. Pavitt (1995), 'Patterns of technological activity', in P. Stoneman (ed.), *Handbook of Innovation and Technological Change*, Oxford: Blackwell, 14-52.

Smith, K. (2005), 'Measuring innovation', in J. Fagerberg, D. Mowery and R.R. Nelson (eds), *The Oxford handbook of innovation*, Oxford: Oxford University Press, 148-77.

12. R&D Internationalisation from an Indo-German Perspective

Rajnish Tiwari

INTRODUCTION

Even though internationalisation of research and development is not a completely new phenomenon with one of its early academic documentations tracing it back to the late 19th century (Dunning 1958), it was long considered to have been effectively centred in the triad of North America, Western Europe, and Japan (cf. Archibugi and Iammarino 1999, Carlsson 2006). R&D activities in the 'emerging economies' of the developing world by global MNEs is a relatively recent trend, especially regarding the scope of the truly 'innovative' work conducted there (Tiwari and Herstatt 2012). Nevertheless, of late, there have been suggestions that the growing and largely unsaturated markets and increasing technological capabilities in some emerging economies are creating lead markets for affordability-driven 'frugal innovations' and acting as a 'pull' factor for FDI in R&D (Asakawa and Som 2008, Tiwari 2013). Even more recent, and still somewhat scattered, is the trend of MNEs from developing countries like India to indulge in outward FDI in the industrialised world for R&D purposes (Dachs and Pyka 2010, Sauvant et al. 2010).

Not surprisingly, the issue of probable differences in the motives of the two sets of MNEs and the resultant implications of overseas R&D for the respective home countries require further research for a comprehensive understanding. For, the internationalisation of R&D may lead to a new division of labour in R&D within multinational companies, and different tasks may be shifted to locations abroad. This might, in some instances, have negative implications for the home country, but on the other hand may also help increase R&D activities in the home country; for example when the headquarter activities can benefit from a higher overall demand due to expansion into new markets.

This chapter seeks to generate some insights into possible motives and implications of this 'North–South' interaction especially with regard to the EU. For this purpose four cases studies[1] are conducted in the specific, bilateral Indo-German context, which is particularly interesting given the fact that in recent years, the two countries have substantially deepened economic collaboration. The level of bilateral trade between India and Germany has increased several-folds within the short span of a decade growing from about 5 billion EUR in 2003 to more than 17 billion EUR in 2012 (Statistisches Bundesamt 2004, 2013). The level of FDI in the bilateral context has also seen considerable scaling on both sides. According to statistics of India's Department for Industrial Policy and Promotion, the cumulative stock of FDI by German firms in India stood at 5.5 billion USD at end of March 2013 and accounted for 2.8 percent of the complete FDI stock in the country (GOI 2013). Data of Germany's central bank (the Bundesbank) indicates an even higher level of Germany's cumulative FDI stock in India standing at 7.8 billion EUR at year-end 2011 (Bundesbank 2013). In the other direction, Indian firms were estimated to have invested a cumulative sum of 4.7 billion EUR in Germany in operations that include R&D activities (Tiwari 2012).

The chapter is structured on the following lines: At first R&D activities of two Indian MNEs in Germany are presented and analysed along the dimensions such as main geographic markets, R&D locations and mandates, modes of FDI, motives, the role of public policy, and the prospective implications for the home country. This is followed by two cases studies of R&D activities German MNEs in India, which take a deeper look into the integration of their India operations in the global corporate business, motives for doing R&D in India, and the implications for the home country.[2]

TWO INDIAN MULTINATIONALS IN GERMANY

This section investigates the motives of two Indian multinational firms to do R&D in Europe in general, and more specifically in Germany. In particular, the case study examines factors that determine the extent of the R&D undertaken by these Indian subsidiaries. In particular, we seek to examine which factors the firms regard as locational advantages of the EU compared to North America or Asian countries, and how they choose between different locations in regard to their future R&D investments.

Two Indian multinationals, viz. Defiance Technologies Limited and Suzlon Energy Ltd., were selected for the purpose of this study. The primary selection criterion was that both firms were known to be technology-driven firms with R&D capabilities in India and Germany as well as one or more member states of the EU.

Defiance Technology Limited ('Defiance Tech') is an India headquartered company offering Engineering, Enterprise Resource Planning (ERP) and Information Technology (IT) services to global customers. It undertakes new product development and design activities on behalf of its customers. Defiance Tech, in its own words, serves 'over 60 active global clients including 20 of the Global 500 and Fortune 1000 companies'. The registered corporate office is in Chennai (erstwhile Madras) in Southern India. The company currently employs close to 1200 employees worldwide.

Suzlon Energy Limited ('Suzlon') is an Indian company listed at Mumbai Stock Exchange and active in wind energy business. It is headquartered in Pune in Western India. Incorporated in 1995 it has grown impressively capturing nearly 50 percent of the Indian wind energy market. The Suzlon Group today belongs to top 5 five wind turbine makers worldwide with a global market share of approx. 10 percent (Bradsher 2006). It employs nearly 13,000 people in 32 countries. The turnover in fiscal year 2010-11 stood at 178.79 billion Indian rupees (approx. 4 billion USD). Even though the firm has faced some problems in previous two years, overall the firm has grown nine-fold in previous seven years. It acquired management control of Hamburg-based REpower Systems, a market and technology leader for wind turbines in Germany and Europe, in 2006 for an estimated price of $ 1.8 billion. In late 2011 Suzlon acquired 100 percent stake turning REpower into a wholly-owned subsidiary.

Main geographic markets

Main geographical markets of Defiance Tech are India, EU and the US. Recent turmoil in Middle East has had some negative impact on business there. The company also expects negative developments in the US in the short run due to recession fears. On the other hand it exudes positive outlook for Asia Pacific, China and India for the coming five years. Defiance Tech sees growth opportunities for itself primarily in Western Europe, since the US market is showing signs of saturation. Accordingly, the firm has made Germany a major point of its operations and established a wholly-owned subsidiary Defiance Tech GmbH as part of its global expansion plan. Cologne is set to serve Defiance as its 'European Headquarters', whereas the development centre in Walldorf is focused on engineering activities. The firm hopes that its 'presence in Germany will help gain better traction with its European customers and make Defiance's presence felt in the European market' (Hinduja Panorama 2010).

Key geographical markets for Suzlon are the US, India, China, Spain, Portugal and Australia. In addition, its subsidiary REpower Systems caters to European markets, especially Germany, Austria, France, Great Britain and Italy (REpower 2011). From the company's perspective the most important markets are expected to remain principally unchanged. However, the company expects that the relative shares of markets would change over time shifting the balance towards India and China. Recently, Suzlon has re-adjusted its market portfolio. REpower Systems focused at higher-end products, and announced withdrawal from China citing a ruinous (price-based) competition and the alleged preferential treatment of domestic firms. From now on, Suzlon with a low-cost base in India and local manufacturing facilities in China would serve that market.

Locations of R&D

The two companies have established R&D activities in several locations around the world. Suzlon has created R&D capabilities in Germany, the Netherlands, Denmark and India. Its 'Technology Group' has a strength of 500 and is headquartered in Hamburg (Germany). R&D locations outside India include Berlin, Hamburg and Rostock in Germany, Århus in Denmark, and Hengelo and The Hague in the Netherlands. Within India, Suzlon has R&D facilities in Pune and Vadodara.

Defiance Tech has development centres in Chennai, Bangalore and Pune in India, and at Walldorf in Germany. Furthermore, it has established state-of-the-art engineering and validation facilities at Troy and Westland in Michigan (US). Development capabilities are also located in South Africa.

There is considerable difference in the path taken by the two firms for internationalising their R&D activities. Overseas R&D establishments, for Defiance Tech, have predominantly resulted from mergers & acquisitions (M&A). This preference has been motivated by the desire to acquire established engineering capabilities and reduce the risk associated with greenfield investments in the service sector. Defiance Tech is reportedly looking for further suitable targets in Europe, US, and Australia (Narasimhan 2011).

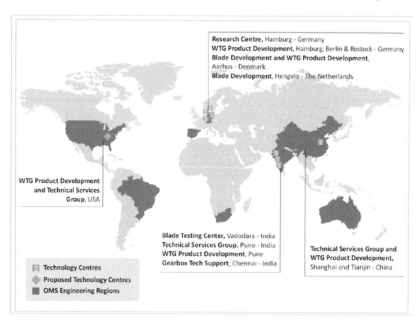

Source: Suzlon Energy Limited Annual Report 2010-11, p. 11.

Figure 12.1 In-house technology and R&D network of Suzlon

In contrast to Defiance Tech, Suzlon has taken both greenfield and brownfield routes for creating R&D capabilities outside the geographic boundaries of its home base. Its original operations in Germany, initiated under the aegis of Suzlon Windenergie GmbH, were greenfield ventures. Later, it acquired REpower Systems. One of the reasons for this acquisition was its desire to access high-end technology. Later, it created a joint venture (JV) with REpower Systems on parity basis. Under this JV a new entity called Renewable Energy Technology Center (RETC) was established in Hamburg and was entrusted with the task of doing basic research in the field of wind energy. Its mandate also includes trainings and project management.

India plays a dominant role in the present R&D setup of Defiance Tech and is poised to retain a strong position owing to factors such as cost advantages and the abundant availability of skilled labour. The company, however, expects a shift of balance in terms of R&D personnel in the next five years with the EU gaining in importance relative to India and the US (see figure 12.2). The firm makes it a point to emphasise that it is a growing business so that it expects the overall numbers to increase across all the locations; it is only the relative share that is expected to change.

The view within the Suzlon Group seems to concur with this scenario. Suzlon intends to further strengthen its R&D engagement in wind energy lead markets, Germany and Denmark (Jacob et al. 2005), and wishes to leverage the existing technological capacities for cutting-edge research. Capacities in these two countries, especially at locations in Hamburg and Rostock, are expected to be strengthened further. The relative share of Europe in the concern-wide R&D might go down nevertheless, as Suzlon intends to create 'dedicated R&D facilities' in countries like China, Singapore, and the US and has already started setting up engineering facilities related to design and development in several other countries such as Brazil.

The two companies in the sample also vary considerably in the assignment of tasks to their various development units. While Defiance Tech has concentrated basic research in India and intends to retain it there at least in the medium run, Suzlon has intentionally created hubs for basic research in Europe and actively shifted such functions away from the home base in India. Product development is carried out at the R&D units, whereas local adaptation is done at several engineering facilities set-up in various key markets including in Brazil and China. Defiance Tech too intends to globalise its applied research and experimental development further. Especially Western Europe, where 'a lot of innovation is taking place' is set to gain relevance, as Mr. Bratin Saha (Defiance Tech's Practice Head Engineering – Europe) puts it.

Present distribution of R&D personnel at Defiance Tech in 2011

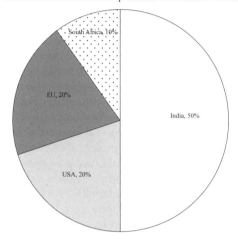

Expected distribution of R&D personnel at Defiance Tech in 2016

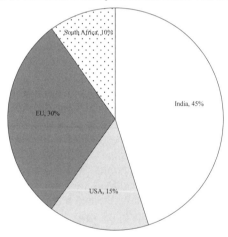

Source: information based on interviews with Defiance Tech.

Figure 12.2 Distribution of R&D personnel at Defiance Tech

Overseas affiliates of Defiance Tech do not have regional mandates as the firm rather prefers to work with product and/or technology mandates. In this scheme Indian units are responsible for matters related to general industrial transportation, the German affiliate is entrusted with the tasks related to aerospace, automotive and SAP, whereas the US unit is responsible for solutions based on Microsoft and Epicor products. Additionally, customer inputs related to the power and energy sector are collected from France and Belgium, for IT sector from the United Kingdom (UK).

Suzlon follows a comparable, though not identical, strategy. Local adaptation and technical support is carried out by engineering facilities in key markets which have a regional focus. On the other hand, R&D units are organized along technology portfolios. Suzlon's German units in Rostock, Berlin and Hamburg working under the aegis of Suzlon Windenergie GmbH concentrate on Systems Simulation, Power Electronics, Design, Drive Systems, Electrical Systems, Software, and Technical Support.

The R&D group in Århus is integrated in the local Danish subsidiary Suzlon Energy A/S and focuses on tower design and the Supervisory Control and Data Acquisition (SCADA) system. The R&D division for Blade Technology is based in Hengelo and The Hague in the Netherlands, and at Pune and Baroda (also known as Vadodara) in India, as well as Århus in Denmark (Suzlon 2011). The RETC conducts material and component testing of critical structures in its specialised laboratories and supports its customers along the entire chain of innovation management.[3]

Locational advantages of the European Union

One of the most important locational advantages of the EU compared to North America and Asian countries lies in what Mr. Bratin Saha calls is its 'centralised location in a happening place'. Distance of travel is comfortable and compatible with work process with one overnight flight to US, India and/or South Africa. Furthermore, EU countries are a growing market in terms of engineering services as outsourcing may be considered to be still in a 'nascent stage' in many EU countries while there is a growing need for European businesses to outsource. Opportunity-wise the EU is therefore seen as a 'young and virgin market' and a 'centre of attraction'.

For Suzlon it is rather the 'lead market' function of Europe, which is the biggest advantage (cf. Beise 2004). 'Germany and Denmark are together without doubt the headquarters of pioneering engineering knowledge and application for wind technology. Active co-operation of wind energy experts, newest scientific innovations, high-end technology usage and highly qualified human resources for selection of materials and production processes make them the 'destination of choice' for Suzlon's R&D endeavours and accomplishments'.[12]

Apart from the desired interaction with the innovation ecosystem in Europe there are also important market related considerations: 'Europe's 20 per cent by 2020 renewable targets, alongside developments like Germany's recent decision to shut down its nuclear plants […] have all put in place strong drivers for the wind sector. With Europe's limitations in land area, the opportunity for this growth is clearly offshore. And with REpower's leadership in offshore wind technology, this is again a market we are well positioned in' (Suzlon 2011, p. 2f). Even though India and other emerging markets such as Brazil, China and South Africa are seen as high growth markets and remain a priority for Suzlon, they are not expected to develop into wind energy lead markets in near future. The same holds true for the US, Suzlon believes.

Locations within the EU, however, do not offer advantages on a platter. Companies are sometimes also faced with certain challenges that need to be overcome for being successful. Suzlon is worried about the current as well as anticipated shortage of skilled labour in Europe. In some instances, Indian firms in Germany – not very familiar with the management practices and cultural settings of the host country – have struggled to keep attrition rates low (Tiwari and Herstatt 2010) and especially Suzlon has faced some issues retaining the REpower management, post-acquisition (Mishra and Surendar 2009). Suzlon has, however, been optimistic and sees this challenge as an opportunity. Mr. Tulsi Tanti, Chairman and Managing Director of Suzlon has been quoted by The Economic Times as saying: 'Europe doesn't have adequate engineers while we have good human resources but not the know-how' (Thakur 2007).

Defiance Tech sees EU markets as 'tough to crack', especially owing to linguistic and cultural issues. English is not the lingua franca in most EU states (unlike in the US and many other Asia Pacific countries). The company is therefore required to customise its products to smaller, culturally diverse markets reducing economies of scale. Moreover, most Fortune-500 companies are concentrated in the US. In comparison, the EU has a higher share of small and medium-sized enterprises which aggravates the scaling challenge leading to 'less volume and magnitude'.

Asked to judge the attractiveness of Eastern European countries such as the Czech Republic, Hungary, or Poland, for doing R&D compared to Western European and Asian countries, Defiance Tech, at present, sees less scope for its services in Eastern Europe which lacks large corporate houses that typically seek outsourcing of business processes. 'Barring one or two major companies there are no big players in our fields of engagement', is the tenor. The company sees some rays of hope in Hungary and Poland, though.

Linguistic issues further complicate the situation in Eastern Europe which has been hit by financial crisis. At the level of technical competencies Eastern Europe is seen at par with India while not offering a similar market advantage. Defiance Tech perceives greater business potential in Asian countries such as Japan and Korea. Owing to these factors Defiance Tech has no immediate plans of establishing direct R&D operations in Eastern Europe and would prefer to consolidate its business in developed economies in Western Europe while adopting a wait-and-watch policy in respect of Eastern Europe. A similar wait-and-watch policy can be observed at Suzlon, which sees great growth potentials in Eastern Europe and has even established a subsidiary in Romania. There are however no immediate plans of setting up R&D facilities in the region.

Drivers of overseas R&D

Both Defiance Tech and Suzlon see market demand as the single most important factor driving the internationalisation of R&D in their respective company. For Defiance Tech, a major factor influencing market demand would be the need for cost-cutting by European companies. Seeking access to skilled personnel is also regarded as a key driver for outsourcing by potential clients and is expected to play an important role in any future developments.

For Suzlon, the drivers of overseas R&D are however a bit broader in perspective, which is probably understandable, since the firm is not a provider of (engineering) services. Rather, it is looking for ways to access and even create knowledge and technologies. For these reasons, it stresses the role of knowledge co-creation partners such as universities and research institutions. Defiance Tech, on the other hand, does not see universities or other knowledge co-creation partners as a major factor for future changes in locations. Similarly, it does not expect initiatives by local managers to play a major role in these future changes, at this stage.

Suzlon, on the other hand, having selected Germany as its R&D headquarters seeks to encourage initiatives by local managers, who are also integrated in the decision-making processes at the group headquarters in Pune. Since one of the primary motives for Suzlon to do R&D in Europe is the desire to participate in the regional and sectoral innovation systems in European wind energy lead markets, it does not see a 'unilaterally decisive role' for cost factors in selecting R&D locations.

One interesting factor mentioned by Mr. Saha as a driver for R&D location decisions in the next five years was the expected foreign direct investments by emerging market firms. According to Mr. Saha, FDI by low-cost country firms such as India will open new business opportunities for collaboration in engineering and product development in Europe.

Role of public policy

Defiance Tech sees itself confronted with 'restrictive immigration policies' in the EU member states, especially Germany. In the opinion of the firm, these policies affect its ability to hire suitable people from various backgrounds and nationalities. The company is therefore of the opinion that public policy can significantly improve the attractiveness of locations for R&D if it implements regulatory changes to make it easier to recognise academic degrees of immigrated population. The company would highly welcome regulatory initiatives to enable cross-country hiring, advocating that the EU should 'follow an open door policy for their own benefit'. Citing the example of 'much more liberal' immigration policies in the United States and the resulting high numbers of Indian-origin scientists and engineers at NASA and other US firms Mr. Saha emphasises positive effects of collaboration for all parties involved, terming liberal immigration policies as 'key to cooperation and collaboration'.

Suzlon expressed its general satisfaction with public policies even while pleading for greater government support for renewable energies. Two areas of policy level encouragement mentioned by the Suzlon representative were: a) need for more liberal visa rules to allow easier and greater exchange with the headquarters, and b) active encouragement of industry-academia collaboration for foreign-owned firms.

Implications for the home country

The impact of the two firms' R&D expansion into Europe, from the perspective of India, the home base, can be summarised as follows:

- Creation of R&D capacities in Europe has helped upgrade the technological base (Suzlon) opening up new higher-end markets, or local development capabilities have helped the firm get access to new markets (Defiance Tech).
- Home R&D and European R&D do not compete against each other due to growing business, even though, as in Suzlon's case, basic R&D has been largely shifted from India to Europe.
- R&D capabilities, when measured in absolute numbers, continue to grow simultaneously at home and in Europe even as India's relative share is expected to go down in the case of both firms. As regards Europe the firms present a mixed picture, while Suzlon expects Europe's relative share to decrease too (since it plans to open new facilities in places like Singapore, China and the US), in case of Defiance Tech) Europe's share is set to increase.
- Both firms actively promote internal transfer of tacit knowledge by active cross-country integration of R&D personnel.

Summarising for this section, it may be stated that both Indian multinationals examined in this study have a positive view and outlook of Europe as an R&D destination. Primary drivers of establishing R&D capabilities in Germany/Europe are:

- Lead market function of Europe in a given field (for Suzlon: wind energy) and the associated knowledge networks, access to advanced technology, and highly skilled experts act as a pull factor.
- Europe is seen as possessing untapped market potential in comparison to saturated market demand in the US (and other Anglo-Saxon countries) in the field of IT services.
- Strong technological competencies in promising future technologies such as aerospace, green technologies, and automotive.
- Outward FDI by emerging market firms (e.g. from India) from manufacturing sector is creating new collaboration and investment avenues

for other firms from related and supporting industries acting as a pull factor.

- Economic and scientific/technological growth in India is encouraging firms to move up the value chain in European markets, still relatively untapped by Indian firms.

Indian companies intending to expand their R&D operations in Europe also face some challenges as they need to find ways to cater to smaller national markets dominated by relatively smaller firms and a more apprehensive social environment. There is also some challenge emanating from immigration policies that are perceived as being far more restrictive than the policy regime in the US.

Finally, and the aforementioned challenges notwithstanding, the ongoing globalisation of R&D has reached also Indian firms, which are increasingly seeking global resources to cater to worldwide demand relying on basically two factors: market demand and technological competencies. In this strategy Europe is set to play an increasingly important role even as the US market saturates and firms seek newer avenues of growth. Markets in Asia Pacific (with exception of Japan) are seen as growth markets with large potential. Europe with its market attractiveness and technological competencies has – for now – decisive lead in attracting Indian R&D investments, if the two firms are any indicator.

TWO GERMAN MULTINATIONALS IN INDIA

This section investigates the cases of two German firms, viz. Bosch and Siemens, doing R&D in India. Both firms are technology leaders and have strong R&D capabilities at the home base as well as in India.

Company profiles

Germany's **Bosch Group** is 'a leading global supplier of technology and services' in the areas of automotive and industrial technology, consumer goods and building technology. In fiscal year 2010 it employed nearly 283,500 people worldwide and generated sales of over € 47 billion (Bosch Group 2011). The group comprises of the flagship company Robert Bosch GmbH and over 300 subsidiaries spread across 60 countries. The group has business interests in about 150 countries. Bosch maintains a worldwide network for development, manufacturing, and sales activities. More than 90 percent of the share capital of Robert Bosch GmbH is held by Robert Bosch Stiftung GmbH, a charitable trust. The remaining shares are held by the Bosch family and by Robert Bosch GmbH (Bosch Group 2011). Table 12.1 shows some key business indicators for the Bosch group.

Table 12.1 Key business indicators of the Bosch Group (2006-2010)

	2006	2007	2008	2009	2010
Sales (billion EUR)	43.68	46.32	45.13	38.17	47.26
Yearly growth in sales (%)	5.40%	6.0%	-2.6%	-15.4%	23.8%
Profit before tax (billion EUR)	3.08	3.80	0.94	-1.20	3.49
Profit to sales ratio (%)	7.1%	8.2%	2.1%	-3.1%	7.4%
Employees (annual average)	257,754	267,562	282,758	274,530	283,500
In Germany (approx.)	110,500	112,300	114,000	112,000	114,000
R&D employees	25,300	29,000	32,600	33,000	34,000
R&D expenditure (billion EUR)	3.35	3.58	3.89	3.60	3.81
R&D intensity (ratio to sales)	7.7%	7.7%	8.6%	9.4%	8.1%
Patent applications filed	>3,000	3,280	3,850	3,870	>3800

With a revenue of nearly 11 billion EUR (23 percent of total sales), Germany constituted the largest market for the Bosch group, followed by the US (5.5 billion EUR) and China (4.2 billion EUR). Region-wise Europe was the primary market accounting for over 58 percent of the sales, followed by Asia (21 percent) and the Americas (18 percent). All other areas (e.g. Africa and Australia) accounted for less than 2 percent of total sales.

The share of individual business fields in the business and R&D in 2010 was as follows:

Table 12.2 Share of individual business fields in Bosch Group's business

(figures in billion EUR)	Sales	R&D expenditure
Automotive technology	28.1	3.0
Industrial technology	6.7	0.3
Consumer goods and building technology	12.5	0.5

With its 125 years old history Bosch is a renowned technology leader. Its 34,000-strong R&D workforce (12 percent of total employees) generates more than 3,000 patent applications a year.

The bulk of Bosch's R&D is based at its home base in Germany. With over 16,000 researchers and developers in 2006, Germany continued 'to be a key research and development location' (Bosch Group 2007, p. 21). Even though its relative share in total workforce has gone down from 64 percent in 2006 to an estimated 50 percent in 2010, the absolute numbers of R&D personnel in Germany has continued to grow. The relative growth has been stronger elsewhere: 'Our R&D workforce showed the strongest growth in Asia, where the number of engineers rose [within one year] from some 7,000 to over 8,000' (Bosch Group 2011, p. 58).

Bosch has been operating in India for 90 years (Bosch India 2011a). First manufacturing operations were established in 1953 (Bosch India 2012a). Robert Bosch GmbH holds 71.18 percent stake in Bosch Limited. Bosch's India operations however also include further 'sister firms', viz. Bosch Chassis Systems India Ltd., Bosch Rexroth India Ltd., Robert Bosch Engineering and Business Solutions Ltd. (RBEI), Bosch Automotive Electronics India Private Ltd. and Bosch Electrical Drives India Private Ltd. The flagship company Bosch Ltd. is headquartered in Bangalore (Bosch India 2011a). Bosch India runs 14 manufacturing and three development centres (Bosch India 2012a). In 2008 it increased its shareholding in the Indian subsidiary from around 60 percent to around 70 percent (Bosch Group 2008, p. 13).

Bosch India is active across all the segments of the parent concern, i.e. automotive technology, industrial technology, consumer goods and building technology. It manufactures and trades products such as fuel injection systems, automotive aftermarket products, auto electricals, special purpose machines, packaging machines, electric power tools and security systems (Bosch India 2011a). In fiscal year 2010 Bosch Ltd. employed 11,700 associates. Group-wide headcount in India stood at 22,500 (Bosch India 2012a).

Table 12.3 Selected performance indicators for Bosch Ltd. in India[4]

	2006	2007	2008	2009	2010
Sales (in millions EUR)	651	751	697	708	1101
Growth (in %, local currency base)	27,1%	13.1%	6.1%	4.6%	39.6%
Profit before tax (in millions EUR)	137	150	132	118	200
Profit to sales ratio	21.1%	20.0%	18.9%	16.7%	18.1%

Bosch has established a 'futuristic Technical Centre' in Bangalore that is supposedly 'the first-of-its-kind in the country' and intends to provide 'world-class technological solutions for the auto industry' (Bosch India 2012b). It is also the first global development centre for the Bosch Group to be set up outside Europe. It works in close cooperation with vehicle and engine manufacturers to develop electronic diesel control and petrol injection systems to match specific needs of new generation vehicles. It has been en-trusted with the global responsibility for designing, developing and manufacturing certain products like single cylinder pumps, multi-cylinder pumps and mechanical distributor pumps for the entire Bosch group (Bosch India 2012b). Over 350 qualified and experienced R&D engineers and tech-nicians work at the Technology Centre (Bosch India 2011b). In addition to the Technology Centre, also an 'Application Centre' has been established which houses a full-fledged application test facility for electronic diesel con-trol, petrol injection, spark plug and auto electrical products. This centre is targeted at Indian auto manufacturers (Bosch India 2012b).

The Engineering and Information Technology division of Bosch in India is the largest development centre of Bosch outside Germany (Bosch India 2012a). RBEI with a headcount of over 9,000 is directly owned by Robert Bosch GmbH and is specialised in offering offshore technical services to global customers 'with a focus on Europe' (RBEI 2011). All employees 'have to undergo basic German language training in addition to intercultural orientation' (RBEI 2011). The company has two state-of-the-art facilities in Bangalore and a development centre in Coimbatore. With proper selection of projects and clearly defined interfaces RBEI claims to be able to offer a cost advantage of 30-50 percent in comparison to developed countries (RBEI 2011). The company has also gone global with own presence in places like the US, Europe and Vietnam.

Siemens AG is a German multinational firm primarily active in business sectors Energy, Healthcare, Industry, and Infrastructure and Cities. It is headquartered in Munich and has business interests in close to 190 countries. Siemens calls itself 'an integrated technology company', because – as the company puts it: 'Our closely aligned business units enable us to offer a wide range of products and solutions that help customers drive competitiveness, enhance business performance, cut costs and reduce CO_2 emissions' (Sie-mens 2011a).

With revenues worth 10.8 billion EUR (14.7 percent of total sales) Ger-many accounts for the second largest market for Siemens, after the US (19.6 percent). China (8.7 percent) and India (3.2 percent) are also rapidly taking an increasingly important role for Siemens with double-digit growth rates (Siemens 2011a). Table 12.5 shows the contribution of individual business fields to Siemens' revenues and R&D expenses.

In fiscal year 2011 there were 27,800 R&D employees at 160 Siemens re-search centres around the globe. Out of these, 11,800 R&D employees were located in Germany and approximately 16,000 R&D employees abroad in close to 30 countries including in China and India (Siemens 2011a). In 2009, Siemens had employed 12,700 employees for R&D in Germany and 19,100 employees abroad (Siemens 2009: 52) indicating a decrease in the number of overall R&D. The decrease in Germany was 7 percent and abroad even 16 percent. The decrease has however also resulted from selling off certain business units.

Table 12.4 Key business indicators of the Siemens Group (2007-2011)

	2007	2008	2009	2010	2011
Sales (billion EUR)	64.24	69.58	70.05	68.98	73.52
Yearly growth in sales (%)	-3.4%	8.3%	0.7%	-1.5%	6.6%
Profit before tax (bn EUR)[5]	3.43	1.57	2.53	4.26	7.01
Profit to sales ratio (%)	5.3%	2.3%	3.6%	6.2%	9.5%
Employees (annual average)	320,000	346,000	333,000	336,000	360,000
In Germany (approx.)	126,100	128,000	128,000	128,000	116,000
R&D employees	32,500	32,200	31,800	27,200	27,800
R&D expenditure (bn EUR)	3.40	3.78	3.90	3.85	3.93
R&D intensity (ratio to sales)	5.3%	4.9%	5.1%	5.1%	5.3%
Patent applications filed	5,060	5,000	4,200	4,300	4,300

Siemens has a very long association with India. Way back in 1867 it laid the 1st Indo-European telegraph line connecting London and Kolkata (Kundu 2005). Siemens' operations in India today are conducted under the flagship of its publically listed subsidiary, Siemens Ltd., headquartered in Mumbai. In fiscal 2011 Siemens AG increased its stake in the Indian 'daughter concern' from 55.3 percent to 75 percent with an express desire 'to continue driving our booming business in India and boost its influence on our operations on the subcontinent' (Siemens 2011a: 48).

Table 12.5 Share of individual business fields in Siemens' business

(figures in billion EUR)	Sales	R&D
Industry (e.g. automation, mobility)	32.94	1.6
Energy (e.g. power generation, transmission)	27.61	1.0
Healthcare (diagnostics)	12.52	1.2
Rest	00.45	0.1

The Siemens Group in India comprises of 17 companies (Siemens India 2012b), providing direct employment to over 18,000 persons, which amounts to 5 percent of the global workforce (Siemens 2011a: 71). Currently, the group has 21 manufacturing plants, a wide network up of Sales and Service offices across the country as well as over 500 channel partners (Siemens India 2012b). In fiscal year 2010-11 Siemens India spent Rs. 555.34 million (€ 9.2 million) on R&D (Siemens India 2011). This was a significant increase from the previous year when total R&D expenditure amounted to only Rs. 86.83 million (€ 1.3 million) (Siemens India 2010).

Table 12.6 Selected performance indicators for Siemens in India[6]

	FY 2007	FY 2008	FY 2009	FY 2010	FY 2011
Sales (in millions €)	1,676	1,885	1,680	1,877	2,353
Growth (in %, local currency base)	69.6%	7.4%	4.9%	5.9%	28.7%
Profit before tax (in millions €)	150.4	156.5	219.8	187.6	211.7
Profit to sales ratio	11.0%	10.4%	16.0%	13.3%	10.5%

While business units at Siemens 'concentrate their R&D efforts on the next generation of their products and solutions', R&D specialists at Corporate Technology 'are focused two generations ahead and prepare the technological basis for that generation' (Siemens 2010: 61). The Corporate Technology division has a total strength of about 5,500.

The Corporate Development Centre, with its 3,160 employees (Siemens 2011c), is an internal solution provider and responsible for software development for Siemens products. It is a part of the Corporate Technology division and has three locational clusters, Central Eastern Europe, India and China. The Development Centre in India is the largest; employing approximately 2,300 engineers and IT specialists (over 75 percent of the global strength) at five locations, i.e. Bangalore, Pune, Calcutta, Chennai (erstwhile Madras) and Gurgaon. 'One of India's great strengths – the very high number of young, highly-trained IT specialists it produces – is therefore also contributing to Siemens' success' (Siemens 2011d: 2). Software engineers in India develop software for all of Siemens' Sectors (Siemens 2011d).

The Bangalore research location of Corporate Technology was established in 2004 and employs 105 researchers. It specialises on software technologies, decentralized energy systems, embedded systems and SMART technologies (see next section). Furthermore, it also operates an innovation centre for renewable energies (Siemens 2011c). Researchers from Corporate Technology in India have developed a low-cost Algae-bacteria based Wastewater Treatment system, which needs about '60 percent less energy for treating wastewater than conventional sewage treatment plants' (Siemens 2011c: 29).

Siemens has launched an initiative called 'SMART', which stands for 'simple, maintenance-friendly, affordable, reliable, and timely to market' products (Siemens 2011a: 134). In this respects SMART products can be considered as 'frugal innovations' that are conceptualised as 'high-tech low-cost innovations that work reliably and, as far as possible, without requiring maintenance' (Siemens 2011c). It is hoped that the capability to design, manufacture and sell SMART products will help Siemens gain market share and increase revenue in strategic growth markets like India and China, 'where customers may consider price more strongly than product features when making a purchase decision' (Siemens 2011a: 134). Recently, there have been suggestions that lead markets for frugal innovations may be emerging in emerging economies outside the classical base of industrialised nations (Tiwari 2013).

Out of a total of 160 SMART projects worldwide (Siemens 2011a: 52) 60 have been launched in India (37 percent) to target an estimated market worth over 7 billion EUR (Siemens 2011b). These 'value-based products' have relevant, functional features and uncompromised quality. Siemens India has developed several SMART products, including a Fetal Heart Rate Monitor, which has been launched also in developed country markets (Siemens 2011c; Siemens India 2011).

Siemens has recently also launched a 'Lighthouse' project in India in the field of medical care in remote areas, which utilizes a scalable IT system. Siemens describes those projects as 'Lighthouse projects', which are considered strategically important for their potential to open up new fields of business for the company through the development of groundbreaking technologies. Worldwide Siemens is working on 10 Lighthouse projects (Siemens 2011c).

Motives for R&D in India

Both, Bosch and Siemens, have significantly globalised their R&D operations in various countries. The two companies have long-standing and relatively large-sized business interests in India, where they have been experiencing steady and sustained growth, even during the recent financial crisis.

The figure below shows that their respective subsidiaries in India have thoroughly outperformed the parent concern in recent years, once the effect of fluctuating exchanging rates is filtered out by using local currencies. This market growth is also an important motive for establishing R&D competencies in India. In the following we highlight a few key motivations for doing R&D in India based on the two cases discussed above:

- Markets in India – owing to several peculiarities: e.g. large (rural) markets, price sensitivity, infrastructural deficits and high customer aspirations of a young and consumption-friendly population – require new solutions that are 'high-tech, low-cost' (Maira 2005, Tiwari and Herstatt 2012). Merely stripped-down versions of existing technologies do not suffice as solutions. Successful MNEs operating in India state that to succeed in the local market, a firm typically requires a product that 'costs 30 percent of the global price and offers 95 percent of the performance' (Tiwari 2013, p. 25).
- Indian market is seeing intense competition from domestic and global players, so that time-to-market plays an important role.

- Firms anticipate new trends (e.g. fuel efficiency, low maintenance, small cars) to emerge in India and wish to participate in these processes, such as Bosch's engagement with the Tata Nano, the world's cheapest car. Firms hope for positive image and business effects.
- High growth in India enables financing of local R&D operations. The subsidiaries are profit centres and do not cause burden on the parent.
- India's low-cost advantage continues to act as a significant leverage instrument. In some instances firms are able to reduce project costs by 30-50 percent. In other instances, it is impressive to see the performance of the Indian subsidiary in the light of their 'meagre' budgets not exceeding single-digit millions in euro.
- Last but not least, firms expect new impulse for internal innovation processes in the form of a 'diversity dividend'. For instance, Bosch says, it profited from coming together of engineers of many nationalities to develop new technologies and products for the Tata Nano. "Such collaboration in international teams is becoming more and more central to our business' (Bosch Group 2010: 63; Schuster and Holtbrügge 2011).

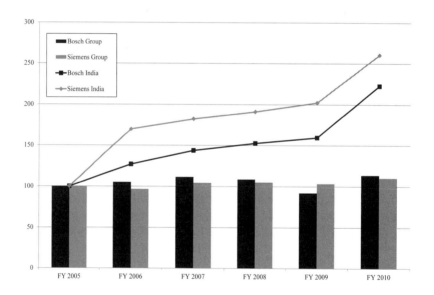

Note: FY 2005 = 100

Figure 12.3 Revenue growth at group level and in India[7]

Implications for the home country

The impact of India's integration into the global R&D networks of the two firms on activities in the home country can be summarised in the following:

- Opening of new markets in India (and other developing economies) has been made possible by the complementary role of a strong knowledge base at the home and new competence centres in India. None of the two could have substituted the other.
- R&D operations in India have been configured in a way that they do not compete against R&D operations at the headquarters, as the growing number of R&D personnel at the home base (Bosch) confirms. Growth in absolute numbers has been possible simultaneously. As in the case of Siemens the home base has been more insulated from layoffs than the overseas operations (7 percent decrease vs. 16 percent decrease within 2 years).
- The relative share of the headquarters in the number of R&D personnel has nonetheless decreased and may be expected to decrease further, even though it is set to retain its key role as a provider of basic research into next generation products, as coordinator of knowledge synergies and transfer, and as formulator of the corporate R&D strategy.
- Basic research, so far, continues to remain largely concentrated at the headquarters. The firms expect, however, that the global development centres coming India shall be entrusted with basic research in foreseeable future. This would be generally focused on new business fields with specific relevance to India and other comparable markets in the developing world.
- The two companies have significant programmes for internal knowledge transfer. Apart from the usual electronic tools of knowledge sharing, both firms reported employee exchange programmes between the headquarters and global R&D units. For example, many Indian and German engineers (and over 2,000 associates worldwide) are currently working on multi-year assignments outside their home country. This is done with an expressed purpose of creating and sharing tacit knowledge.

Overall speaking, the case studies of two German MNEs do not provide indications to suggest any significant trend of offshoring of R&D jobs to India. Rather, they indicate towards creation of new jobs as a result of emergence of new markets in India with positive effects on headquarters. The growth challenge could not have been mastered, had the respective companies insisted on retaining the locational proportion of R&D employees at the headquarters.

As the indicators of business performance for both firms demonstrate, the R&D engagement in India has largely had a substantially positive impact on the competitiveness of the parent firm, opening new markets in India and other emerging economies. Many products developed in India could be commercialised also in developed countries since it has emerged as a lead market for affordability-driven frugal innovations targeted at price-sensitive customers (Tiwari 2013). Cost reduction has helped strengthen the competitiveness of the parent units. Moreover, India as a low-cost location with a large pool of skilled labour has helped firms to react flexibly to market developments both during upswing, when the developed countries faced shortage of skilled labour owing to demographic changes (Müller 2006: 38-48), or during market turbulences, as the low-cost basis in India is financially more manageable and acts as a strategic asset once the market picks up because capacities do not have to be re-created (Doval and Nambiar 2011).

The two examples also show that both the home and host country capacities can grow simultaneously, as is the case with Bosch. In case of Siemens, this effect is too ambiguous to give a straight answer, since Siemens has sold some of its business units in the period under discussion leading to fluctuation in the number of employees owing to external events. In the past there have also been certain reports of acceptance issues at the Siemens headquarters (cf. Buse, Tiwari and Herstatt 2010: 224). The present study, however, did not find any indication of such discord.

SUMMARY AND CONCLUSIONS

This chapter examined cases of two German MNEs, i.e. Bosch and Siemens, which have deliberately established and carefully cultivated engineering and development capacities in India; and of two Indian MNEs, viz. Defiance Tech and Suzlon, which have done the same in Germany. The study could identify several examples of successful product and process innovations for the local and global markets in the firms examined. These innovations have been initialised and developed by the respective foreign-based subsidiary.

We can observe positive correlation between the home country R&D activities and the overseas R&D engagement of the firms examined here. The results are in line with other academic studies, e.g. (Asakawa and Som 2008; Herstatt, Tiwari, Ernst et al. 2008; Bruche 2009; Ernst, Dubiel and Fischer 2009; Tiwari and Herstatt 2012). The crucial difference however seems to lie in the key motivation of the two sets of MNEs:

Firms from the developed world chiefly seem to (a) develop affordable 'frugal innovations' that target untapped and unserved market potential in emerging economies, such as India, with their local R&D operations, with the purpose of securing growth prospects outside their saturated home market, and (b) seek cost arbitrage in order to ensure competitiveness in a globalised world, and (c) stem the existing shortage of skilled labour at their home base.

Firms from emerging economies when establishing overseas R&D operations in an industrialised nation engage primarily in technology seeking in order to upgrade their innovative capabilities to tap global markets outside their price-sensitive home bases. The Lead market function of some European nations such as Germany seems to act as a catalyst in this endeavour. The added advantage is that the technology procured in Europe can be used to create frugal products for the home market by reducing technological uncertainties and utilising analogies. Finally, they follow a strategy based on exploiting the strengths of their already established low-cost home base and the rather abundant supply of skilled labour in combination with high-tech capabilities in Europe.

The strategy of combining high tech infrastructure in Europe with growth prospects in emerging economies endowed with skilled labour seems to be the unifying and underlying fundament for the both sets of MNEs. Finally, these findings, based on a small sample of four firms, are of preliminary nature and need to be ascertained in a more detailed empirical study.

NOTES

1. Case studies are regarded to be particularly suitable for researching an emerging field (Yin 2003).
2. Apart from accessing a host of company documents, press reports, and other secondary literature, the study has benefited from a total of seven semi-structured personal interviews of about 90 minutes lengths with senior-level management at the firms concerned. Two of the interviewees were managers of Indian MNEs in Germany, whereas five interviews were conducted in India with managers of German MNEs. Interview partners wish to remain anonymous.
3. The integration process of REpower Systems in the Suzlon concern is still on, so that it is too early to speculate what shape the restructuring will take place. Reportedly, a leading management consultancy is currently working on a concept to reorganise the responsibilities between existing Suzlon units and REpower.
4. Based on: Bosch Ltd.'s Annual Report 2010. Values converted from Indian rupees to euro, using the Reserve Bank of India's official average exchange rates for the respective fiscal years (RBI 2011: Table 147). The original extent of growth in rupee terms was much higher as suggested by the growth rate in row 2 (through-out positive). It has been however impacted by the depreciation in the rupee's exchange rate vis-á-vis euro.
5. Refers to 'Income from continuing operations'
6. Revenue data varies considerably across Annual Reports due to sell of various business entities by Siemens, source for sales data: (Siemens 2009, 2010, 2011a). Furthermore, some fluctuation in the growth is caused by volatile exchange rates. Data source for growth and profit: (Siemens India 2011). Profit before tax has been converted from Indian rupees into euro, using RBI's average exchange rates for the respective fiscal year (RBI 2011: Table 147).
7. The graphic is intended to illustrate only the growth trend of recent years, since the definitions of the respective fiscal years are not necessarily identical across the four entities.

REFERENCES

Archibugi, D. and S. Iammarino (1999), 'The policy implications of the globalisation of innovation', *Research Policy* **28**(2-3), 317-36.

Asakawa, K. and A. Som (2008), 'Internationalization of R&D in China and India: Conventional wisdom versus reality', *Asia Pacific Journal of Management* **25**(3), 375-94.

Beise, M. (2004), 'Lead Markets: Country-Specific Success Factors of the Global Diffusion of Innovations', *Research Policy* **33**(6-7), 997-1018.

Bosch Group (2007), *Annual Report 2006*, Stuttgart: Robert Bosch GmbH.

Bosch Group (2008), *Annual Report 2007*, Stuttgart: Robert Bosch GmbH.

Bosch Group (2010), *Annual Report 2009*, Stuttgart: Robert Bosch GmbH.

Bosch Group (2011), *Annual Report 2010,* Stuttgart: Robert Bosch GmbH.

Bosch India (2011a), *Annual Report 2010,* Bangalore: Bosch Limited.

Bosch India (2011b), *Bosch Limited: Profile 2011,* Bangalore: Bosch Limited.

Bosch India. (2012a), *Bosch in India*, retrieved 23.01.2012, from http://www.boschindia.com/content/language1/html/7310.htm

Bosch India. (2012b), *Research and Development*, retrieved 23.01.2012, from http://www.boschindia.com/content/language1/html/4427.htm

Bradsher, K. (2006), 'The Ascent of Wind Power', *New York Times*, 28.09.2006.

Bruche, G. (2009), 'The emergence of China and India as new competitors in MNC's innovation networks', *Competition & Change* **13**(3), 267-88.

Buse, S., R. Tiwari, et al. (2010), 'Global Innovation: An Answer to Mitigate Barriers to Innovation in Small and Medium-sized Enterprises', *International Journal of Innovation and Technology Management* **7**(3), 215-27.

Bundesbank (2013), *Bestandserhebung über Direktinvestitionen*, Statistische Sonderveröffentlichung 10, Frankfurt am Main: Deutsche Bundesbank.

Carlsson, B. (2006), 'Internationalization of innovation systems: A survey of the literature', *Research Policy* **35**(1), 56-67.

Dachs, B. and A. Pyka (2010), 'What drives the internationalisation of innovation? Evidence from European patent data', *Economics of Innovation and New Technology* **19**(1), 71-86.

Doval, P. and P. Nambiar (2011), 'Big Bosch not just cog in the wheel', *Economic Times*, Mumbai. 08.01.2011.

Dunning, J. H. (1958), *American investment in British manufacturing industry*, London: Allen and Unwin.

Ernst, H., A. T. Dubiel, et al. (eds) (2009), *Industrielle Forschung und Entwicklung in Emerging Markets: Motive, Erfolgsfaktoren, Best-Practice-Beispiele*, Wiesbaden: Gabler.

GOI (2013), *Fact sheet on foreign direct investment (FDI): From April 2000 to March 2013*, New Delhi: Department of Industrial Policy and Promotion, Ministry of Commerce and Industry, Government of India.

Herstatt, C., R. Tiwari, et al. (2008), 'India's national innovation system: Key elements and corporate perspectives', *Economics Series Working Paper No. 96*, Honolulu: East-West Center.

Hinduja Panorama (2010), 'Defiance continues global expansion', *Hinduja Group Newsletter* **1**(28), March.

Jacob, K., M. Beise, J. Blazejczak, et al. (eds) (2005), *Lead Markets for Environmental Innovations*, Heidelberg: Physica-Verlag.

Kundu, K. K. (2005), *German FDI to India: Untapped potential*, Frankfurt am Main: Deutsche Bank Research.

Maira, A. (2005), 'Aspiration alignment: a hidden key to competitive advantage', *Journal of Business Strategy* **26**(6), 12-18.

Mishra, A.K. and T. Surendar (2009), 'Saving Suzlon', *Forbes India*, 18.05.2009.

Müller, O. (2006), *Wirtschaftsmacht Indien: Chancen und Herausforderungen für uns*, Munich; Carl Hanser Verlag.

Narasimhan, T.E. (2011), 'Defiance Tech eyeing buys in US, Australia', *Business Standard*, 06.05.2011.

RBEI (2011), *Robert Bosch Engineering and Business Solutions (Company Profile)*, Bangalore: Robert Bosch Engineering and Business Solutions.

RBI (2011), *Handbook of Statistics on the Indian Economy*, Mumbai: Reserve Bank of India.

REpower (2011), *Jahresabschluss zum Geschäftsjahr vom 01.04.2010 bis zum 31.03.2011*, Hamburg: REpower Systems SE.

Sauvant, K. P., J. P. Pradhan, et al. (eds) (2010), *The rise of Indian multinationals: perspectives on Indian outward foreign direct investment*, New York: Palgrave Macmillan.

Schuster, T. and D. Holtbrügge (2011), 'Tata Nano: The Car for the Bottom-of-the-Pyramid', in Zentes, B. Swoboda and D. Morschnett (eds), *Fallstudien zum Internationalen Management: Grundlagen – Praxiserfahrungen – Perspektiven*, Wiesbaden: Gabler: 83-102.

Siemens (2009), *Annual Report 2009: How can we ensure sustainability while generating profitable growth?*, Munich: Siemens AG.

Siemens (2010), *Annual Report 2010: Our path to sustainable value creation*, Munich: Siemens AG.

Siemens (2011a), *Annual Report 2011: Creating Sustainable Cities*, Munich: Siemens AG.

Siemens (2011b), *The Company: Siemens 2011 – Status: October 2011*, Munich: Siemens AG.

Siemens (2011c), *Global Research at Siemens*, Munich: Siemens AG.

Siemens (2011d), *Global Software Development at Siemens*, Munich: Siemens AG.

Siemens India (2010), *Annual Report 2010: Answers for India*, Mumbai: Siemens Ltd.

Siemens India (2011), *Annual Report 2011: Strong roots, sustainable growth*, Mumbai: Siemens Ltd.

Siemens India (2012a), *Research and Development at Corporate Technology*, retrieved 23.01.2012, from http://www.siemens.com/corporate-technology/en/facts-figures.htm.

Siemens India (2012b), *Siemens in India*, retrieved 23.01.2012, from http://www.siemens.co.in/en/about_us/index.htm

Statistisches Bundesamt (2004), *Außenhandel: Rangfolge der Handelspartner im Außenhandel der Bundesrepublik Deutschland – 2003*, Wiesbaden: Statistisches Bundesamt (Federal Statistical Office).

Statistisches Bundesamt (2013), *Außenhandel: Rangfolge der Handelspartner im Außenhandel der Bundesrepublik Deutschland (mit Umsatz und Saldo) – 2012*, Wiesbaden: Statistisches Bundesamt (Federal Statistical Office).

Suzlon (2011), 'Annual Report 2010-11', Pune: Suzlon Energy Limited.

Thakur, M. (2007), 'Suzlon to set up R&D institutes', *Economic Times*, 06.11.2007.

Tiwari, R. (2012), 'Indian Investments in Germany: A Win-Win Proposition', in

Indo-German Chamber of Commerce (ed.), *Annual Review 2012*, Mumbai, 123-25.

Tiwari, R., and C. Herstatt (2010), 'The Emergence of Indian Multinational Enterprises: An Empirical Study of the Motives, Current Status, and Trends of Indian Investment in Germany', in K. P. Sauvant et al. (eds), *The rise of Indian multinationals: perspectives on Indian outward foreign direct investment*, New York: Palgrave Macmillan, pp. 233-53.

Tiwari, R., and C. Herstatt (2012), 'Assessing India's Lead Market Potential for Cost-effective Innovations', *Journal of Indian Business Research* 4(2), 97-115.

Tiwari, R. (2013), *Emergence of Lead Markets in Developing Economies: An Examination on the Basis of 'Small Car' Segment in India's Automobile Industry*, doctoral dissertation, Hamburg: Hamburg University of Technology.

Yin, R. K. (2003), *Case Study Research: Design and Methods*, Thousand Oaks: SAGE Publications.

13. R&D Internationalisation and the Global Financial Crisis

Bernhard Dachs

In 2008, the global financial crisis hit the world economy, causing a sharp decline in economic growth and even more severe reductions in FDI and international trade. Export volumes decreased from 2008 to 2009 by 25 percent in Japan, 18 percent in Canada, 15 percent in the European Union, 14 percent in the United States, 11 percent in China, 8 percent in South and Central America, and by 3 percent in India (WTO 2010, p. 8).

This chapter asks if – and how – the global financial crisis has affected the internationalisation of business R&D. The first section discusses possible linkages between business R&D internationalisation and the crisis. The crisis may have reduced the level of R&D performed abroad, but may have also changed the distribution of R&D expenditure of multinational firms between countries.

In a second step, the chapter reviews the existing empirical evidence on the development of R&D internationalisation during and after the crisis. This section is based on patent data, data on outward BERD of US firms and data on inward BERD in various European countries. The chapter closes with some general remarks on future directions of R&D internationalisation.

HOW THE CRISIS (MAY) HAVE AFFECTED R&D INTERNATIONALISATION

Today it is widely accepted that R&D and innovation are major determinants of long-term economic growth. However, fluctuations in economic growth can also affect the propensity of firms to invest in R&D and innovation. There are several transmission mechanisms (OECD 2012, p. 24): First, economic downturns may reduce the actual demand for products and increase uncertainties as to future developments which probably lowers incentives to innovate. Second, an economic crisis reduces liquidity in the financial system and funding opportunities for R&D and innovation. Third, countries may change public expenditure during an economic crisis, which may also include changes in public funding for R&D and innovation.

Theory predicts that innovation activity tends to cluster in upswings of the business cycle, and decreases in recessions. Patterns of BERD growth, however, reveal a different picture the global financial crisis of 2008-09. The OECD (2013 p. 42) has collected data on trends in business R&D expenditure for the years 2000-2011. Between 2007 and 2009, business R&D expenditure *decreased* in Canada, the Czech Republic, Israel, Japan, Luxembourg, the Netherlands, and the UK. Business R&D expenditure in Austria, Estonia, Hungary, Korea, Ireland, Poland, Portugal, the Slovak Republic and Turkey, however, was *higher* in 2009 compared to 2007. One can also add China to this group, where business R&D expenditure increased by 27 percent between 2007 and 2009.

All other OECD member states show no or only small changes in this period. 2010 marked another decrease in Canada, Finland, Luxembourg, Mexico, Portugal, Spain, Sweden and the United States. There is no data for Greece, Iceland, Switzerland, and New Zealand.

In addition, there is a considerable degree of heterogeneity in terms of impact of the crisis across sectors, firms, and different types of innovation activities (Cincera et al. 2012; Rammer 2012; Archibugi et al. 2013). According to Cincera et al. (2012) the automotive industry and other medium-technology manufacturing sectors were most severely affected, while low-technology manufacturing sectors faced only modest reductions. Rammer (2012) reveals that R&D intensive sectors in Germany had larger decreases in innovation expenditure than all other sectors. Both sources indicate that R&D and innovation in services seems to have suffered less than in manufacturing.

With respect to firm characteristics there is also evidence that innovation activities in smaller firms and in export-oriented firms were more severely hit by the crisis (Paunov 2012; Rammer 2012; Archibugi et al. 2013). Credit constraints may have posed considerable problems for the funding of innovation projects in smaller firms; large firms, in contrast, have larger internal means to finance those activities. Exports dropped faster than domestic demand such that exporters where hit hardest by the crisis. Moreover, younger firms, firms with no or little access to public funding and suppliers to foreign multinational firms were more likely to stop on-going innovation projects (Paunov 2012). Moreover, the economic crisis may have hit different types of innovation activities to a different degree. Luccese and Pianta (2012) point out that firms have stronger incentives to introduce (labour-saving) process innovations in recessions, while product innovations find market acceptance more easily in upswings. Moreover, German data indicate that non-R&D innovation expenditure (including investment in process technologies, design, organisational and marketing innovation,) dropped faster than R&D expenditure during the crisis (Rammer 2012).

Some firms even saw the crisis as an opportunity to distinguish themselves from competitors and increased innovation expenditure: Archibugi et al. (2013) observe for the UK that the crisis led to increases in innovation expenditure in fast-growing new entrants and firms with high sales from market novelties before the crisis, which the authors regard as a sign of high innovativeness. A similar development can be observed in Germany, where 34 percent of all firms intensified innovation activities between 2008 and 2009 (Rammer 2012).

The empirical literature reveals a considerable degree of heterogeneity in the impacts of the crisis on R&D and innovation. What about foreign-owned firms? Did the crisis hit them harder than domestically owned firms, leading to a backslash for the internationalisation of business R&D?

There is some reason to believe that this was indeed the case, although firm-level evidence is still largely missing. One exception is a study by Kinkel and Som (2012) who compare R&D offshoring of German firms between the period 2004/06 and the period 2007/09. They find a sharp decrease in the propensity to offshore R&D. In relative terms, locations in the EU gain shares at the expense of Asia and America.

As discussed above, various authors point out that export-oriented firms in technology-intensive sectors were more severely hit by the crisis. There are two important characteristics in which foreign-owned firms differ from their domestically owned counterparts (Markusen 2002; Bellak 2004). A higher exposure of foreign-owned firms to international markets and their sectoral affiliation (e.g. in high-tech industries) may have led to a more severe drop in R&D and innovation activity of foreign-owned firms compared to domestically owned firms. Moreover, there may be a preference of multinational firms to cut R&D and innovation expenditure abroad instead of at home. This may have even amplified decreases in R&D and innovation expenditure of foreign-owned firms in the host countries. Some characteristics of multinational firms, however, may have also stabilised R&D and innovation activities in affiliates abroad. Foreign-owned firms as part of large multinational groups are less dependent on credit markets and have larger internal funds for R&D and innovation. Moreover, foreign-owned firms are not only oriented towards the growth prospects of their host country, but also towards the global growth outlook. In addition, multinational firms have better means to spread the risks of R&D projects a large number of countries.

A second effect of the crisis on R&D activities of multinational firms may be a re-distribution of outward BERD across countries. It has been mentioned above that different countries were affected by the crisis to a different degree, and countries also differed in terms of their policy response to the crisis (Filippetti and Archibugi 2011; OECD 2012, Annex 1A). This may have led to different expectations of future market growth and unequal incentives to invest in R&D across countries. As a consequence, foreign affiliates in countries with expectations of high future market growth increased R&D expenditure, while subsidiaries in countries with weak expectations decreased R&D expenditure. The literature points out that foreign subsidiaries in OECD countries today evolve to a considerable degree on the initiative of the local management that makes use of favourable framework conditions, subsidiary autonomy and capabilities (Birkinshaw et al. 1998; Frost et al. 2002). Corporate headquarters may have amplify this effect by re-allocating funds for R&D to countries with higher growth expectations. This may have led to a re-distribution of overseas R&D and innovation activities across various locations. Based on the observed growth rates during and after the crisis, one would therefore expect that the crisis has accelerated the shift towards emerging economies.

Re-distribution effects may have also occurred in the composition of inward BERD of a particular country, because MNEs from countries that were more severely hit by the crisis may have reduced R&D activities disproportionally.

EMPIRICAL EVIDENCE FOR THE EFFECTS OF THE CRISIS ON INWARD BERD

Five years after the global financial crisis reached its climax in 2008 there is sufficient data available to evaluate its effects on aggregate R&D activities of foreign-owned and domestically owned firms. This analysis will be based on BERD data collected by the OECD and the US department of Commerce and on patent data. The crisis is defined as the period 2007 to 2009; a two-year period seems appropriate since most countries perform their business R&D surveys bi-annually; moreover, the adaptation of R&D activity to a changing business outlook may involve a time lag.

Table 13.1 gives an overview of inward BERD, domestic BERD and total BERD between 2007 and 2009 for. Countries in the table have been divided into highly internationalised (share of inward BERD on total BERD is higher than 50 percent), medium internationalised (inward BERD share is between 25 and 50 percent), and moderately internationalised (inward BERD around 25 percent or below). Overall, it seems that foreign-owned firms suffered more from the crisis than their domestic counterparts, which confirms some assumptions from the previous section. The median change of inward BERD in the period 2007/09 is 1 percent, compared to 6 percent for domestic BERD. There are only five countries where inward BERD grows faster than domestic BERD, and ten countries where domestic BERD grows faster. In Canada and Israel, inward and domestic BERD decline.

This is a considerable difference to the development in the period 2003 to 2007 (see Chapter 4), when the shares of inward BERD on total BERD increased in nearly all countries observed which indicates a faster growth of inward BERD. From the data presented in Table 13.1, it seems that R&D internationalisation came to a halt or even changed into reverse gear during the crisis. The overall degree of R&D internationalisation in a country is not related to the size of the effect of the crisis.

A surprising result from Table 13.1 is that changes in inward BERD and domestic BERD are not related in most countries. The correlation coefficient between both variables is only -0.05, which indicates that there is virtually no relationship between the two variables. This contradicts the finding from Chapter 11 that inward BERD and domestic BERD are positively related over time. This finding may be an indication of the asymmetric impacts of the crisis on R&D in foreign-owned and domestically owned firms.

Table 13.1 Changes in total BERD, inward BERD, and domestic BERD (2007-2009)

		Total BERD	Inward BERD	Domestic BERD
Highly international-ised countries	IE	25%	20%	36%
	AT	7%	5%	11%
	BE	6%	-4%	21%
	CZ	-1%	-4%	2%
	IL	-5%	-5%	-6%
Medium internation-alised countries	PL	25%	80%	1%
	UK	-2%	15%	-13%
	DE	7%	12%	6%
	HU	44%	11%	68%
	IT	13%	1%	17%
	AU	8%	-5%	16%
	CA	-6%	-12%	-3%
	SE	1%	-14%	9%
Moderately interna-tionalised countries	FR	10%	48%	0%
	JP	-10%	11%	-11%
	US	5%	-1%	6%
	ES	4%	-25%	10%
	Median	8%	8%	10%
	Mean	6%	1%	6%

Source: OECD (2013).

Data available for specific countries allows to dig deeper into the effects of the crisis on firms in different sectors and from different countries of origin. Germany is a good example to study effects at the country level, because it is the largest host country for R&D activities of foreign-owned firms in Europe. With a BERD increase of 7 percent between 2007 and 2009, Germany mastered the crisis quite well (see Table 13.1 above). Inward BERD grew faster than domestic BERD during the crisis.

Inward BERD in Germany is concentrated in transport equipment, electrical, electronic and optical equipment and pharmaceuticals (Table 13.2). In 2009 these three sectors together accounted for two thirds of total inward BERD. The three big sectors took different routes during the crisis. While inward BERD increased by 17 percent in pharmaceuticals, it decreased in electrical, electronic and optical equipment and stagnated in transport equipment. Overall, changes in inward BERD and domestic BERD were remarkably similar, which may point to the importance of sectoral influences. One potential explanation for the big differences in the changes of inward BERD and domestic BERD found in Table 13.1 may therefore be the sectoral composition of individual countries as it seems that R&D intensive manufacturing sectors suffered more than less R&D intensive manufacturing sectors.

Table 13.2 Domestic and inward BERD by sector (Germany, 2009 and change 2007-2009, million EUR)

NACE Rev. 2		2009		Change 2007-2009	
		Domestic BERD	Inward BERD	Domestic BERD	Inward BERD
20	Chemical products	2,752	440	6%	-19%
21	Pharmaceutical products	1,851	2,044	18%	17%
22-23	Rubber and plastic prod., non-metal mineral prod.	703	430	1%	3%
24-25	Basic metals, metal prod.	914	292	7%	37%
26-27	Electrical, electronic, optical equipment	4,923	2,225	-4%	-5%
28	Machinery	3,565	932	0%	11%
29-30	Transport equipment	12,081	3,796	1%	1%
10-19, 31-33	Other manufacturing	1,225	525	14%	-1%
58-63	Information and communication	2,024	534	19%	298%
69-75	Professional, scientific, and technical activities	1,910	715	14%	110%
10-33	Manufacturing	28,015	10,685	2%	3%
A, B, D-U	Services, other sectors	6,965	2,711	11%	41%
A-U	Total	32,682	12,273	4%	10%

Source: Stifterverband für die deutsche Wissenschaft (2013).

The big winner of the crisis in terms of R&D expenditure growth is the service sector, in particular information and communication and professional, scientific and technical activities. The two sectors together constitute the majority of knowledge-intensive business services (see also Chapter 10). Starting from low levels in 2007, inward BERD in these two service industries both increases by more than 100 percent and nearly 300 percent, respectively. The growth of these sectors is driven by a higher knowledge intensity in the economy, but also by outsourcing (Peneder et al. 2003). Firms may find it advantageous to buy in various KIBS, instead of producing them internally. A number of firms in commercial R&D services are even affiliated to multinational enterprises and act as corporate R&D centres. Based on the German data, it seems that the trend toward a stronger internationalisation of R&D in services which could already observed in the years before 2007 (Chapter 6) remains intact.

Another trend which remains intact despite the crisis is that of geographical de-concentration. Chapters 4 and 8 have already demonstrated that the number of countries involved in R&D internationalisation increases and the shares of the largest countries of origin decrease in most host countries, although R&D internationalisation still mainly takes place between neighbouring countries.

Table 13.3 Inward BERD – country of origin (Germany, 2007-2009, million EUR)

		2007	2009	Change 2007-2009
EU-27		5,140	5,276	3%
	Netherlands	*2,089*	*1,934*	*-7%*
	France	*1,327*	*1,632*	*23%*
Non-EU Europe		1,483	1,576	6%
	Switzerland	*1,416*	*1,534*	*8%*
NAFTA		4,125	4,528	10%
	United States	*4,049*	*4,442*	*10%*
Asia	Japan	305	477	56%
	South-East Asia	22	29	34%
Other countries		133	387	190%
Country not specified		139	28	-
All countries		11,208	12,273	10%

Source: Stifterverband für die deutsche Wissenschaft (2013).

This is also true for inward BERD in Germany during the crisis (Table 13.3). Inward BERD from the EU-27 and Switzerland – which dominates total inward BERD in Germany – grows slower than inward BERD from the US and from Asian countries in particular. These growth differentials, however, were too small to cause a large change in the shares of individual countries of origins. Japan increases its share on total inward BERD in Germany only from 2.8 percent to 3.9 percent.

The share of other South-East Asian countries including China and India increases by 34 percent, but is still far below 1 percent of inward BERD. It seems that firms from these countries did not take the opportunity of the crisis to increase their engagement in Germany. This is in line with the assumption that markets with a higher growth potential during the crisis envisage also stronger increases in R&D expenditure. It may have been less beneficial for firms from South-East Asian countries to invest in R&D in Germany compared to investment opportunities at home.

EFFECTS OF THE CRISIS ON OUTWARD BERD

How has the crisis affected R&D activities of firms abroad? This section employs EU patent data and data on US outward BERD from the US Department of Commerce to provide a more detailed picture. The use of patent data is a compromise, since patents have some serious shortcomings as an indicator for R&D (Patel and Pavitt 1995; Smith 2005). First, the propensity to patent differs considerably between sectors. Patents are a reliable proxy for R&D only in high-technology manufacturing sectors such as pharmaceuticals, semiconductors, or chemicals. Innovations in services are hardly protected by patents. Second, there is a gap between invention and the date of the filing of a patent, which has to be considered in the interpretation of patent results. Third, patent counts for some countries may suffer from 'home advantage' bias (Criscuolo 2005), because domestic applicants predominantly file patents at their home country patent office.

One feature, however, makes patents useful for studies of the internationalisation of R&D: since a patent protects both the owner's and the inventor's rights, it contains information on the location of the applicant (owner) and on the inventor's place of residence. By comparing these two locations, one can derive an indicator for the internationalisation of R&D activities (Guellec and van Pottelsberghe de la Potterie 2004). This section utilises this approach with a sample of patent applications to the European Patent Office filed between 2006 and 2010. This approach may underestimate patent applications by US and Japanese residents, since their home patent offices are not included in the analysis. Data has been provided by the OECD REGPAT database. The seven countries selected for this chapter all have considerable overseas R&D activities in total or relative terms.

The data reveal that the propensity to file a patent have suffered considerably during the crisis. The number of patent applications based on overseas inventions decreased between 2007 and 2009 by 1 percent for German and Swiss firms, by 8 percent for Finnish firms, by 16 percent for US firms, by 18 percent for Swedish firms and by 24 percent by UK firms. Only Japanese firms raised overseas patent inventions during the crisis by 8 percent. In 2010, overseas patent applications by Sweden, Switzerland, the UK and the US were lower compared to 2007.

Did this drop in overseas patent inventions and associated R&D activities imply a concentration of R&D at home? Such a development may be the result of uncertainty during the crisis and the wish to keep the utilisation of R&D facilities high in the home country.

Table 13.4 shows the share of domestic inventors on total patent applications of a country. The value for Switzerland in 2006, for example, indicates that 46.7 percent of all patents applied for by Swiss applicants at the EPO are based on domestic inventions. The figures of Table 13.4 indicate that the ratio between domestic and overseas patent inventions is remarkably stable for all countries except Finland. Changes between the years are mostly within a range of 1 percentage point. Hence, there is no sign that firms have reduced overseas activities in favour of domestic activities during the crisis relative to domestic R&D activities. Measured by patent applications, it seems that the crisis has affected domestic and overseas R&D activities in the same way. There was neither a concentration of R&D in the home country because of uncertainty and utilisation motives, nor an acceleration of outward BERD due to forced investments in less affected countries or relocations of R&D activities to low-wage countries.

Table 13.4 Share of patent applications by domestic inventors on total EPO patent applications for selected countries (2006-2010)

	2006	2007	2008	2009	2010
CH	47.9%	46.2%	46.5%	45.6%	48.4%
DE	89.2%	89.6%	89.3%	88.9%	88.6%
FI	77.3%	71.3%	70.1%	71.7%	70.1%
GB	88.8%	88.0%	88.8%	89.1%	88.4%
JP	97.5%	97.9%	97.9%	97.9%	98.2%
SE	72.6%	71.7%	69.9%	72.7%	72.4%
US	90.6%	90.6%	90.5%	90.5%	90.4%

Source: OECD REGPAT, own calculations.

Did the global financial crisis change the distribution of overseas R&D activities between host countries? The answer is – probably yes. As discussed in Chapter 7, the EU-27 is the most important host country region for overseas R&D activities of US firms, but also for firms from EU countries. This has not changed during the crisis, as can be seen from Figure 13.1. The EU-27 still holds a share of more than 50 percent on total overseas patent inventions of five of the seven countries of the figure. The share of the EU-27, however, increased in most countries until 2008, and decreased afterwards, with the exception of Japan. In other words, the trend of rising shares for the EU-27 did not continue during and after the crisis in most countries. Whether this development has been caused by the crisis, however, is difficult to say. Figure 13.1 shows that the share of the EU-27 on Swedish and US overseas patent applications gently decreased already in the years before the crisis, so the development after 2007 there may be part of a longer trend.

Data not presented here show a similar trend for North America where the share overseas patent inventions decreased since 2007 for all countries except the United Kingdom and the US.[1] This trend started well before the crisis, and did not accelerate after 2007.

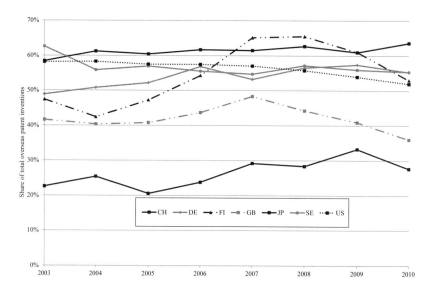

Source: OECD REGPAT, own calculations.

Figure 13.1 Share of the EU-27 on total overseas EPO patent inventions of various countries (2006-2010)

Asian countries, in contrast, did comparably well during the financial crisis. It seems reasonable to assume that this good economic performance has led European, US and Japanese affiliates in these countries to increase their R&D efforts. Empirical evidence presented in Figure 13.2 confirms that overseas patent inventions of all countries in China and India have increased considerably during the crisis. Compared to the years 2003-2007, it seems that this growth has even accelerated since 2007/08. Finnish firms, for example, almost doubled the share of patents invented in India and China on total overseas patent inventions between 2007 and 2009. An acceleration can also be observed for the UK, Germany, and Switzerland since 2007 and for the US and Japan since 2008. In 2010, the share of China and India on overseas patent inventions was higher in all countries than in 2007.

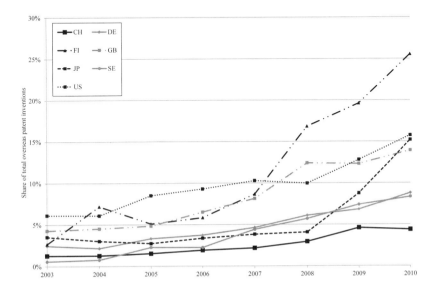

Source: OECD REGPAT, own calculations.

Figure 13.2 Share of China and India on total overseas EPO patent inventions of various countries (2006-2010)

Level and re-distribution effects can also be observed in data on outward BERD of US multinational firms (Table 13.5). US outward BERD declines sharply from about 42 bn USD in 2008 to 39 bn USD in 2009, the largest decrease since data is available. In 2010 there is again a slight increase in US overseas R&D expenditure.

US outward BERD drops in all major host regions including Asia between 2008 and 2009 (Table 13.5). The magnitude of this reduction, however, is different across regions. The EU-27, the largest host region, accounts for 1.7 bn USD or about 2/3 of the decrease in absolute terms between 2008 and 2009. In relative terms, the share of the EU-27 on US outward BERD drops by 0.5 percentage points between 2008 and 2009 and by 5 percentage points over the longer period 2007-2010. A similar decrease can be observed in overseas patent inventions of US firms in the European Union.

US outward BERD to non-OECD Asia including China and India decreases by 74 Mio USD. However, the region can increase its share on total US outward BERD by 0.5 percentage points due to the fact that losses are larger in all other regions. Over the longer period 2007-2010, US outward BERD to Asia increases by 70 percent, and expenditure growth takes up much faster after the crisis between 2009 and 2010 than in the EU-27.

The figures indicate a re-distribution of US outward BERD from the EU-27 and Japan to emerging economies during the global financial crisis because US outward BERD in these countries grows faster than in the European Union where it remains stagnant. Whether this re-distribution has been caused by the crisis, however, is unclear, since this trend can already be observed between 2003 and 2007.

Table 13.5 US outward BERD by host region (1998-2010, million USD and share of total)

Year	EU-27	Japan	Other OECD	Non-OECD Asia	Rest of the world	Total
2003	14,249	1,649	4,332	1,782	781	22,793
2007	21,365	1,919	7,380	2,801	981	34,446
2008	25,130	2,001	8,761	4,546	1,261	41,699
2009	23,435	1,835	8,112	4,473	1,350	39,205
2010	22,579	1,885	8,428	4,805	1,773	39,470
2003	62.5%	7.2%	19.0%	7.8%	3.4%	
2007	62.0%	5.6%	21.4%	8.1%	2.8%	
2008	60.3%	4.8%	21.0%	10.9%	3.0%	
2009	59.8%	4.7%	20.7%	11.4%	3.4%	
2010	57.2%	4.8%	21.4%	12.2%	4.5%	

Source: Bureau of Economic Analysis, own calculations.

From a sectoral perspective the reductions in US outward R&D are confined to the manufacturing sector, in particular again to high-technology manufacturing industries. Low-technology and medium-low-technology manufacturing experienced stable levels of US outward BERD, while overseas R&D expenditure in services even increased during the crisis. This was entirely caused by an increase of more than 50 percent in the research and development services. A similar trend could already be observed for German inward BERD data.

SUMMARY

The global financial crisis of 2008/09 has severely affected the internationalisation of business R&D. Inward as well as outward R&D activities declined during the crisis in a number of countries. Empirical evidence indicates that R&D activities of foreign-owned firms suffered more from the crisis than R&D expenditure of their domestic counterparts. This may be explained by the higher export intensity and a different sectoral affiliation of foreign-owned firms. R&D intensive manufacturing industries – the sectors where foreign-owned firms mostly operate – suffered more during the crisis, while R&D internationalisation in the service sector has even accelerated between 2007 and 2009.

There is also evidence for a re-distribution of R&D activity between host countries and a further de-concentration of inward and outward BERD during the crisis. The shares of the EU-27 and North America on overseas R&D activity gently decreased between 2007 and 2010, while shares of emerging economies, in particular China and India, increased. However, it is difficult to constitute a causal relationship between the global financial crisis and this decline; these trends existed already well before the crisis and the existing time series are too short to infer a structural break. Overseas R&D expenditure of European firms in the US and vice versa is still multiple times larger than R&D expenditure of US or EU MNEs in emerging economies.

Overall, it seems reasonable to assume that R&D internationalisation will also continue to evolve over the next years. The main drivers of R&D internationalisation are still in place: rising incomes and rising knowledge intensity in various parts of the world which give multinational firms an incentive to locate R&D abroad, together with decreasing cost of exchanging information and knowledge over distance.

NOTE

1. Overseas R&D activities of US firms in North America are basically R&D activities of US affiliates in Canada.

REFERENCES

Archibugi, D., A. Filippetti and M. Frenz (2013), 'Economic crisis and innovation: Is destruction prevailing over accumulation?', *Research Policy*, **42**(2), 303-14.

Bellak, C. (2004), 'How Domestic and Foreign Firms Differ and Why Does It Matter?', *Journal of Economic Surveys*, **18**(4), 483-514.

Birkinshaw, J. M., N. Hood and S. Jonsson (1998), 'Building Firm-specific Advantages in Multinational Corporations: the Role of Subsidiary Initiative', *Strategic Management Journal*, **19**(3), 221-41.

Cincera, M., C. Cozza, A. Tübke and P. Voigt (2012), 'Doing R&D or Not (in a Crisis), That Is the Question', *European Planning Studies*, **20**(9), 1525-547.

Criscuolo, P. (2005), 'The "home advantage" effect and patent families. A comparison of OECD triadic patents, the USPTO and the EPO', *Scientometrics*, **66**(1), 23-41.

Filippetti, A. and D. Archibugi (2011), 'Innovation in times of crisis: National Systems of Innovation, structure, and demand', *Research Policy*, **40**(2), 179-92.

Frost, T. S., J. M. Birkinshaw and P. C. Ensign (2002), 'Centers of Excellence in Multinational Corporations', *Strategic Management Journal*, **23**(11), 997-1018.

Guellec, D. and B. van Pottelsberghe de la Potterie (2004), 'Measuring the Internationalisation of the Generation of Knowledge', in H. F. Moed, W. Glänzel and U. Schmoch (eds), *Handbook of quantitative science and technology research*: Dordrecht: Kluwer Academic Publishers, pp. 645-62.

Kinkel, S. and O. Som (2012), *Changing patterns of R&D relocation activities in the course of the global economic crisis*, Copenhagen: Paper presented at the DRUID Summer Conference 2012.

Lucchese, M. and M. Pianta (2012), 'Innovation and Employment in Economic Cycles', *Comparative Economic Studies*, **54**(June), 341-59.

Markusen, J. R. (2002), *Multinational Firms and the Theory of International Trade*. Cambridge [Mass.]: MIT Press.

OECD (2012), *OECD Science, Technology and Industry Outlook 2012*, Paris: OECD.

OECD (2013), *Main Science and Technology Indicators 2/2012*, Paris: OECD.

Patel, P. and K. Pavitt (1995), 'Patterns of technological activity', in P. Stoneman (ed.), *Handbook of Innovation and Technological Change*, Oxford: Blackwell, pp. 14-52.

Paunov, C. (2012). 'The global crisis and firms' investments in innovation', *Research Policy*, **41**(1), 24-35.

Peneder, M., S. Kaniovski and B. Dachs (2003), 'What Follows Tertiarisation? Structural Change and the Role of Knowledge-Based Services', *The Services Industries Journal*, **23**(2): 47-67.

Rammer, C. (2012), *Schwerpunktbericht zur Innovationserhebung 2010*, Mannheim: Centre for European Economic Research.

Smith, K. (2005), 'Measuring Innovation', in J. Fagerberg, D. Mowery and R.R. Nelson (eds), *The Oxford handbook of innovation*, Oxford: Oxford University Press, pp. 149-77.

Stifterverband für die deutsche Wissenschaft (2013), *Interne FuE der Unternehmen in Deutschland nach Konzernsitz*, Essen: Stifterverband.

WTO (2010), *International Trade Statistics 2010*, Geneva: World Trade Organisation.

Index